What Critics Had to Say "Learning to Talk Bear"

"...combines research, suspense and good story-telling to help the reader understand Grizzly behavior. It reminded me of two other books, John McPhee's *Coming Into The Country*, about Alaska, and Sebastian Junger's *The Perfect Storm*."

Franklin Marchman
(amazon.com review)

"Few writers have ever done so masterful a job in explaining why hunters hunt while also providing an enjoyable text on how to hunt."

Coeur d'Alene Press

"Roland Cheek's talent is an ability to entertain while sharing information. *Learning To Talk Bear* is such a book."

Beverly Magley, Editor
Montana Magazine

"Not just a hunting book, this collection of accounts, gleaned from the author's love affair with the elk, is also a family-oriented book; an elk hunter's basic manual but also one of the most entertaining books on the market today."

Brookville (OH) Star

"Provides a treasure trove of information for any wishing to understand the nature and science of the grizzly bear. . ."

The Midwest Book Review

"Roland Cheek probably has forgotten more about elk hunting than many of us ever will know. But what the veteran outfitter, guide and outdoor writer remembers and packs into his new book makes it worthwhile for anybody who pursues the elk."

Great Falls Tribune

"Cheek is at his best when he's describing bears in action, and at his best he's excellent."

*News Tribune/*Tacoma, WA

More Comments About Roland Cheek's Last Two Books –
"Learning to Talk Bear" and "The Phantom Ghost of Harriet Lou"

"New book paints perfect picture of grizzlies."

Billings Gazette/Montana

"In reality, the *Phantom Ghost* is a blueprint for how someone becomes an outdoors expert."

Explore! Magazine

"A major literary contribution in an effort to save the magnificent grizzly."

Marin Independent Journal
San Rafael, CA

"*The Phantom Ghost of Harriet Lou* is the book for those who want to understand everything from … grazers and carnivores to mosquitoes and hop toads, but most especially, about the wapiti."

Midwest Book Review

"A heartwarming tale of interaction between the hunter and the hunted."

Independent Record/Helena

"[Roland Cheek] is a born storyteller."

The Register Herald/Eaton, OH

"To simply say that Roland Cheek's new book, *The Phantom Ghost of Harriet Lou*, is a deeper read than one expects to find in a work about animals is an understatement."

The Shelby Promoter

"As in his book, *Learning To Talk Bear*, this new book, *The Phantom Ghost of Harriet Lou*, is as much about the human/animal relationship as it is about the animal itself. It is the intangibles of elk hunting that set this book apart from other hunting stories."

Rural Montana

"A compelling read."

Morning Call/Allentown, PA

Dance on the Wild Side

Dance on the **Wild** **S**ide

A True Story of Love Between
Man and Woman and Wilderness

Roland and Jane Cheek

a Skyline Publishing Book

Cover design assisted by Bill Lepper and Laura Donovan
Text design and formatting by Michael Dougherty
Typesetting by Type & Graphics, Bozeman, Montana

Publisher's Cataloging in Publication
    (Prepared by Quality Books, Inc.)

Cheek, Roland.
        Dance on the Wild Side / Roland & Jane Cheek. —
1st ed.
        p. cm.
        LCCN: 98-91129
        ISBN 0-918981-05-0

        1. Cheek, Roland. 2. Cheek, Jane. 3. Naturalists—West (U.S.)
        4. Couples.   I. Cheek, Jane. II. Elman, Robert. III. Title.

QH26.C44 1999   508.73'092'2
                                           QBI99-25

Published by   Skyline Publishing
                      P.O. Box 1118
                      Columbia Falls, Montana 59912

Printed in The United States of America

ATTENTION SCHOOLS, ORGANIZATIONS, AND NON-PROFIT GROUPS: Quantity discounts are available on bulk purchases of this book for educational purposes or fund raising. For information, please contact Skyline Publishing, P.O. Box 1118, Columbia Falls, MT 59912. Phone: (406) 892-5560.

TABLE OF CONTENTS

Roland

Jane

Dedication

To Roland, the man who not only brought me to the dance, but taught me to see, understand, and unite with life. I love you.

Jane Cheek

To Jane, the woman who allowed me to live wild and free. You'll do to take home for dinner.

Roland Cheek

"Life is either a daring adventure
or nothing."

Helen Keller

Introduction

It was her idea to compete in a man's world.

That's the way Jane refers to her growing involvement and enchantment in outdoors adventure—"competing in a man's world."

That concept infuriates me. I understand that people must struggle with everyday problems and relationships. I realize love must be learned and earned, and that it can be lost through mistakes or choices made during life. Some might applaud the thought of a woman determined to become "her own woman" in a man's world. Not me.

What bothers me is not that my petite wife wants to compete in outdoors proficiency, but where in the hell did she or anyone get the idea that it's a *man's* world—that all in nature belongs to men? What makes us—all men and most women—assume the outdoors is the male's domain?

Jane and I recently visited a hunting camp deep within the Bob Marshall Wilderness. We swung from our horses and lashed them to the hitchrack. A man came from a tent to meet us, introduced himself as the cook, and left an unspoken question hanging: *Who in the hell are you, where did you come from, and what are you doing here?*

The camp was like dozens of others—the spitting image of most folks' perception of a typical male-dominated realm. There was nothing unusual about the five men lounging around camp: some were short, some tall. One wore glasses, another's hair was distinctly curly beneath his baseball cap. One man's soiled jeans were held up by a single red suspender while the other hung loose. Beneath suspenders and jeans, the man wore what had once been white long underwear. All were unshaven.

"I'm Roland," I said, "and this is Jane. We just thought

we'd drop by and say hello."

We accepted a cup of coffee and sat on stools to chew the fat. The men eyed Jane—but why not? Most discriminating men do—she's pleasant to the eye. But when we rode out, Jane said she was uncomfortable. "By their body language, I felt they resented my intruding into their world."

I doubt that her perception was correct. I think the guys simply stared in amazement that a *woman* of any kind, let alone one so petite, could stand the rigors of the long trek into their domain.

I chuckled at the thought. If these guys only knew that petite woman *walked* half the distance leading her saddle-horse at a trot—and that she used to do it dozens of times each year—they would really be stunned.

With either theirs or Jane's perception, of course, the outcome is the same: both have the connotation that it's a *man's* world.

But it isn't. Not today. Not with the fair sex understand-

A scenic panorama of the Northern Rockies high country where our story takes place.

ing that they can comprehend nature at least as readily as the macho half, that wholesome outdoors exercise is healing, and that food for the soul can be had free for the taking by venturing beyond road's end.

Once Jane and I encountered three women backpackers near the top of the escarpment called the Chinese Wall. As it happened, the women were only six

Roland and Jane Cheek. This is a love story.

miles from the site of the hunting camp mentioned above. The women looked to be in their fifties or sixties. Their loads were certainly bulky and appeared quite heavy. We paused to talk with them and discovered they'd begun their journey at Benchmark and planned to hike through the Bob Marshall from east to west, exiting at Holland Lake, some fifty miles away. They'd already traveled twenty-five.

"Three ladies backpacking seventy-five miles across the wilderness!" I said. "And alone. I'm surprised."

"Oh, there's a man with us," one said. "He's a couple of miles back."

"Yes," another said. "He can't keep up."

We met their man a few minutes later. He labored under a pack that appeared no larger than those of his female companions. The man wore a scowl and he never so much as glanced up at our horses, let alone paused for pleasantries. Perhaps to him there were none. A man's world? Go figure.

Both Jane's and my name are on this book. The voice is mine, but it is *our* lives that the book covers. Jane collaborated in every way with the creation of the volume you hold in your hand. She offered thousands of suggestions, many in written form; I merely reworked them for flow. She helped reconstruct events that occurred many decades before. She edits. And she clears schedules so I can concentrate on the job at hand.

This book, then, is about two people in love sharing a life of exciting adventure. What makes the storyline remarkable is how many times they fell on their butts while doing it. ■

Chapter 1

Everybody's Favorite

There was but one certainty in the world of my child-hood: that all existence was controlled by two powers. The first was a terrible, vengeful Creator with direct authority over an unspeakable horror called hell, a creator who delighted in consigning even an innocent child to the flames of eternal damnation for the tiniest infraction. The second was a mother who wielded a seven-foot piece of broken driving rein with such relish that risking God's displeasure was preferable to even a baleful glance from His most prominent challenger.

In fairness, my mother's determined forcefulness may have bubbled so near the surface because of a perceived need to compete in a world peopled with males. If so, she succeeded remarkably well, tolerating little dissent from her husband and less from her three sons; especially the youngest, who failed from the outset by arriving via Cae-sarean section in the midst of the Great Depression, and with the wrong orifices.

My brother Hillburn, the oldest of the three boys, was six months into his nineteenth year when the attack came on Pearl Harbor. He wanted to enlist before the oil slicks cleared and he would have done so, but mother ordered him to wait for the draft. Not even her favorite in the full flush of young manhood dared test that outthrust jaw and piercing eye.

There was little doubt the eldest *was* the apple of my mother's eye. Such favoritism wasn't misplaced, however, as few individuals I've known in the decades since could match Hillburn's natural synthesis of hand and tool. An accomplished wood craftsman, the lad used our father's prized power tools to turn out fine furniture and bowls and lamp bases from the many types of hardwoods growing near our home. He handled mystifying electrical repairs with ease, and he became an excellent mechanic, tackling difficult repairs on compression engines, outshining our father who was engaged in the trade (a point mentioned repetitiously by mother to any who would listen).

But the skills of mother's eldest son that appealed most to her youngest were his deftness with a flyrod and his ability to outthink deer. He was uncanny.

In a sense, my brother was unique during those pre-war Depression-era days when fish, fowl, and game provided rural folks not sport, but food. For some families, fresh-caught fish or wild game was their only basic tablefare; therefore little regard was given to how it was acquired: jacklighting deer in an apple orchard at midnight, pitch-forking sea-run salmon and steelhead trout from spawning streams, ground-sluicing mallards in a grain field. With survival on the line, observing luxuries such as legal seasons for hunting, fishing, or trapping was not considered a realistic option. Yet my brother developed a sense of outdoors ethics that seemed out of place and time.

Hillburn took up fly fishing, using a split-bamboo rod he crafted himself, searching among his own hand-tied fly patterns for the one to match whatever hatch might be kissing the dark pools near our home. He was the first deliberate trophy hunter I knew. True, Teddy Roosevelt and Ernest Hemingway and Grancel Fitz preceded him, but their kind was as alien among our Oregon hill-country people as Sadducees to Hunkpapa Sioux. He was as woodswise as a bushman, with the stamina of an Apache. And the guy could drive barn nails with a rimfire .22.

Best of all, he shared his survival skills, animal instincts, love for the outdoors, and moral convictions with his baby brother. Then he received his greetings from Uncle Sam.

The day my brother left for induction, Mother cried and clung to him, while Father, stern-faced and a little proud, clasped his hand and patted him on the shoulder. Hillburn shook our middle brother, Duane's hand, just as though he was twenty instead of twelve, then tousled my cotton hair and stuck a tiny Australian shepherd pup in my arms. "Take care of Skippy for me, will you, squirt?" he said. He'd brought the pup home only the week before.

The pup promptly peed on my arm and I glanced quickly up at Mother. I knew and Duane knew and Hillburn knew and Dad knew she didn't want the dog around, but she only stared a moment at the black and white fur ball, then glanced away, and finally clasped her eldest to her and cried some more. From a half-century vantage, I now understand that Hillburn brought the pup home for me, then presented it as a *fait accompli* in a way mother could not refuse. I cried, too, and Hillburn gave me a little shove and I ran around the house to dry my tears and rough-house with Skippy.

I don't remember where Hillburn took basic training, but we weren't surprised when he scored "Expert" with the rifle. Neither were we dismayed that he proved equally proficient with a machine gun.

His skill with the .50-caliber weapon got him into the Army Air Corps—the branch in which he would have enlisted the week after Pearl. Further training took him to Sheppherd and Lacklin Fields in Texas, then to Mountain Home, Idaho, for parachute training.

By today's standards, Mountain Home wasn't so far from our southwestern Oregon farm, and mother desperately wanted to visit her eldest son there. But in those wartime days, travel restrictions and our family's precarious financial position meant a few hundred miles might as well have been the moon.

Just before he was posted overseas, Hillburn returned home on furlough. The county road past our place served three other families and dead-ended just a couple of miles farther. Traffic was infrequent enough that rural dwellers ran to their windows to gawk at any vehicle traveling the isolated road. I paused from my marbles game as a gray Dodge pickup braked to a stop at the end of our lane. A man in uniform, obscured by a cloud of dust, stepped out. Skippy broke away from our game to charge for the road, barking. I stood up to see better. The man jerked a suitcase from the pickup box, and the Dodge rolled away in another cloud of dust. Then the man squatted, arms wide, to catch the dog and the screen door banged behind and my mother ran past, crying.

Hillburn spent most of his leave building an addition to our tiny two-room home—Mother wanted the added space and Dad was fifteen hundred miles away, working for several months to earn a portion of the four hundred dollars he'd agreed to pay for our small farm.

Duane and I tried to help with the construction. But it was obvious we were poor substitutes for a father with whom the young man yearned to visit before marching off to war. Finally the addition was roughed in and its shake roof in place. I worked the pump handle while Hillburn scrubbed his rich black hair and splashed water across his bare chest. "Tomorrow, squirt, we go fishing," he said as he toweled dry.

"Mother says I got to weed the strawberry patch."

"You don't hear too good, do you? I said tomorrow we go fishing."

We left home in midmorning, he wearing a pair of worn jeans and a sleeveless U.S. Army-issue undershirt, I in the hated hand-me-down knee pants and a flour-sack-pullover mother had sewn. We hiked the tiny creek that flowed through our property, following it downstream through neighboring farms until it was joined by other branches to form a stream with pools a seven-year-old could skip flat rocks across.

Hillburn grinned and poked me with his rod tip when I

picked up a skipping stone, then began working the rod, feeding out doubletapered fly line, developing the sensuous casting magic I'd seen him use once or twice before. Neither leader nor line had a chance to follow his fly onto the water as the surface exploded and a twelve-inch rainbow did a rhumba to the shallows at my brother's feet.

He released the fish, winked at me, and again worked out line. This time, the fly kissed the surface at the vee above the pool's exit riffle, and he had another rainbow. "Okay," he said after releasing the second fish, "go ahead. Let's see how many times you can make that rock skip."

I looked down at the flat stone still clutched in my hand and dropped it. "Uh-uh. I want to fish."

He chuckled. "All right, short stuff. We'll move down to the next pool and you can catch our supper."

At the next pool, he handed me his rod. First I was into the brush behind, then tangled around a piece of driftwood at my feet, finally coiling the bucktail amid several loops and knots and flinging the mess to plop near the middle of the still pool.

"Here, squirt, let me see the rod." After retrieving the line and shaking out the knots, he said, "Look, it's like this—you've got to keep the rod tip up. Think of a clock. Your rod should work someplace between ten and…"

I learned a lot about fly casting at that pool and the next, though my ungainly efforts must have left any lurking trout gasping with glee. But I snagged an eight-incher in the next pool and a six-incher in the next, losing both through excitement and bungled rod handling.

We came to a long narrow pond, studded with boulders and shrouded by stately Douglas firs. A slow current moved through the rocks, leaving tiny eddies behind each one. Hillburn took the rod, gently dropped the Coachman behind the first two rocks, one after the other, and pulled a fat trout from each. Then he handed the rod back. "Here you go, Roland. You ought to catch supper here."

I tried to imitate his wizardry, and indeed there was at least one fish behind every rock in that pool. But it took a half-hour before I landed my first fish. When I dropped the rod and ran back to show my brother my coveted first fish, squeezing the squirming rainbow in both fists, Hillburn was asleep, his head resting on a tree root.

Much later, with the sun stumbling toward the western horizon, I found him leaning against a rock outcrop, a daisy with half-plucked petals in his hand. "Whatcha doing?" I asked.

"Huh? What?"

"Don't you want to fish?"

He looked up at me, then at the mess of trout I carried threaded onto a forked willow stick—just as he sometimes did. "Naw, short stuff. Looks like you got plenty." He looked down at the flower and another petal fell from his fingers.

"What're you doing?" I asked again.

"Seeing if she loves me."

I didn't have to ask who, so I said, "Why?"

"Because I want to know."

This mystery was explained on Hillburn's last day home, when *that girl*—the cute blonde who ribbed me one minute, then treated me as an adult the next; the one with whom I was secretly in love—came to dinner. She wore what mother said was an engagement ring.

※

Hillburn Cheek was posted to England in 1943, as one of the men and women making up the Eighth Air Force, entering combat as a gunner on a B-24 Liberator bomber. He wrote regularly, but his letters were heavily inked out, with entire passages lost at the censor's table. Newspapers and radio accounts fleshed out the scanty information in his letters enough so we knew he was in the thick of an air war raging at its worst over Germany. Then a letter arrived that had somehow escaped censorship. It told of his flak-and-bullet-riddled airplane crashlanding in Belgium, and how its crew hid out for a week to escape enemy patrols before discovering they were, in fact, in territory held by the Allies.

Promotions came regularly for my brother, and soon he

was flight engineer and Technical Sergeant. I thought they should have made him a general.

* * *

Meanwhile, on the home front, all America mobilized for the war effort. Gasoline and tires were rationed. Most automobiles carried a sticker posted prominently on the windshield, asking its driver and passengers, *Is This Trip Necessary*? Meat was also rationed. And blackstrap molasses became a despised substitute for the sugar we once used to sweeten oatmeal.

School openings were often delayed to permit the children to help gather harvests. It was child labor pure and simple, but it's not likely that many children of my generation wound up developmentally stunted because we had to work. And I took considerable pride in knowing I, too, was helping smash Hitler, Tojo, and that fat guy from Italy.

Our family was lucky. Mother was a good cook. But even her culinary talents might have been challenged had she not raised a mammoth garden and canned its surplus. Roadsides weren't sprayed with chemicals in the Oregon of my youth, so blackberries and wild hazel nuts were abundant and easily accessible—if we could beat the birds and squirrels to them. In addition, Dad milked a cow and raised a fatted calf. And each fall, when the weather turned cold, we butchered a hog.

Then Dad got the job caretaking the Kofferberg place.

What a fabulous home: two stories, hardwood floors, antique furniture. We weren't allowed in except when Mother opened the padlocks and entered to dust. The house sported metal-framed windows that cranked open with a handle, and not one but *two* bathrooms—the first I'd ever seen. (Ours was a two-hole outhouse, cobwebbed in the summer, frigid in the winter, complete with a "Monkey Ward" catalog missing the softer, tissue-like yellow pages.) The Kofferberg toilets each had water closets fastened to the wall above, and they'd empty with an easy tug on a chain hanging within reach of even a child. I spent a lot of time cranking windows or sitting on one or the other of those toilets pulling chains—until Mother caught up to paddle my hinder and send me stumbling outside.

The place belonged to a wealthy auto-industry executive from Detroit who'd planned to retire to the remote Oregon countryside, only to be frozen on his job for the war's duration. He needed someone to watch over his far-off retirement home and somehow heard that Dad was an honest and reliable workman. The deal they struck was that my parents were to take care of the place in return for fruit produced in its orchards. It proved to be a lucrative arrangement. For me, too.

There were perhaps ten acres in orchards on the Kofferberg place: Bing, Royal Anne, and Black Republican cherries; Jonathon, Winesap, and Red Delicious apples; two types of peaches—one I think a Hale; two types of pears I can't remember; prunes I came to detest; and English walnuts I loved for the way the husks stained my hands to a rich, dark brown. All trees were mature. There were more prune trees than all others combined—a good thing, too, for prunes were easily dried, kept well, and were in demand for America's armed forces.

Roland and his mother, Viola, at their home in Oregon, 1940.

Cherries ripened first, followed in swift succession by peaches, pears, prunes, apples, and walnuts.

"Rolie," Dad said when it came time to pick prunes, "your mother and I have decided you've done so well picking cherries and peaches that we'll let you have everything you make picking prunes. We'll open a savings account in your name and you can deposit your money in it. That will begin your college fund."

So I picked prunes. I picked prunes until I was sick of prunes. Dad would shake the trees, and Mother and my second brother Duane and I picked and sorted prunes from daylight to dark, day after day, until we finished. I wound up with over a hundred dollars in my bank account—unheard of for a stripling boy back in a time when grown men did well to earn three dollars for a day's work. But I've not been able to look at a prune since.

❧

At last it was March, 1945, and Hillburn's crew had served their full duty tour. They volunteered en masse, however, to continue until the end of hostilities. More missions and it was May; Germany surrendered. Both Mother and Dad cried with relief. Then a letter came from Hillburn. He said they were to return to the States in early June. "With luck," he wrote, "I'll be home for my birthday"—June 22nd.

We couldn't have been more excited. One or another of us walked the half-mile to our mailbox every day, hoping always for additional word that never came. My parents said it would be like their eldest son to walk in one day unannounced.

Then a day came when our family traveled to town in order to lay in a few last-minute birthday gifts for the returning hero. On our way home, my parents stopped to visit friends. It was upon taking their leave, while sharing parting words before we clambered into Father's '36 Chevrolet, that the taxi turned into our friend's lane.

To a ten-year-old kid from rural southwestern Oregon, taxicabs represented the ultimate in sophisticated city life.

I'd only seen them a few times—always from a distance—and was in awe of the people they carried. "Hillburn?" Mother whispered.

I glanced at Mother, who for some reason seemed less forbidding, then at Dad, who still shook the hand of his friend in goodbye. He stopped chattering abruptly and I saw his eyes narrow to slits against the noonday sun. The neighbor lady slipped an arm around Mother's shoulder. Time stood still.

The taxi pulled up in a cloud of dust. It carried only the driver. He stepped out. "The Chevy," he said. "I saw it from the road. Is the Cheek family here?"

Father seemed to shrink. Mother's lower lip trembled. Their farmer friend said, "Yes, these are the Cheeks. Can I help you?"

The cabdriver nodded. "I was told to look for a brown Chevrolet sedan. I have a telegram for them."

Father turned away, so the driver handed the telegram to Mother. She took it hesitantly, her eyes wider than I'd ever seen. The driver backed away, clambered into his cab and roared off, his haste unseemly even to a ten-year-old puzzled by his parents' actions.

Dust from the departed taxi had settled before Mother turned and thrust the unopened telegram to her friend. "Please!" she whispered.

Mother's friend opened it as if in slow-motion. She glanced at the telegram, then again put her arm around Mother and said, "Come inside." She began weeping.

The date was June 22, 1945.

Hillburn Leon Cheek had died nine days earlier, along with his fellow flight and ground crew—fifteen men, all told. Their B-24 crashed, for reasons unknown, into mountain country in northwestern Scotland. After scores of missions over hostile Germany; after—as we later learned—crashlanding their crippled airplane once behind advancing Russian lines, as well as once in Belgium; after returning to England numerous times with holed wings and fuselage; after their war had ended, they died on their way home.

My brother was dead—that's all I knew. After God knows how many medals and campaign ribbons, including two Purple Hearts, he wasn't coming home! There'd be no more casts at twilight with him standing at my elbow, smiling and frowning and talking about techniques or how to outthink fish. Never again would he whisper about the enchantment of frost on a spiderweb or dewdrops on salal leaves or the excitement of discovering bear tracks near

Hillburn Cheek just before marching off to do battle with the bad guys.

our home. There'd be no more monster buck antlers for me to trail fingers along and ogle with wonder; no more daisies to pluck, rods to build, flies to tie.

When we arrived home, I took my brother's dog into a dense fir thicket hiding-place and wept unashamedly while Skippy whined and licked away the tears, pawing at me as if he understood.

And a few days later, I received a spirited beating with the broken driving rein for playing Marines on Okinawa in the dust of our front yard. ■

Chapter 2

Irish Eyes Are Smiling

My brother's death destroyed our family. Whatever mutual accommodations our parents had made ended shortly thereafter amid bitter acrimony. Within a year they were separated, and finally, after more years, divorced. Neither of them remarried. Their open hostility estranged my surviving brother and he ran from home, from our lives, never to return. I lived with my mother by court decree, but only for a time. Living with her seemed always to be dwelling under the shadow of the son she would never again see, a reminder that I was a poor substitute for the daughter she'd always wanted.

As might be expected, I, too, metamorphosed; formerly a model kid, I turned rebellious, a gifted student turned truant.

I came to hate most things at which my eldest brother had excelled simply because no matter how much effort went into a project it was always found wanting by a mother who had thrilled to her favorite's talents in woodcraft, mechanics, carpentry.

But outdoors adventure was something else. Our hardworking father had never found time to indulge in the luxury of outdoor activities, and mother considered such pursuits frivolous. So hunting, fishing, a love for nature—those were interests Hillburn and I had shared. And they beckoned amid the present void....

To a country boy awakening to an outdoors world, town school was a considerable contrast. There were more boys in my sixth grade class than the number of kids in the entire eight grades at my country school. Whereas I'd been the fastest boy in scratch football games at rural Lookingglass, at least two of my classmates at Fullerton Elementary were more fleet of foot. And a half-dozen proved tougher.

Escape from the trauma of town life wasn't easy. There'd been dozens of secret hiding places amid the woods and brambles of our hardscrabble farm. And a delicious marsh full of polliwogs, frogs, and garter snakes beckoned from across the Lookingglass school fence.

A bicycle helped, though. With its added mobility, I sought new hiding places at ever-increasing distances. Some of those places were high in the hills surrounding town, others in the brush along the meandering South Umpqua River. I learned to climb like the feral goats on Mount Nebo (watched with religious intensity by townspeople who claimed their elevation on the flagpole hill was an indicator of coming weather) and swim like an otter above and below the city's sewage-outflow pipe.

I paid for the bicycle—a second-hand beater—with money from my own savings account, tapping into the college fund with the excuse that the bicycle was essential in order to acquire a paper route and earn even more money for my future education.

The paper route proved to be a demanding taskmaster, however, as was the shoeshine stand the summer before; both kept me too often from exploring the surrounding countryside.

My mother's home was a "spec" house Dad built on one of three lots he'd purchased in a new subdivision in 1945, counting on the coming end to hostilities. The spec house was to be a stepping stone to financial betterment. Instead, Mother and I moved in, while Dad stayed on the hardscrabble farm.

Dad had been right about the war's end, but he couldn't

have guessed at the coming explosive growth throughout the entire Pacific Northwest. Soon subdivisions sprouted around ours like mushrooms after a rain. The two vacant lots north of Mother's home turned into a gathering place for pick-up ball games among neighborhood kids. During the summer of 1949 an Arkansas family moved in on a street nearby. The father had a hook where one hand had

Me Tarzan, where's Jane?

been—lost in an industrial accident. The kids were two boys, both slightly older than me, and a rat-bag of a daughter a couple of years younger, painfully shy, skinnier than a bundle of pick-up sticks, and with green Irish eyes as round as saucers in a tea set.

It's possible that Mother saw the unusually shy, skinny girl, so innocent and demure, as the daughter for whom she'd always yearned. At least the girl seemed underfoot a lot.

A year went by. It was a period in which I grew increasingly lackadaisical about school and rebellious at home. I was about to enter high school, and the girl-next-door was about to begin the eighth grade. By now she'd become enough of a fixture around our house that on one particularly hot August day I asked if she wanted to walk a mile to a soda fountain for a milkshake. It was the first date for either of us—one shake, two straws. Neither of us proved adept at social graces, however, and long silences fell between us.

I moved from Mother's home shortly after the soda-fountain fiasco, opting to return to the farm and live with Dad. Mother sold her home in 1951 and moved to southern California to be near relatives. She died a year later. Then Dad sold the old home place and took his small sawmill to a tract of timber he'd purchased in northern California. I dropped out of school in my senior year, squandered my savings on alcohol, wrecked two cars, and turned worthless.

My father took a financial beating in the California woods and returned to Oregon in 1953. The house he moved into was a rental belonging to Sam and Myrtis Wingfield. Sam was the man with a hook for a hand. Their daughter, Jane, was the girl with green, saucer-sized eyes I'd last stared into across a mutual milkshake. She'd developed nicely to complement those fascinating eyes.

I still wasn't worth wheeling across the street in a casket, however. The girl's father took a look at the punk who was to share his rental with the kindly Mr. Cheek and told his daughter that she was to have nothing to do with me.

I labored in the woods felling and skidding timber, driving a truck. The hours were long, and anyone working with my father either knew how to work or damned soon learned. I was coming nineteen, however, and in the full blush of indestructible youth. Dad was nearing his mid-fifties—the years taking their toll. In addition, my old man suffered from a plethora of past injuries resulting from an ingrained habit of laboring to exhaustion, an inherent atti-tude of "damn the torpedoes, full speed ahead," and a total lack of safety consciousness.

The summer of 1953 was hot and dry. In order to avoid the heat, we left home long before daylight, greased the Caterpillar tractor just as a tint of rose touched the east, then roared to work as soon as daylight struck. Ten hours later, we knocked off and, tired and dirty, headed home.

The girl next door carried a basket of fresh-washed clothes out her kitchen door as we drove into our yard. "Hi," she said across the back fence as I struggled from our truck, carrying a lunch bucket. I nodded in return, hurry-ing for the house. Later, after showering, I peeked out our kitchen window. The girl was still hanging wash. To a man conditioned to get a job done and get on to something else, she seemed terribly slow. While I watched, she glanced toward our house, clothespins in her mouth. Probably not very bright, either, I thought.

The next day was Saturday, which meant the next night was Saturday night. Jane was sitting on her back-porch stoop shelling peas when we returned from work in midafternoon. "Hi," she called. Again I nodded. She was still there an hour later, head down, working slowly and methodically. I thought of my evening's date and decided the coming attraction was not half as pretty as the girl next door. But the devil I knew promised a great deal more excitement.

Sunday I hiked the mountains where the weather goats roamed. It was good to be back in familiar country. I sat near the top, under the spreading limbs of a white oak tree, eating a sandwich and contemplating the bustling val-ley below. My eyes wandered to a perfectly round hole under the oak's roots and off to the left. I wondered if the hole belonged to mouse or snake.

As if in answer, a deer mouse popped from the hole, second guessed himself and reversed direction without stopping. I sat very still. Within ten seconds, the mouse's head and ears thrust out. He, too, was motionless for another ten seconds, then popped on out, only to stampede again back to safety. And again he popped from the hole. (I refer to him as "popping" from his hole because that is precisely what it seemed. The hole appeared no more than an inch, perhaps an inch and a half, in diameter. The mouse, fully emerged, seemed twice that size.)

This time the rodent paused, pondering many of the world's most agonizing questions before scampering back inside. I joined him in weighty deliberation. The next time he emerged, it was less a "pop" than an explosion. He charged straight on across the veldt at my feet to reach a fallen, half-rotted tree fifteen feet to the right. He did not reappear during the two additional hours I engaged in problem-solving. I still think of that mouse as lacking the necessary dedication to effect real change in his mouse world.

On Monday, it happened that Jane again hung out wash as we drove into our yard. As usual, she said, "Hi." This time I paused, conscious of my grease and grime. "You folks must soil an awful lot of clothes." I was very serious. She laughed. Somewhere during the intervening years between our milkshake date and now, she'd learned to put music into her laugh. I again peeked from our kitchen window. The girl wore light pink pedal-pushers and a gray blouse with its tails tied across her midriff. She wore them well. The sheet she pinned must have been a little awkward because she turned to get a better grip and saw me watching.

The next day the girl sat in a lawn chair reading a book. I walked to the divider fence to ask what she was reading. She held it up. It was too far for me to read the title, so she said, "It's about a young girl who loses her family on the way West."

I shifted my lunch bucket and said I liked to read, too.

"Oh?" she said, but didn't ask what kind of books most interested me. Unfortunately, she'd located her chair to face our kitchen window, inhibiting my studying her undetected. Near sundown, the girl was still in her lawn chair as I left for my evening's entertainment. She didn't appear to be especially swift at reading either.

The girl next door sunbathed atop a beach towel on Wednesday. But her head was averted when we drove in, and during the entire hour I spent glued to the kitchen window she didn't once glance my way to gauge whether or not she made an impression. Although I thought her a little lean for my taste, her bathing suit had an impact: one-piece blue with light tan flowers, ruffles at her thighs, and a sort of folded bib at her bosom. Although her suit was not as revealing as some I'd seen, I was, even then, convinced *something* should be left to a man's imagination.

On Thursday evening, after cleaning up and eating supper, I went out to tinker with my old Plymouth. She wandered from her house. "I've just made a pitcher of lemonade. Want some?"

I hate lemonade, so I drank two full glasses. When at last I returned the empty tumbler, I said, "Someday I'd ought to buy you another milkshake."

"This time, can I have a whole one for myself?"

I put on my most pained expression. "And not drink together?"

"We could take them one at a time."

The following Sunday afternoon, we played croquet while my father visited with her parents. "Nice form," I said, after the girl made an especially nice shot.

She paused in midstride. "Meaning?"

"In every way I can think."

With the reputation I'd earned, there were a lot of strikes against me when it came to pursuing this girl. But I had one great asset: my father.

Dad had no enemies. A kindly, thoughtful, well-read man, he was easy to engage in debate, but never dogmatic. He was slight of build but ramrod straight—most people thought of him as taller than his five-ten. He was so honest he squeaked, his word his bond. Hardworking to a fault, he'd gambled in business and lost several times through no fault of his own. Failure didn't bow him, however, and he believed firmly in what America is all about: the right of an individual to rise (or sink) to the level of his own abilities. He had convictions and lived by them. He believed in God, country, and his fellow men. Nothing else counted.

Best of all, he attended the same church as Jane's parents. And I was quick to see the advantage of riding in on his coattails, so I went to church.

The following week was a continual round of sunbathing, hanging out wash, reading, car tinkering, mowing the lawn, finding excuses to exchange glances and pleasantries. But when Sunday rolled around, I responded to a second siren and went fishing. She was not without her own resources, however, and the following Sunday my kindly father received an invitation to dinner. As an adjunct, the invitation included his son.

And thus it was that nature took its course over an afternoon long Scrabble game, under the benevolent eye of my father and the baleful glare of hers. ■

Chapter 3

The Blind Side of Love

In a committed outdoorsman's career, there is no point more fraught with peril than when casting about for a lifelong mate. I wasn't on the way to Damascus when I received that blinding flash of light, but I never once doubted its verity. With that fact as a given, the question then became how to satisfy the need for continuing adventure after pledging my troth. It was a crucial question of compatibility, and instinct said beating around the bush wouldn't help, nor could smoke and mirrors be a lasting solution. But instinct also whispered that avoiding the issue of my affinity for outdoors adventure might be fatal to standing on frosted ridgetops during buck season.

On the other hand, when you've marked an attractive but skittish young filly as a possible, it's not usually a sound plan to stand in the shadows while she kicks down the stall planks.

Your best tool for successful denouement lies in understanding that the skittish filly has her own set of affinities and objectives—and that tumbling from the womb, her gender automatically equips her with a doctorate in feminine wiles. That's why it may be easy to assess your target's current outdoors knowledge but impossible to discover her proclivity for future adventure. Meanwhile, as you're trying to discern the viability of togetherness, her own evaluation process is usually nearing completion. And if your filly still hangs around, as mine did, after fall elk and deer season, winter trapping, and spring steelhead fishing, *then* is the time to strike.

"Jane, how about driving up in the mountains for a picnic?" I asked my gal in May of 1954. I already knew she loved picnicking. What I didn't know was whether she would enjoy real adventure: searching for wildlife along steep, muddy forest roads far from civilization; if she would in fact dare to go where others feared to tread?

There wasn't a cloud in the sky as we drove from town via the river route, heading west toward the low-spreading Coast Range Mountains. Verdant corn waved knee-high from the fields. Farmers strung wire for advancing bean runners. And melon vines crept along the ground. As we entered the mountains, wildflowers were plentiful. I told Jane that she impressed me with her ability to identify a number of varieties.

"Silly," she said, "columbine grows in our yard at home. So do rhododendron and azaleas."

The lass sat in the middle of the seat as I braked and accelerated up and down the undulating road, her pedal-pushered left thigh resting against the rough jeans of my right leg. We'd passed a dozen abandoned homesteads where families had eked out an existence during the Depression, abandoning that squalid lifestyle as soon as wartime prosperity beckoned.

Another bend and we passed another ramshackle homestead falling into disrepair. Elk grazing in a tiny roadside meadow threw up their heads in alarm. They began to mill at our intrusion.

Elk, for those unfamiliar with them, are oversized deer with dark necks, lighter-colored bodies, and still paler tan rump patches. When curious, they'll mill, lifting their heads atop outrageously long necks, pointing their ears toward suspected danger. Surprise was complete all the way around.

"Look at the camels!" Jane blurted.

I slammed on the brakes, forgot the elk, and looked at

the woman I was measuring for futurity. The elk fled. She turned red. "I … I knew they weren't camels. I don't know why I said it. They … they were elk, right?"

I hugged her.

"I just got excited," she added. "They were beautiful and … and I got excited."

I hugged her again.

She pulled back and deliberately widened her eyes. "How much mileage do I get for this one blunder?"

I laughed and hugged her again.

It was August and Jane and I sprawled alongside the river at one of my favored swimming holes where, years before, I'd played hooky from school. Minutes earlier I'd crossed the road and picked a flower from the garden of a walled estate. I began plucking its petals. She sat up, clasped her knees to her breast, toecaps of her shoes peeking from the hem of her flowered, pleated skirt.

"Why are you doing that?"

"No," I said. "You're supposed to ask *what* I'm doing."

"Okay. What are you doing?"

"Seeing if she loves me."

"That's nice. She does."

"No, now you're supposed to ask why."

"Why?"

"Because I want to know."

Marriage proposals, in the movies, are class acts full of charm and pageantry. In real life—at least in my one single real-life experience—a decision of such consequence as with whom will I share a bathroom for the next fifty or sixty years was hardly a Cecil B. DeMille production. Instead, it sort of grew like Topsy:

"Maybe we'd ought to get married."

"Sounds okay to me."

"Money might be a problem."

"They say two can live for the price of one."

"Your dad will be a problem."

"He'll be a problem."

"So, what do you think?"

"I don't know. You'll have to ask him."

"And if he says you're too young, what then?"

"Both my brothers married young."

"But what if he says no?"

"Let me handle him."

"Then why should I bother to ask him, if you're going to handle him?"

"You have to ask."

"When do I do that?"

"It's up to you."

A gentle breeze wafted through the open car windows. Early evening lights from the city winked below. I leaned an elbow on the steering wheel and cupped chin to palm. *Something's not right here, Roland. Have you thought this thing through?*

Instead of chasing the thought, I said, "How soon could we pull it off—get married?"

"It'll take a little time. Mother will want to make the dress. Perhaps the bridesmaids' dresses, too."

"Then you want a church wedding?"

She laid her head on my shoulder. "Don't you?"

"I'm not exactly overwhelmed by the idea."

"I can't imagine getting married someplace besides in a church."

Thus, I made an appointment with her father and asked what he thought of my marrying his daughter. He said it was the stupidest thing he'd ever heard. Then he pushed himself from his easy chair and left the room.

But with my well-liked, painfully honest father working my corner for a top-quality daughter-in-law he'd all but despaired of my being able to snare, and with Jane's shy, kindly, and loving mother working her corner for a son-in-law she knew her daughter loved, Sam Wingfield was simply rolled on the way to our altar. The best he was able to negotiate was that if he walked his little girl down the aisle, I had to deliver her to the podium the following spring, when high school diplomas were handed out—a promise made and kept.

The wedding was set for November 27, 1954, after elk season—I was adamant about that. Two weeks prior to the nuptials, Jane and I were invited to a dinner party honoring the bride-to-be. I was to pick her up at a quarter to seven. It was eight-thirty before I got back to my partner's Jeep after taking my first elk.

She married me anyway.

Memory serves the actual wedding poorly. But I do recall the highway patrolman who stopped us for speeding down Interstate 5 on the way to our first night's motel.

Highway patrolmen worked singly in those days, even at midnight, walking with impunity to an offender's car to peer inside. If he thought liquor contributed to my erratic driving, he was wrong, and he knew it the moment the beam from his flashlight picked up Jane in her wedding dress.

"Congratulations," he said.

"Yes, sir. Thank you, sir."

"Where you headed?"

"Grants Pass, sir."

"Know how fast your were going?"

"No, sir, I don't."

He slipped his ticket book back in his pocket, snapped off the light, and

Here's Jane!

turned away. "Keep it between the lines," he said.

I've always wondered what he meant.

Jane and I were too young for marriage: she was but seventeen, I was nineteen. We had little money and spent most of that on a week-long honeymoon to Grand Canyon, where it rained and snowed for our entire stay.

Upon returning home, we rented a furnished room in a run-down apartment complex. Three weeks after we settled in, a slick-talking salesman showed up at our door, spent a few minutes explaining his program, and left with a contract. It was a couple of hours after he'd gone before we figured out that the creep did not *give* us a set of Collier's encyclopedias; instead, we were to pay $8.94 per month for the next two years.

Jane, oddly enough, never begrudged the transaction. Instead, she seemed a little pleased and a whole bunch awed that I would read encyclopedia volumes for entertainment.

I couldn't handle town life, so we started building our own home on a couple of acres of land ten miles into the country. We moved into the home when it was little more than unfinished walls, roughed-in plumbing and wiring, and a tarpaper roof. Then came the washing machine, stove, refrigerator—all second-hand, all on the installment plan. Then came our first daughter, Charlotte Selene.

My hours working for my father in the woods and in his sawmill were long. As I matured, I shouldered more and more of the workload from my father. Ours was a role reversal as I brushed him aside to tackle the heaviest lifting, the hardest jobs. Sometimes I crawled from bed as early as one o'clock in the morning to drive fifty, sixty, perhaps eighty miles to get to the jobsite before daylight, worked ten to twelve hours before afternoon dry winds and lowered humidity raised the threat of machinery-ignited, accidental forest fire so high it drove us from the woods.

My father still bid the timber, signed contracts, was the skilled sawyer who converted my logs into his lumber and our profits. But age was telling on him day by day.

Dad built a home a short distance from ours. Now that I'd settled down and had what he figured was the perfect wife, he seemed content. And he doted on his only grandchild. Life was good and my father and I became closer than we'd ever been. He worried about us, though; worried that we were moving too far into debt. I knew many survivors of the Great Depression who were like that—afraid to incur risk for fear of future loss. I laughed at my father. "What have you ever lost to foreclosure?"

He surprised me by staring down at his sandwich. It was

during lunch break at the mill site. A Steller's jay called from a tree to the left, and two digger squirrels perched nervously nearby, tails flitting, waiting for their ritual pieces of bread crusts. "Three lots," Dad said at last. "They were just down the street from where we lived in Sweetwater. I put money down on them in 1929, managed to pay off about half, then lost them before you were born."

We never talked about the subject again.

My dad believed in God. His God was not at all like the firebreathing, revenge seeking, architect of damnation I'd known as a child. His God was a forgiving, loving, powerful force for good against evil; a bulwark on which the righteous could lean during their travails. As much as he truly *believed*, however, the man never tried to impose his will on others. I considered him a Christian of the highest order.

I never knew alcohol to pass my father's lips and cards were not allowed in the home of my youth. When Dad first saw me sprinkle tobacco from a Prince Albert can onto a cigarette paper, his face grew long, but he only said—and that mildly: "I don't want to see you smoke. But if you must, for gosh sakes, smoke Sir Walter Raleigh."

He must have led an interesting early life. As a young man, he'd been in on some of the big West Texas oil booms. He told of bringing in a gusher in Ranger, Texas, a sleepy little farming community of three hundred. Within three months, according to my father, Ranger contained sixty thousand people, few of whom he regarded as credits to society. He told me this story while driving through Ranger, Texas, in 1951. Its city-limit sign read:

RANGER Pop. 300

My father also told of teamsters hauling pipe to the oilfields on great high-wheeled wagons, pulled by several spans of mules. He told of midwinter mud up to the wagon hubs and midsummer dust at least as deep. He told of sitting in a barber's chair, holding his coat and hat on his lap—otherwise neither would be there for him when the time came to leave. He told of downwind gushers blown in during the night and how every morning he'd awaken to find a thin film of oil over everything in his tent.

And one Sunday afternoon he walked next door to visit us and play with his granddaughter. Jane and I were playing two-hand pinochle. After a few minutes, my father rose and headed for the door.

"No reason to leave," I said.

He paused, his hand on the doorknob. "No. Looks to me like all you're going to do is play with them filthy cards."

I grinned. "Come on back, Pa. We'll teach you to play pinochle."

He actually weighed the offer. "Nope," he said, opening the door. Then he closed it, turned and said, "Now if you'd play pitch...."

So that afternoon Jane and I learned to play pitch. I studied my father as he shuffled and dealt, wondering what other secrets might be hidden beneath his inscrutable shell. I was never to find out.

***

Our second daughter, Cheri was born just nine days before Jane turned twenty years old. Dad was tickled pink.

Exactly one week later, he and an employee buttoned up our mill for the day as I made one last turn for a load of logs. Usually, I drove the loaded lumber truck from the woods, but today he was impatient, already in the driver's seat, gunning the engine. I'll never guess why I shouted, "Go ahead!" and leaped atop the load of lumber instead of climbing into the cab. The truck lurched forward with its heavy load.

My father missed gears at the top of a steep pitch, then lost control of his truck as it gathered speed. I leaped from atop the lumber as the truck left the road to careen through small oaks and firs, flattening and uprooting them as if they were matchsticks. I could hear my father still grinding gears, trying desperately to slow the truck, when it slammed into the ditch at the bottom. Then, as I picked myself from the ground and limped down the hill, everything turned deathly quiet. ■

Chapter 4

Choosing Direction

The local daily newspaper I once delivered, The News Review, with press runs upwards of 20,000, paid my father a higher compliment in death than he'd ever received in life. The two-inch-high headline across the top of the July 26, 1957 front page read:

H.S. CHEEK DIES IN TRUCK CRASH

My father's death did not warrant the lead story in the county's top newspaper because he was politically powerful or had the ear of those who were. Neither was he a repository of old money, or hardly any money at all. His ancestors had not settled in southern Oregon with the Applegate pioneers of the 1840s, nor had he founded a business dynasty employing hundreds. Though he supported noble causes, my father was hardly a visible club or community leader, organizer, or fundraiser. He lived in the area for only seventeen years, made no waves, moved no mountains. Yet the newspaper's editors felt he had so many friends and was known by so many of the area's people that his untimely death was the day's top story.

I took—and I still take—a lot of pride in my father's reputation. And so should others, even though the man may have passed on decades before many of them were born.

How so? Maybe it sounds corny, but there's still hope for us as a nation and a people if a quiet, friendly, honest, hard-working, God-fearing man who always placed the welfare of others before his own can rise to prominence without knowing—or caring—that it happens. What a class act for a son to follow!

─────────

When, after a time, I recovered from the trauma of my father's death, I calculated my many friends, neighbors, schoolmates, and acquaintances who had been killed while working in the woods, and I had no heart to return to such a dangerous occupation.

Now what? I was twenty-two years old, a high-school dropout with no appreciable job skills I was willing to use, an anxious wife, two small children still in diapers, a mortgage on a half-finished home, and car payments to be met—not exactly a foundation on which you'd care to bet the farm.

I took a job working in a small sawmill only a couple of months before the mill closed. Jane's father put in a word for me at the mill where he worked. Then that mill laid off a shift and I was once again pounding the street.

It was during this period that we discovered our eldest daughter was severely retarded. And our world fell apart.

I was without work for three months during that winter of '57-58, at one time reduced to scrounging through threadbare clothes hanging in our closets, searching for enough pocket change to buy a loaf of bread or quart of milk. Finally, in April, I was hired at a new plywood mill in Roseburg. I *wanted* to work; desperately *needed* to work; we were at the end of our tether!

I was employed by U.S. Plywood for over six years, starting on the midnight shift, working every bit of overtime possible, seizing each opportunity to learn machinery and process. To my credit, advancements in shift preference, responsibility, and pay came steadily. Gradually our economic situation improved, and we were able to finish building our home.

Throughout this period, the stress on Jane was considerable, focusing as she had to on a struggling husband and the demands of two infants—one mentally impaired and growing increasingly unmanageable. Finally we had no choice but to accept the advice of medical experts and hospitalize our eldest. Jane again became pregnant.

❦

My love for the outdoors continued unabated. It was an inclination that, if not encouraged, was certainly accepted by a young wife wise enough to believe a husband who spent his idle hours amid distant mountains would be too tired to be attracted to more shameful diversions.

As the outdoor inclination flourished, a vague, indecipherable yearning grew—a yearning to accomplish something more in the outdoors, though I had no inkling what that something might be. It was during this period that a friend and I hiked thirty miles of the Skyline Trail, along the crest of Oregon's southern Cascades.

Near the end of our week-long journey, we clambered over a high pass and dropped into an idyllic place called Seven Lakes Basin. A U.S. Forest Service District Ranger was accompanying his packer and mule string and chanced to camp at the same lake. For some reason, the ranger and I struck responsive chords in each other, and we talked for hours about outdoor recreation, backcountry travel, and where forest management was headed. The two government men invited us to breakfast the following morning. I'd never seen the like on an extended packtrip: fresh eggs, flapjacks, and bacon. The ranger stood nearby smoking a crooked-stem pipe as I wolfed pancake after pancake.

"So what do you do, son?" he asked.

"We both work in a plywood plant." I glanced at the man to see if he really was interested. "I'm a glue mixer. Gary works on the spreaders."

"Like it?"

I toyed with my fork. "Yeah, I guess so. Beats going hungry."

"Ever considered working for the Forest Service? This outfit needs young men like you."

I shook my head. "College? I haven't even finished high school."

He took a draw on the pipe and blew a perfect smoke ring. "You think about it."

Forestry. Was it possible? I discussed the idea with Jane. She sounded encouraging. A high-school dropout? With a young family? I made an appointment with a guidance counselor at my old high school.

Ms. Randall pored over my records. "It says that you failed English."

I nodded.

"Twice."

I nodded again.

"In fact, it looks as though your marks are somewhat subnormal throughout high school."

"Yes ma'am, that's true. I wasn't worth much then. But college is out of the question unless I go back and pick up those English credits. So that's what I'd like to find out—if it's possible for me to return to high school for those classes."

"I wouldn't advise it."

My heart sank.

"What I would advise is taking a high-school equivalency examination."

"Beg your pardon?"

"Are you familiar with G.E.D.—the General Educational Development Test?"

"No."

The counselor I had feared most in high school, the one with the world-class scowl and a gruff voice who could scald the hair off a cat, smiled. "Just talking to you, Roland, I believe you might score well on that test. That would give you high-school equivalency and allow you to enter college. If you'd like, I'll arrange for you to take the test."

I worked the graveyard shift—eleven at night to seven in the morning. Ms. Randall set up the test for the following week—one subject each morning at eight: literature, social studies, math, natural science, and English. To pass, I would have to average 70 percent correct answers throughout the test—and results below 40 percent in a single subject meant a flunk.

Mentally I was charged; but by test time each morning, after working my regular shift, I was physically bushed. Nevertheless, of a possible 100, I scored 90 in literature, 99 in social studies, 96 in math, 98 in natural science— and 46 in English.

"Well, I must say there's good reason for you to fail English," Ms. Randall said, staring at my test results. "I'm surprised. I really am surprised. What happened?"

When I didn't answer, she sighed. "You passed the test. You passed the test with very high scores, except for English. Obviously if you want to enter college you'll have to do some remedial English studies. I recommend a correspondence course."

So I signed up for an English correspondence course. I did not complete a single lesson. By then, Jane and I had returned to reality: we simply couldn't face four struggling college years.

Still, discontentment rattled within me.

I worked with a fine bunch of men at the Roseburg plywood mill. Most of them became friends, and three became hunting and fishing buddies—the highest commendation any outdoorsman could grant another. Each of the three was, at one stage or another, my mentor at the mill. First, there was a brief apprenticeship under Ted Armstrong on the plywood press, then a longer study period under Mark Worsley as a mixer of the vital bonding glue essential to plywood manufacture, and finally, a period of learning from Jim Wright, who was night-shift supervisor.

Looking back, it was a strange relationship. I was the youngest, the least experienced in the trade, the one with the shortest tenure with the company. But I worked hard, was unusually willing and reliable, earned advancement, and, when friendships blossomed into outdoors partner-

ships, was most knowledgeable about adventure potential
and most willing to do the necessary legwork to find out
where bull elk roamed or rainbow trout abounded.

There are many forks in the pathway of life. Some are
obvious enough to make us pause and choose the one we
wish to follow. Others are less apparent until years later
when, with the benefit of hindsight, we can see that some
course corrections were made via subconscious drift. One
such drift came because two of my hunting and fishing
companions—Ted and Mark—were originally from Montana and had fond memories of that land and its people.

"This is all right," Ted said one day, as he gunned his old
surplus Jeep up a muddy forest road. Rain pelted down in
sheets. I swiped at a windshield fogged with condensation
from our wet clothes. "But I just wish I could have packed
into the Bob Marshall Wilderness with my dad and brothers."

"Why didn't you?"

His mouth twisted. "They said I was too young. Said my
time was coming. I've always thought what they really
wanted was somebody to stay home and do the chores."

The Jeep skidded on a hairpin turn and Ted geared
down before continuing. "Then when I did get old
enough, the war came along and we moved to Portland so
Dad could work in the shipyards."

"Why didn't you go back on your own?"

My friend slowed to wheel onto an obscure track over-
grown with fiddlehead ferns. "I did. When I mustered out
of the Marines, I headed right back to Montana. Got a job
working on clearing the reservoir behind Hungry Horse
Dam."

He fell silent as the Jeep crawled through the under-
brush, whining toward the fallen-in homestead shack
where we planned to park for the afternoon hunt. I waited
for him to continue, scanning the roadside for fresh elk
tracks. I glanced around just as he shook his head. "Spent
a year there in a camp at Sullivan Creek. The Bob Marshall was just a little ways farther up the road."

"So did you go?"

He grinned. "Hell no. I spent every weekend in the bars at Martin City."

I was fortunate to come to manhood in the 1950s, during the heyday of Oregon elk and deer hunting. Roosevelt elk, almost unknown in the Coast Range mountains to the west of my childhood home, were multiplying to the point where they were said to be eating themselves out of house and home. And deer hunting—on the west side of the Cascades for Columbian blacktail and to the east for mule deer—was so superb that veteran hunters sneered when they mentioned someone taking less than a four-point (western count) buck.

Fishing was also great. It was an era when accelerated timber harvests were just beginning, and men and machinery had not yet shaved the forests from the land. Streams ran clear and cool beneath spreading limbs of ancient forests, their spawning gravels unsilted from eroded soil pouring from massive clearcuts. Spawning chinook and silver salmon ran from the oceans up those streams in the thousands, as did steelhead and sea-run cutthroat trout. Rainbow and cutthroat trout and little brookies inhabited the waters, too.

I began exploring the Cascade Mountains to the east of my home, and found the myriad lakes dotting its maps. Many of those lakes were accessible only by trail during the late '50s and early '60s. To my hunting group's delight, I discovered that elk were also moving into that portion of the central Cascades. And in 1961, when Fish & Game opened a limited elk season on a permit-only basis for the area, we were among the few to apply.

Mark Worsley is long and lanky, an Iowa farm boy who grew up wanting to be a cowboy. Upon graduation from high school, Mark headed west, eventually signing on with the Shellhammer Ranch, near Livingston, one of Montana's great pre-war horse ranches.

When World War II came along, the young cowboy headed out to do battle with the bad guys. After the war, he returned with a young wife to the isolated and wind-swept Shields River Valley, northeast of Livingston. He bought a small wheat ranch and prospered as grain prices escalated during the late 1940s.

But the isolation of remote south-central Montana, along with the constant keening wind peculiar to the Shields Plateau, proved tough on a young city-bred wife. "I'd be there yet," Mark said one day as our families picnicked, "if Mary could have stood it. We paid off the ranch in just three years. Federal supports had gone into place, stabilizing wheat prices. Everything was coming up grand. I was in Montana, where I really wanted to be. There were mule deer and elk in the hills around the farm and whitetails and pheasants and Huns in the wheatfields and pastures."

My friend peered at me and smiled—but the pupils of his eyes were magnified through his horn-rimmed glasses and it was easy enough to see the smile failed to carry up to them. "If only Mary could have been happy there ..."

❦

Circumstances made me the chief strategist of our group's fishing and hunting adventures. I was the one who planned where we fished, how we executed our hunts, and usually where we camped. If we failed to draw elk permits for the Cascades' North Umpqua area, the burden of a fall-back plan to hunt the Coast Range Callahan country fell to me. Usually I did the legwork necessary to discover the areas elk used before opening day. And as a group, even during those halcyon days of the '50s and '60s, we were more successful than most.

But the private timber companies, Bureau of Land Management, and U.S. Forest Service were building roads into remote forested regions of Oregon faster than I could explore. We watched in dismay as new haul roads were punched squarely through beautiful alpine meadows where, in previous years, we had stalked bull elk. Entire mountainsides where the wily wapiti retreated for shelter were scalped of forests.

"This can't be happening in Montana," Ted said one day as we sat dejectedly atop the berm of a newly-dozed haul road and stared at a shiny Chevrolet pickup, doors swinging in the wind, parked, keys still in the ignition, astride the tracks of the small band of elk we'd been following for two hours. It was easy enough to see what had happened: pickup truck rounds bend just as elk, milling at the side of a new road that had not been there a few days before, breaks for safety. Pickup slides to a stop and hunters pile out.

My friend voiced our thoughts: "At least in Montana, there's some wild places set aside where they can't build roads or clearcut the whole damned forest."

That was in 1962—the same year our son, Marc, was born.

Roads and clearcutting weren't the only problems. Driven by massive expansion in timber harvesting, a benign climate, and a westering spirit inherent in much of the rest of America, the population of the land where I'd come to maturity continued an explosive growth. Gradually an idea began to take root in my mind.

"You've been quiet all week," Jane said. "What are you thinking?"

I shoved my cup across the table, and she reached for the coffee pot. "About moving."

"Moving? Whatever for?" She poured a cup for herself, then pulled out a chair and plopped down across the table from where I stared out the window at huge oak trees and the bank of a meandering creek. "You say you're the best paid workman in your plant. We're almost out of debt. Why would we want to leave all that?"

My eyes came back to her. *Still looks like a teenager*, I thought. *Still looks like I robbed the cradle.* Beautiful enough for any man. "I don't know, Jane. It's sort of hard to explain. I just get this feeling in my gut that we're not going anywhere."

She started to say something and I held up a hand. "It is a good job. I do have the best-paying job in my plant. On top of that, I'm on straight day shift, we have loads of friends, we live in a good neighborhood, and I suspect we'd be secure and comfortable clear into our dotage."

"So why …"

"Look around you. They built three homes in the field behind this house just last year. The country is growing like crazy. It's a far different place than when you and I were schoolkids. I'm not enamored with the idea of our kids growing up in a place with the kind of environment this will be when they hit their teens. Nor do I think it best for them to attend a high school that had too many kids in it when we were there."

I reached down and grabbed two-year-old Marc by the diaper as he crawled past. "I guess I'd like our kids to grow up in a small town like we did, go to small schools. Be bigger frogs in littler ponds than just another tadpole in a lake." I released the kid and he scampered to his mother. She took him to her knee.

"What do you have in mind?"

"I'd like to take a little more control of our lives. I'd like to see Montana."

"Just like that?"

"No. I'd like to visit there on our vacation. There are three plywood plants in the state now, and Mark Worsley told me they're building another in a place called Columbia Falls. I've got enough work experience now that I should be able to get on at any one of them. But most of all, I guess I'd like to look at the country, visit the plants, talk to their people."

Her silence was awkward. So I added, "I'd like you to see the area, too. See if you think you could like to live there." She bounced Marc on her knee, staring at me, saying nothing. So I lamely added, "And Columbia Falls is near Glacier National Park." Then she surprised me. "It's also near the Bob Marshall Wilderness, isn't it?" ■

Chapter 5

Treasures of the Treasure State

Some men talk as if their search for a personal destiny and the American yearning for adventure were limited to males alone. Jane, too, was smitten by the Rockies. As a result, I left job applications at all three operating plywood-manufacturing plants in Montana, and even applied at the one under construction in Columbia Falls.

Jane may have merely dabbled with thoughts of adventure, choosing to humor my dreams. Perhaps she didn't yet know that, with some people, dreams are first steps to reality, never an end. But when the fruit farmer's ancient flatbed nosed into our yard with me behind the wheel, she at last grasped that I was willing to push all our chips to the center of life's table.

"Got it for a song," I said. "A hundred and fifty dollars. Runs like a top."

My wife, arms folded across her chest, walked three times around the 1941 ton-and-a-half while I trailed along babbling. "Most everybody calls these old Internationals 'cornbinders,' I don't know why."

She paused. "And we will join the rest of the wagons at Independence?"

I was called back for a job interview at Columbia Falls in late October. As luck had it, Jane and I arrived for that second interview on opening day of Montana's general hunting season. By the plethora of nimrods on the road—driving trucks or pulling trailers loaded with horses or herding four-wheel-drive pickups with tagalong campers—I saw in a heartbeat that Montana was my kind of place.

The new plant, its construction not yet completed, appeared well designed. And its builders, Plum Creek Lumber Company, had an excellent reputation throughout the wood-products industry for stability, product quality, and employee relations. The company offered a foreman's job, to start December 1. I accepted.

My old hunting buddy with Montana roots, Mark Worsley, whooped with delight when I told him I'd been hired by the Columbia Falls company. Then he said something I

The wagon train on way to the "Promised Land." At least it's our old "Cornbinder" International, vintage 1941, on way to Flathead Lake and our new Columbia Falls home.

dismissed with a laugh: "After you get settled in, Roland, you'd ought to take a look at becoming a hunting and fishing guide. You'd be a good one."

We easily sold our home in Oregon. For the first time in our married lives, Jane and I were out of debt.

The break from the homeland of our youth was— except for Buck and Arlene Fritts—painless. The Fritts family were neighbors and, yes, friends, but not close. That's why we were surprised when they showed up on our doorstep to help us load furniture into the old truck. Then they popped the tops on a couple of beers, toasted knowing us, and blubbered at our leaving. It was touching; especially so when we were little more than kids and they were both nearing railroad retirement.

Buck's uncle had been my father's best friend.

I rented a house on a quiet street in Columbia Falls. Our front door faced a public tennis court, the rear looked out over a river bottom. Deer passed beneath our windows. We lived only a few blocks from my work. I was content. Jane was unhappy.

"I don't want to rent," she said shortly after moving to Montana.

"Honey, we haven't even been here two months."

She picked at her breakfast eggs. "I don't care. It's so foolish. We should be building equity in our own home instead of paying it out in rent."

I refilled my coffee cup and hers, chuckling. The woman really did have a fly up her rear.

"Besides," she continued, "we could build another home."

I slammed the pot back on the stove. "Absolutely not. I'll never build another house. There's more to life than all work. You know I'm no handyman-carpenter."

"Then we'll …"

"No. I'm not even going to remodel our next house. That's it. Final. Finis. Forget it!"

She glared over the rim of her cup. I tried tact: "Look,

Jane, it makes no sense for us to even *think* of looking for a place until we've lived in this valley long enough to decide exactly where we'd like to locate."

She set her plate in the sink. Dishes rattled. With her back still turned, she said, "You were the one who wouldn't live in town. Now why are you so set on it?"

"I'm not, dammit. I want a few acres in the country as much as you. But not now. It'd be crazy to buy anything, especially before the snow melts in the spring. How could we tell what kind of ground we'd be getting?"

She opened the hot-water tap, squeezed in dish soap, and turned for my plate. Her eyes met mine. "I boxed the Christmas decorations. They're in the living room. Please take them to the garage."

"Jane, we are not buying a place now—that's final!"

Within two weeks, the woman found a small farm along a highway five miles south of Columbia Falls and talked me into taking a look. Another week and we'd signed a purchase agreement on an old farmhouse and fifteen acres. We moved in at the end of February and, within two months, poured the foundation for an addition that would double the size of our new home.

It was a day in early May. Jane was inside the old house tearing out cracked plaster walls. I cut rafters for the new addition. An unfamiliar car with Oregon license plates nosed into our driveway. Then I recognized our former neighbors, Buck and Arlene Fritts.

In keeping with their personal philosophy of living life to its fullest, the couple had, on a whim, taken a Sunday drive to eastern Oregon's high desert. As afternoon waned, they came to a road junction. "Right or left?" Buck had said.

"Huh?"

"Right or left?"

Arlene pondered as Buck tapped the steering wheel in cadence with the country music from their car radio. "Home is left," she said at last. "What's right?"

"Montana. The Cheeks."

She giggled. "Let's go right."

So they showed up on our doorstep without a change of clothes or a toothbrush. On the surface, their arrival seemed to come at the worst possible time for us. But Buck Fritts was an accomplished handyman-carpenter. He spit on his hands and began carrying rafters while Arlene rolled up her sleeves and joined Jane in the nastiest work imaginable. Four days later, the addition was framed.

❦

I had this dream of being a latter-day frontiersman in buckskins. We dwelled in a mountain valley that snuggled hard against the main chain of the northern Rocky Mountains. I was twenty-eight years old, in the prime of young manhood. There was a Jeep wagon in the garage, a horse in the pasture, and parked by the barn was an old cornbinder truck capable of hauling a bunch of ponies to a trailhead. I purchased a used saddle for thirty-five dollars and picked up a second-hand lariat rope. I was *ready*!

Two months after we brought the mare home, she threw a colt. "What the hell is this?" I demanded of the man from whom I'd bought the horse."

Walt laughed. "I didn't know she was bred, Roland. If I had, I'd have wanted more money for her."

Jane and the kids thought the colt cute; I not only found him a four-legged delinquent, but his mother, formerly a docile old mare, turned aggressively protective. In short, it quickly became apparent that becoming a modern Jim Bridger required a modicum of rudimentary horse know-how.

That's about the time John Bullock turned up, looking for work at the plywood mill. John was fifty years old when he was assigned to my crew as a laborer. The guy was a stove-up cowboy who could neither read nor write. But he knew how to work. And, as it turned out, the old man knew a bunch about horses and the handling of them.

John Bullock had run away from his home on Oklahoma's Cherokee Reserve to try his luck in rodeos. He developed into a saddlebronc rider of merit, moving eventually to the big circuit: Cheyenne, Calgary, Pendleton,

Fort Worth.... Rodeoing in the 1930s was tough love, however, even for the best. The half-Cherokee youth won some and lost more. Ultimately, he wound up bent and broken by broncs from New Mexico to New South Wales. In between rodeo seasons, John worked on ranches all over the West, topping off their rough strings. If a man could be said to know horses, I thought my workman was that guy.

Truth will out, and John discovered I had a novice's burning interest in learning about horses. Since the old bronc stomper knew more in one fingernail than most folks learn in a lifetime about ponies and how to use the ropes needed to control them, he took me under his advisory wing. John taught me to braid and splice rope; the difference between a hackamore and a smooth curbed, spade, or snaffle bit. And I learned the rudiments of shoeing a horse. As I began picking up second-hand tack, my mentor showed me their proper use and applications: how panniers and pack covers were usually utilized with diamond hitches thrown over sawbuck saddles; how the iron-ringed Decker saddle was easier to sling packs and use where trails were wide and grades gentle.

I learned a dozen different ways to hobble or picket ponies, how to keep their ropes twist-free, and the value of bells, breaklines, and pigging strings.

John explained horse conformation: how the proper build for a mountain horse is sturdy withers to hold a saddle from slipping forward when traveling downhill and a little pot-gut to hold the cinch in place when clambering uphill. He was a believer in a broad chest for good wind, muscled-up quarters for power, and sturdy long legs for negotiating fallen trees.

John couldn't care less whether a horse was white, black, brown, gray, or polka dot. Neither did he care much about breeding—except where breeding might affect desired confirmation.

In time, John and I planned a short weekend packtrip into alpine country. The idea was to give me some real hands-on experience. We expected to find windthrown trees and perhaps tumbled-down rocks in our trail. But we did not expect to encounter snowfields during mid-July.

The huge expanse of snow lay atop a boulder field. I'd hiked the area previously and knew approximately where the trail snaked through the boulders. So, guiding the gentle old mare, I rode onto the packed and frozen snow and she pussy-footed her way across, followed by the docile big-footed packhorse. After we reached the far side of the snowfield and my two horses once again stood on bare ground, I twisted in the saddle to watch John and his skittish, high-stepping horse cross.

About a third of the way across the drift, one of Trixie's hind legs went through the crust. She began plunging, breaking through with every leap. I caught my breath as the pony bucked off the trail, across the hidden boulders, breaking through, scrambling to regain her feet, breaking through again. Twice the mare went to her belly, only to keep on kicking and floundering until she regained her feet and bucked off in another direction.

Twice John shook boots from stirrups and leaped onto the snow while the mare floundered, holding onto the bridle reins until the horse regained her feet; then the old cowboy leaped back to the saddle, sticking like a leech and fanning the horse with his hat, spurring her on through the snowfield. It was a masterful ride, probably as good as any the old bronc stomper ever made in Pendleton or Cheyenne.

Finally they busted over, under, around, and through the drift to my side. When John's pony finally bucked to a stop, I sputtered and whooped. Peals of laughter. Belly-thumping laughter.

At last I calmed down enough to blurt: "John, didn't I see you grab leather?"

"That horn was put there for somethin' besides ropin'," the crusty old veteran of twenty years' rodeoing growled.

⸻

I was proud to work for Plum Creek Lumber Company. But three years after I began with them, the outfit was sold to the Northern Pacific Railroad.

From the land-grant railroad's standpoint, it was a perfect marriage. They had vast undeveloped timberland resources, but no manufacturing expertise. With the acquisition of Plum Creek, Northern Pacific obtained both a highly skilled work force and a manufacturing arm with a top notch reputation. Later, through mergers, the company metamorphosed into one of America's largest rail lines: Burlington Northern Railroad.

My personal fortunes advanced. I started as shift foreman, then moved to department trouble-shooting, and finally was charged with starting a company-wide safety program. It was a sound management move. As a result, Plum Creek had an active safety program in place throughout five plant locations when Congress passed the Occupational Safety and Health Act (OSHA) in 1971.

As safety director for one of the Treasure State's largest wood products firms, my credentials were advanced out of all proportion to experience or training. I was appointed to several statewide boards and advisory councils. Plum Creek had enough confidence in my performance to supply a vehicle and an expense account. And they gave carte blanche for me to design my own work and travel schedule. I had sufficient salary to keep us in our modest style.

Like wives all over the world, Jane bubbled with ambition for her husband's continuing corporate rise. We were sitting on top of the world. Only an idiot would rock such a splendid boat.

Meanwhile, my thirst for outdoors adventure remained unslaked. ■

Chapter 6

The Price Was Steep

The memory of the kindly forest ranger at Oregon's Seven Lakes Basin stuck in my mind. Though I didn't follow his advice and pursue forestry as a profession, I understood that his effort to recruit me to his agency had another purpose than merely to staff the outfit with eager young men. The ranger was among the last of a breed who had little use for foresters without fundamental woods knowledge. He scoffed at mechanical technology replacing the diamond hitch amid wild country. And he was particularly dismayed that his outfit was turning forests into tree farms.

Somehow I'd made an impression on that man and, although I didn't even know his name, the Butte Falls District Ranger's ideas of proper forestry had made an impression on me.

Also at work in my head was the belief that during the years I came to manhood, national forest road building had exploded, becoming monuments to engineering gone mad. Vast timbered tracts where elk had once roamed degenerated into wastelands of clearcuts. Streams where salmon and steelhead had once spawned in the thousands now had their arterial lives choked and blocked by mud flows and debris from those same clearcuts.

Yet I had come to manhood working in those forests,

felling trees, skidding them, cutting them into logs and hauling the logs to mills. I dozed roads with no thought of erosion. And I'll confess that my heart beat faster when the crawler tractor I operated drove its blade into a mountain's soft belly. Moving from woods to manufacturing served to lessen the visual impact, but the results were still there each time I visited forest or stream.

Montana was still raw land, however; still the way God made it. That was one reason why I lobbied hard for moving to the northern Rockies. But as the years passed, it became apparent that the same rush to develop forests was getting under way in the Treasure State. In order to justify accelerating road construction and expanded harvest programs, the Annual Allowable Cut (a supposedly sustainable harvest rate replaced yearly by new tree growth) on the Flathead National Forest was arbitrarily increased from 80 million to 150 million board feet per year, then to 212 million.

Curious about the increases, I did some research. The year I checked, the Annual Allowable Cut (AAC) was set at 212 million, but 280 million were actually harvested. And there was talk of raising the AAC again!

I was more than merely troubled. I began visiting forest managers, asking questions, writing letters, and attending forest management discussion groups. I'd had previous doubts about the way forestry was being practiced on public lands, but I'd never before questioned forest management from my present heady position in the wood products industry.

⚜

I had a problem in equine understanding, so I sought help. By then I had a half-dozen horses grazing in our pasture, and my friend John Bullock had a leather-repair shop behind his home. I found him there, cutting long strips from a side of cowhide.

John waved at a stool and I pulled it close, waiting while the old horseman concentrated on the task at hand, his tongue thrusting through toothless gums. Finally he laid down the gauge knife and squinted over his wire-framed glasses.

"John," I said. "I've got six horses, and the law of averages says some of 'em must be good. But as good as they are, every single one of them has at least one bad trait. For instance, Old Yeller is as honest as the day is long, but slower than molasses. Rocky is young and powerful and can run like the wind. But on occasion, especially when he's excited or heated up, he'll take the bit between his teeth and run away. What's more, he reins like an out-of-control truck."

John nodded as he gummed his tongue with concentration.

"Buck and Joker," I continued, "are agile and athletic and powerful with youth. But they're only green-broke, and the buckskin, well, he's learning to buck faster than I'm learning to ride."

John picked up his gauge knife. "Go on."

"Blondie, of course, is short and stout and pure of heart. But she stays too fat to carry a saddle well."

A thin strip of leather fell from John's knife, and he began cutting another.

"John, you rode hundreds—maybe thousands—of horses, and owned dozens. Right?"

The old man nodded.

"So, in all the horses you owned, or even among the ones belonging to someone else, did you ever know of one that was perfect in every way?"

The old man laid his gauge knife down and swung his toothless, gray-stubbled face to the sooty shop window for what seemed forever. It didn't take much imagination to see the pictures flitting across the old man's memory: roans and sorrels, buckskins, bays, and pintos; Appaloosas and quarterhorses and Arabs; chestnuts, blacks, palominos and browns; walkers, Morgans, thoroughbreds, and mustangs—they were all there. Rodeo horses, parade horses, bucking horses, cutting horses, and bulldogging horses; range horses and race horses and stable horses and draft horses; big horses, little horses, fat horses, skinny horses;

roping horses and packhorses and pacing horses and trotting horses....

Just when I feared he'd forgotten I was there, John, still staring out the window, broke into a broad grin, murmuring:

"Hit shore woulda been a goodun, wouldn't it?"

My primary class in practical equine utilization took quantum leaps during the third summer in our new home-

A packstring toils up Larch Hill Pass, with the Chinese Wall in the background.

land, with an overnight journey into the backcountry of Glacier National Park and a couple of weekend trips into wild country of the Flathead's Middle Fork. Later, in the fall, I led Jane's father elk hunting into a picturesque basin off the Spotted Bear River. It was on that trip when, for the first time, I actually put foot into my dreamed-of Valhalla —the Bob Marshall Wilderness. That first look was merely a foot-across-the-boundary-line thing. But by the following summer I was ready to do more than just dip a toe into the Bob Marshall. And I talked Jane into tagging along for the ride.

Jane, ironically, was frightened of horses. Most members of the female gender, it has been my observation, jump at the chance to ride horses, but not Jane. She loved the brutes, loved to watch them in the pasture, loved to see them at play. But straddle a saddle with a thousand pounds of horseflesh beneath? Uh-uh.

She'd always enjoyed camping. And she loved beautiful mountain landscapes, appreciated the magnificence of wildlife, and became ecstatic over meadows full of wildflowers. But wasn't there some way to see these things without climbing atop a horse to ride for days into a stretch of wildland sixty miles wide by one-twenty long?

Not to me there wasn't. To me, only a wild-eyed lunatic could suggest alpine scenery was as beautiful from Going-to-the-Sun Highway in Glacier Park as the vistas unfolding from the back of a horse on even the meanest of switchback trails in my Bob Marshall dreamland.

Not being a dabbler-type, I opened a map of the Bob Marshall and stuck my finger on the exact center. *That's* where I wanted to go. We had five days. Let's see, a route allowing us to view the famed Chinese Wall would require traveling around forty trail miles to reach the central wilderness valley. Then taking the shortest distance out would be another thirty. In five days? Obviously there were some things I dared not tell Jane.

Later, after I'd acquired the fundamental horsepacking expertise and upgraded the quality of my horse string, the twenty-three miles Jane and I had to cover during our first day's packtrip into the Bob became little more than routine. But during that first adventure, it was brutal. We began long before daylight, loading horses into the old cornbinder. Then it was a three-hour drive to road's end. To make matters worse, my packing left much to be desired and we stopped often to relash loads, straighten packs, adjust saddles. Those twenty-three first-day miles seemed first cousin to laying the trans-Siberia roadbed from Baikal to Vladivostak. Jane later told me if she'd had a gun she would have cheerfully used it on me.

"But," she added, "what then? I couldn't have made it back to the truck alone. And even if I had, there was no way I could have loaded horses and manhandled that ancient piece of junk down a crooked forest road."

At last we found a place to camp in a grass-filled glade. I unpacked the ponies, then hobbled and turned them out to graze. Jane had unwrapped enough canvas packs to locate her sleeping bag, and she lay atop it glaring. While I kindled a fire, she asked, "How much farther is it tomorrow?"

I shrugged. "I don't know, honey. According to the map, just a little."

This was unlike her—not to pitch in around camp—but I put it down to exhaustion. I prepared supper, and she fell asleep while eating. I tucked her into the sleeping bag just as full dark fell.

The next day was equally tough, but far more picturesque. Our trail snaked out of the forested canyon bottom, through a low pass and on into alpine country. We stopped for lunch along the shore of a small lake that had Jane, even in her blue funk, searching for superlatives.

"Can't we stay here?" she asked as I held her saddle-horse, beckoning for her to mount.

I laughed. "No, Jane. The Chinese Wall is just a little farther, then we'll drop down to White River, where we'll camp. Besides," I said gazing around, "there's not enough grass here for our horses."

The famed cliff formation that forms the crest of the Continental Divide in this section of the northern Rockies opened to view just as soon as we rounded a couple of trail bends. The sight was indeed as spectacular as I expected it would be.

Trees were stunted and scattered at this elevation: whitebark pine, limber pine, and alpine fir were interspersed with beargrass covered meadows and talus fans from the cliffs above. Our eyes were on the towering "wall"—that's the only way I could have missed all the telltale signs that a great number of elk were in the area. Then the hillside about us erupted!

It began with my saddlepony doing a two-step. A packhorse charged past until he was brought up short by his leadrope. Then elk broke across the trail in front and behind, racing past, cows calling, bulls bugling.

I twisted in the saddle and grinned back at my partner. "Look at the camels!"

Jane's face was pale as she gripped the saddlehorn for all she was worth. Fortunately, her pony had danced between the two packhorses and was hemmed tightly in. "Get me out of here," she said in a deceptively low voice.

The sun sank below the western horizon as we dropped into the valley of the North Fork of White River. We made camp at the first place affording clear water, firewood, and good grass for our ponies.

"Do you realize we're within five miles of the geographic center of the Bob Marshall Wilderness?" I called while setting up our tent.

My wife of fourteen years didn't answer. She sat atop a high bank, hugging her knees and staring at the little creek gurgling below. I came to stand beside her, turned a three-sixty and said, "Isn't this a gorgeous place?"

A tear trickled down her face and she murmured, "I'm just thinking of having to ride out of here."

So I plopped down and draped an arm over her shoulder. "Tomorrow we're staying put. I might go for a day ride. Maybe take a hike or two. But you can stay in camp if you'd like."

"I'd like."

The ride out of that wild White River country was even

more brutal than our journey in. I'd intended to take the trail out in two days, especially since the first half was down an abominable, mudfilled trail. But storm clouds gathered and it looked ominous as we reached the Spotted Bear River and passed the Pentagon Guard Station. It was actually Jane who, through gritted teeth, insisted we go on.

It was a wise decision. We arrived at road's end near nightfall, unpacked our ponies, and loaded them into the stock truck. We'd just begun our three-hour drive back to civilization when the heavens opened to pour buckets.

We drove into our yard at midnight. As she stumbled from the truck, Jane said, "If you ever want to go again, don't call me, I'll call you."

I took the lady at her word. And many years were to pass before she actually called. Those were crisis years for our marriage and our lives. ■

Chapter 7

Disastrous Adventure

One way to explain the phenomenon might be to call it spirit—or perhaps intrepidity, audacity, or defiance. Or it could be I was simply stupid. How else can I explain carefully crafting a life upon longed-for goals and ideals, then dismantling it just as methodically as it was constructed? Somehow I'd made an impression on that man and, although I didn't even know his name, the Butte Falls District Ranger's ideas of proper forestry had made an impression on me.

Life in the Montana of my middle years proved to be everything I'd dreamed of—one long adventure. My work was satisfying. Surrounding our valley were vast tracts of wildlands encompassing more places of incredible beauty than I was likely to visit throughout a lifetime. Wildlife was abundant, their species varied: elk, moose, whitetail deer and mule deer, bighorn sheep, mountain goats, black bear and grizzly bear, mountain lion, wolverine. Some people even said these northern mountains harbored woodland caribou and the timber wolf. I didn't believe them. But they turned out to be half right.

Word crept out. I had no deliberate intention of tilting with windmills, but word seeped out about my sympathy for conservation. My employer was not of the Scrooge school, however, and some of my superiors even chortled about having their own in-house treehugger.

Still, though naive about my drift in the beginning, I'd begun a one-way slide. The slide was of my making, of course, brought about by my own growing convictions that one generation should not preempt resource decisions for future generations.

My wife had a difficult time with my growing environmental activism, though, especially when she learned I was the only salaried staff member in all the company who did not receive a pay increase.

✺

Bill Krejci was at loose ends. The man's family had recently come unglued and he was searching for new direction. He was an unusually fine welder and master mechanic, employed by the same outfit for which I worked. He was also an excellent horse trainer and a fair to middling horseshoer. But the damned fool decided, at age thirty-two, that he would become a famous saddlebronc rider.

Bill was a friend of John Bullock, and one day I happened to be sitting in the old cowboy's shop when Bill dropped by. Just a couple of weeks before, I'd watched him ride to a three-second disaster at our local hometown rodeo.

"What happened at Columbia Falls, Bill? You didn't ride long."

He laughed. "Caught a knee coming out of the chute. Never did get my balance after that."

"And how did you do up at Eureka last weekend?"

This time the smile was tight. "That one might take some explaining. For some reason, I never got settled into the saddle right."

"How long did you ride?"

"I think I'll take 'the Fifth' on that one."

John listened to our give-and-take in silence, patiently braiding a set of bridle reins from several strands of split rawhide.

Bill turned to the old bronc stomper and began asking

questions. The old man nodded in most of the right places and grunted in others. Finally Bill said, "Darn it, John. I'm here trying to pick your brain. I want you to tell me how to ride saddlebroncs."

The old man never looked up from his work. A burned-out, handrolled cigarette stub hung from the corner of his toothless mouth and a salt-and-pepper three-day stubble covered his jaw.

"The only thing I'm gonna tell you," he said, "is don't!"

<hr>

Sometimes a person wants something so badly nothing will deter him from his goal. He'll endure insult or injury, accept torment or torture, trial or terror. Nothing can break his spirit or dim the desire. After all, what Christian would've bemoaned being cast to the lions if his lifelong dream was to see a lion?

My dream was to hunt elk in the Bob Marshall Wilderness. By early October of 1968 I was ready. And by any stretch, that journey was an unmitigated disaster.

It began with the loss of my sleeping bag from the trailer on our way to the trailhead.

("Hell no, I don't want to return home for another sleeping bag. That would mean delaying this trip for a whole day and I'm not delaying it for even one minute.")

Our trail was blocked by a single snowdrift across a perilous switchback, directly above a precipitous cliff. We encountered the drift after climbing eight miles to the spine of a narrow ridge. The view from the snowdrift was spectacular, clear down into our destination valley.

("Hell no, I'm not going back. We're going through this snowdrift if we have to chop through it with an axe and scoop it out with a serving spoon.")

It was in the small hours of the morning when our little cavalcade finally shuffled into our campsite. Stars were out by the millions and it was bitterly cold. Five minutes after the horses were loosed to graze, Bill was snoring peacefully in his down-filled sleeping bag. Meanwhile I tossed fitfully under a pile of smelly horsepads and canvas manty tarps.

Elk hunting was lousy—the result of gilded, sunshiny days and crisp, frost-filled nights. My partner took his hunting casually, sometimes sleeping until the raucous cries of whisky-jacks flitting from sunbeam to sunbeam became too annoying to ignore. Other times he returned to camp in early afternoon to read one of the several paperback books he carried in his duffel. Once I chanced into him dozing in a meadow, head propped against the bole of a jackpine, hatbrim pulled over his eyes.

I was more serious: out of my boar's nest of canvas and horse pads long before sunup, preparing breakfast by fire-light, trotting at a fast lope all day across ridgetops and through valley bottoms, pushing through spruce thickets and doghair lodgepole, creeping along cliff ledges, search-ing for the illusive wapiti, until night swallowed the last vestiges of day.

So where's the justice in Bill finding the elk of his dreams, while day after day I came up blank?

After he took his trophy bull, my partner was ready to go home. By then the sheer injustice of this entire adventure

The packstring winding up a hill, sans one sleeping bag.

weighed on me—that and the fitful sleep that had been mine for a week. The next morning Bill trotted out to bring in our loose-grazing ponies while I broke camp. It was but a few minutes before I heard bells jangling and the animals galloped into camp. I managed to catch and halter four before the rest sped away. (We had bells on four. Guess which four I caught?)

We saddled a couple of ponies, and I joined Bill in his search for what had suddenly become wilderness-wise, un-belled horses. It was three in the afternoon before my partner finally located the delinquent band in a tiny off-trail meadow, three miles from camp.

("Hell no, we're not going to spend another night in this godforsaken place. We made up our mind to leave today and leave today is what we're going to do!")

It was past four in the afternoon when we *began* our long packtrip home. The homeward journey continued our trip from hell.

The odyssey began during the blistering heat of midafternoon, when there was no need for a coat. But knowing night was certain to fall while we were on the trail, I tucked mine under a lash rope on my first pack-horse.

Having been weaned of snowdrifts on the high trail, we opted for a different, mud-infested route. Halfway through the worst bog in this abominable trail, the tail packhorse—the one carrying the heaviest load—turned upside down.

("Hell yes, we must wade out in that mud to our knees and pull the pony's packs so he can get to his feet. And hell yes, we must carry those elk quarters out of that mud to solid ground where we can repack the nag.")

It was black-dark when we finished. Wet to the knees from mud, and to the skin from sweat, I went for my coat. "Bill, what did you do with my coat?"

"Huh?"

"I thought I tied my coat right here," I called. The beam from Bill's flashlight shot up and down the packs on our string. No coat.

"Want to go back looking for it?" he asked.

("Hell yes, I want to go back—if it's only a hundred yards. But it might have been jerked from the pack ten miles back. No way. Stupid—just plain stupid. I deserve what I get. Face it, Roland, you are dumber than a box of rocks. But never mind talking to yourself, you got no choice except to tough it out. With crime, there's punishment. No sleeping bag. No coat. Will I ever again be warm?")

I stomped back to my saddlehorse and swung aboard amid pitch blackness.

For a time, I rode with my hand raised in front of my face to ward off unseen branches. I tried riding with my eyes closed, but that works about as well as trying not to grow pimples.

Bill shouted over the backs of the packstring to tell me our flashlight quit. A tear trickled out.

("What else can go wrong? Up since long before daylight. Now it's two hours after dark and we're still many hours from the truck—*days* maybe, the way things are going! Renegade, runaway horses. Little sleep and no bed for a week. Cold? God, yes. No flashlight. Horse down in a bog. If I had two oars, one would be a ping-pong paddle.")

"What are you mumbling about?" Bill called. He began whistling. Naturally, it was off-key.

A full moon rose above the mountains and it really turned cold. At least we could watch our packs through each patch of moonlight filtering through the trees. We could also see onrushing branches bent on taking out an eye.

Finally we reached a better trail and, with enough moonlight, I could swing from the saddle and lead the string on foot, once more getting my blood pumping. We reached the Forest Service Guard Station an hour before midnight and discussed camping there. But unpacking and setting up camp after dark never really appealed to either of us, especially since we'd have to repack everything the next day. And when I thought of another night under manty tarps and horse blankets I clucked at my saddle-

horse and pointed him down the trail toward road's end.

We reached our truck at three-thirty in the morning. I hurried to pull packs and saddles and throw them in the trailer. Soon we'd be driving down the road and I'd finally get warm. Bill lashed the trailer gear down. I climbed into the old cornbinder truck, twisted the key, and pushed down on the foot-pedal starter. The truck groaned—its engine so cold it wouldn't turn over.

("Hell yes, we'll wait until daylight and try to catch someone driving by to give us a tow. You got any brighter ideas?")

Bill clambered into the cab, pulled up the collar of his nice, thick, wool coat and snuggled into a corner. In just seconds, he was snoring.

A logger friend chanced to drive into the campground just after daylight. He gave a pull to start our truck, and a half-hour later we were loaded and headed out.

"God, I'm glad to have this trip behind us," I muttered while double-clutching to a lower gear. An hour later, the inside dual on the right rear blew.

"Arghhh!" we both cried.

It was one-thirty in the afternoon before our crippled

None of my elk had antlers.

outfit limped into my yard—*the day after we'd begun the journey.* Jane, who was not expecting us at midday, ran to meet us. "What are you boys doing home so early?"

I leaned across the steering wheel glaring at her while Bill swung down from the passenger side.

"What's wrong, dear?"

I shook my head.

"Hey! Where's my rifle?" Bill called from behind. "I tied it right here on top of this load." ■

Chapter 8

Role Model for John Wayne

To a lot of people familiar with horseback travel in the northern Rockies, I suppose I appeared to be a quick study. They might have thought differently if they'd watched me coping with the packstring wrecks, runaway horses, dog-tiring days, and short sleepless nights. Still, I learned. I learned to pause when my little string met another on a mountain trail, to hook a leg around the saddlehorn, and pass pleasantries with craggy-faced old-timers who had probably hung in their diapers from a sawbuck packsaddle.

For their part, those long-jawed, stubble-faced men—and a few women—seemed to regard anyone who could win, place, or show on a remote Bob Marshall Wilderness mountainside as their equal. And none snickered, at least in my presence, at the busted packsaddle harness I may have lashed together with binder twine two switchbacks before.

Gradually I *did* learn. I learned to balance packs and lash them high and snug to my Decker packsaddle rings. I learned to watch for hot spots on my horses' backs and for wear spots from tight breeching and cinch and breast collar. My ponies learned, too, and gradually there came mutual trust and respect. Eventually, we even evolved into a respectable *team*.

To my discredit, I learned what my horses could *not* do before learning what they could do. I learned some were more agile and sure-footed than others, some could pack heavier loads, some were more prone to excitement when they stepped into a yellowjacket nest. And I learned not to expect as much distance in as short a time when tiptoeing tough trails or climbing tall mountains.

I learned not to expect to use horses to reach some places I wished to go. Instead I learned to ascend or descend via shanks' mare. But I learned, too, of tiny basins and pockets elk used. And I learned of hard-to-reach fishing holes not well known by others.

First, I earned respect from friends, then from acquaintances, and eventually even gained name recognition from strangers.

So hungry was I to unlock the secrets of the largest undeveloped section of northern Rockies wild country that deliberate excursions into new regions became commonplace. Unfortunately, Jane demonstrated no apparent interest in again exploring with me. But, on the other hand, without her encumbrance, I was able to set my discovery goals higher and higher:

Eighty-eight trail miles in four days.

One hundred and eight in five.

Sixty-three in four.

One hundred and twenty-three in a week.

Jane not only showed no further interest in joining my wilderness odysseys, she started denigrating my lust for adventure to her friends. At first I ignored the barbs.

"You really don't appreciate your wife, do you?"

"Huh? Wha …"

"You don't properly appreciate all your wife does for you, do you, Mr. Cheek?"

"Yes ma'am, I believe I do."

The plan was to make a 110-mile circuit in five days, from the Holland Lake trailhead to Big Prairie, Danaher Meadows, Murphy Flats, and Big Salmon Lake. Independence Day fell on Thursday that year, and the mill where I worked planned to close Wednesday through Sunday for much-needed maintenance.

"You can't be planning to leave us on the Fourth of July!" Jane protested.

"Five days, honey. I've not yet been to Big Prairie and The Danaher. What better time?"

"You don't appreciate your family, do you?"

"That sounds a lot like what Margaret said."

She stamped her foot. "You're not the man I married."

"God, I hope not."

"If I'd known how you were going to change, I would have …"

I waited.

Jane spun toward the house, heels clattering on the sidewalk. She wheeled back long enough to say, "You're infuriating!"

My friend Al Gardner and I loaded stock and equipment, drove the old cornbinder to the trailhead Tuesday evening, unloaded horses and tack, then slept under the truck during an entire night of driving rain. We were up and saddling at first light. The rain tapered to a drizzle. Twenty-seven miles and fourteen hours later, we tied tired horses to the hitchrack at the isolated Big Prairie Ranger Station and, wide-eyed as toddlers in a circus tent, accepted a ranger's offer of a cup of coffee.

"Boy, this may be the most remote ranger station I've ever visited," I said, stripping off my gloves.

The kitchen was spacious, with a big plank table. Windows lined two sides. Light from those windows reflected from well-scrubbed, cream-colored linoleum. The effect was to turn the room unexpectedly bright.

By way of making conversation, I said, "I expected a bigger crew at the most important work center in the Bob Marshall. Where is everybody?"

The ranger slid a heavy enamel mug my way, saying, "Part of the crew is clearing trails around Danaher. But four of 'em went out on that flight that left just before you boys got here. I guess they want to be out where they can celebrate their independence tomorrow."

Big Prairie in those days was still supplied by cargo planes flying out of Missoula or Kalispell. We had indeed heard a heavy plane take off just before we reached the station, but didn't see it for the forest. Sometimes, apparently, when they weren't loaded, the pilot would take hitchhiking forest employees who yearned for a return to the ecstasy of flush toilets.

My eye fell on a paper lying on the kitchen table. It was my hometown newspaper, the Pulitzer Prize winning *Hungry Horse News*. But I couldn't recall seeing this edition. I picked it up and dropped it in surprise! It was tomorrow's paper—July 4, 1969!

"What the hell is going on? This is one of the most isolated spots in America and tomorrow's paper is on the table."

The ranger smiled and shrugged. "Came in on the plane is all I know. Probably pushed up their print schedule because of the holiday, then just happened to hit the right connections to catch the supply plane."

I've never recovered from the shock of riding back into yesterday only to read about today in tomorrow's paper.

⚬⚬⚬⚬⚬

Our kids could hardly have been more different. The boy, Marc, was seven and his sister Cheri was 12 at the time of my grueling Independence weekend forced march into Big Prairie Ranger Station. Where Cheri was an extrovert, Marc was a quiet, introspective kid who seemed quite content to be left to his own devices.

One of my most insistent memories was how the lad would lie patiently on a Lake Blaine dock for hours, watching perch swim the shallows, jigging for them with a line equipped only with a bare hook.

When I suggested he should bait his hook, he said only, "Don't want none."

Wishing to help the boy, I took his little casting rod. "You'll never catch a fish that way," I said. "Here, let me show you." He rolled over and watched while I stuck a piece of corn on his hook. I laughed. "Careful you don't trip over that lower lip, boy."

Marc took the rod when I handed it back, stripped off the kernel of corn, rolled back to his belly without a word, and continued fishing his way. And when the shadows lengthened and our picnic ended, the little runt carried three perch to the car.

Cheri was the opposite: gregarious, always surrounded by friends. She loved sports, was a good student with an inquisitive mind, and was considered reliable by her teachers and her mother. She didn't fool me, though. The girl was, in fact, always testing the limits to her world. She had her daddy's spirit of adventure and was thus, I knew, not to be trusted.

Much to her mother's discomfort, though her daddy didn't spend a great deal of time with her, Cheri was her daddy's girl.

***

"Dad, I want to go with you on the horses."

I looked over the top of the newspaper I was reading at the twelve-year-old, then laid the day's *Missoulian* on a footstool.

"Good. I'm glad to see you take an interest in riding, Cheri. We can figure something out. Maybe a day ride up Columbia Mountain. What do you say to that?"

The girl slid the paper from the footstool and plopped down. "I don't care. But I want to go overnight, with the packhorses."

"That's different. I'm not sure your mother would want to go. She told me the last time we went on a long horseback trip that if she ever wanted to go again, she'd call me. And Marc is still pretty young, too. He may not want to go if Jane doesn't."

"It's okay if they go, Dad, but I don't care whether they do or not. I'm asking for me."

"Then let's go next weekend."

Hauling ponies to the jumping-off point into Elk Creek is a snap. Unlike most backcountry trailheads, the route is an all-weather, surfaced highway along the southern boundary of Glacier National Park. It was a couple hours after daylight when I backed the old cornbinder truck to the unloading chute.

I'd just purchased a young, seemingly gentle, grossly fat palomino mare, and this was to be her trial run. We grained the ponies while brushing and saddling them. Then I slung the two light packs on our packhorse. I had trouble getting my saddle in place on the fat mare—sort of like trying to settle a derby on a bowling ball. That was the day I learned excess fat is no more appropriate on a hard-working trail horse than it is on a competitive athlete.

Blondie was so fat there was only dimple where her backbone should have been. My friend John Bullock took one look at her and mused, "A man fill up that backbone crease with water, he could take a bath in it."

My saddle is a single-rig, slick-forked Visalia purchased for $35 second hand. It's a western saddle, made for raw-boned western horses and hard-riding western men. What it wasn't made for was perching on a horse as flat-backed as a landing barge. Finally I gave up trying to position the narrow-gusset Visalia atop the oil tanker with legs and decided the only logical way to keep it in place was to cinch it as tight as I dared.

It was ten a.m. when I swung into that saddle and pointed our string at the river ford marking the trail to Elk Creek. The ford across the Flathead's Middle Fork is a bad one under the best of conditions and downright dangerous during high water. It was mid-August of a dry year, however, and my most pressing concern was how well the new horse would work, particularly on what might well be her first major water crossing.

The mare waded right in to her knees and paused to drink. I twisted in the saddle to study how my twelve-year-old daughter was doing. The fast river ran so loudly here that I didn't try words of encouragement, contenting myself with a cheerful grin. The girl waved across the back of the packhorse.

Traffic seemed heavy on the highway, cars and trucks whizzing by on U.S. 2, heading to and from Glacier. I pitied the occupants who could in no way be as fortunate

as we riders. An auto pulled into a roadside turnout overlooking the river. Its doors flew open and kids spilled out to run and play. One child pointed our way as Blondie lifted her head and started for midriver and all the urchins crowded the retaining wall to watch. Another car pulled into the parking area and its driver leaped out with a video camera.

I sat up a little straighter and tugged my hat brim into a jaunty angle. Then I noticed something going amiss; my saddle was shifting to the left with Blondie's every stride!

I suppose it had to do with the horse's muscle action working on a saddle improperly constructed to fit her obese back. Whatever the reason, that confounded saddle was marching to spill me into the water as steadily as our little packstring plodded toward midriver.

The time-honored procedure for shifting a saddle upright is to rein your pony to a halt, clamber down, and readjust it. But with a river current running belly-high on the ponies, that wasn't an option. My next-best choice was to bounce all my weight in the opposite-side stirrup—not exactly as dignified as John Wayne in *True Grit*, but under the circumstances what else could I do?

I bounced. It didn't help. I bounced again. Still it didn't help. Apparently the cinch was too tight to allow me to jerk the saddle upright, but not too tight to allow the animal's muscle action to work it farther to the side.

Another tourist vehicle pulled over. And another. Another video camera joined the first. We were at midriver now, with my dignity and saddle both slipping fast. The left-side stirrup trailed in the swirling current. With no other choice, I kicked free from the stirrups and clambered atop the horse even as my saddle continued to

In later years, Blondie became a mainstay horse in our "dude" string.

twist inexorably beneath. *Hell*, I thought, *I'll be pitched into the river!*

What's that? Cheri? Is that damned girl laughing?

More tourists, attracted to whatever attracted the first, pulled into the parking area. And it seemed every damned one of 'em carried binoculars, camcorders, or point-and-shoot cameras. They were lined up gawking my way like crowds at a Roman Triumph.

If this was a triumph, I'd hate to participate in a disaster. The left-side stirrup was completely submerged now, and the saddlebags on that side hung straight down, only inches from the water. My only choices were to *get off* or *fall off*. But wouldn't Rooster Cogburn rather ride to ignominy than make a fool of himself by dismounting in waist-deep water?

As my discomfort mounted, so did Cheri's peals of laughter.

I don't know what the tourists saw, or what they thought. Neither do I know what their cameras recorded. I only know I tried to sit stoically atop that wading horse while the saddle slid inexorably around the mare's barrel.

The saddlehorn was cocked at a ninety-degree angle to Blondie's back while my legs dangled free and the face of a would-be mountain man flamed scarlet. Thank God, though, for small favors—the pony waded into the shallows, then onto the shore. Just as she did, gravity conquered all and the saddle flipped beneath the mare. I was dashed unceremoniously to the rocks.

I bounced up to give my cheering observers a one-finger salute, then whirled to confront my daughter. She sat her horse, completely absorbed by the manicure of her nails.

By the time I had the saddle back in place, I'd begun to chuckle, too. ∎

Chapter 9

Grasshoppers And Vampires

Perhaps it's carved in stone somewhere that when a man finally finds a parade going his way his zipper is stuck and he's got to pee. When he thinks the worst of his problems are finally behind, others pop up in front. So it was when Jane and I inexplicably began drifting apart.

Each of us naturally laid blame at the other's feet. Jane thought, just when our debts were paid and things were coming up roses, that I'd changed the unwritten ground rules of our marriage. She seemed to revel in the prestige of my being appointed to committees by the governor of the entire damned Treasure State. And just as my star was rising within a growing, forward-looking company, she bitterly sensed that I cared little for money, authority, or prestige.

For my part, I suspected the woman I married placed an unwholesome value on unnatural things. Diverging interests led to argument.

Perception, of course, may differ a great deal from reality. In truth, we loved each other deeply. But just as surely as the world spins, burrs started working under both of our blankets. Soon the burrs began to fester, and then came the inevitable slights and psychological hurts humans sometimes inflict upon those they most love. Along the way, she cultivated a sharpened tongue and I discovered a latent talent for tavern shuffleboard. In our domestic struggle, it's probable we involved innocents—our children.

Competition between parents for their children's affection may simply be a universal problem of parenthood, I don't know. In our case, the use of children against spouse may not have been intentional—at least I hope not.

⚜

I missed gears, tried again. This time the ancient stock truck lurched ahead. I glanced at the boy and his cocker spaniel. Both were curled asleep beside me. I wondered about the lad. Does his mother coddle him too much? Will he ever amount to anything? I glanced at a Glacier National Park traffic sign:

SPEED LIMIT 35 -
WATCH OUT FOR ANIMALS ON ROADWAY

I grinned. At the speed this old cornbinder of a truck is capable of, would we be ticketed for moving too slow? Few other vehicles were out at sunup on this early August morning. I yawned, stretched, and leaned over to peer out the passenger-side window as the ton-and-a-half International crawled up the winding road. Several mountain goats dotted a natural mineral lick on the hillside far below.

Should I wake the kid and show him the goats? No, let him sleep, there would be more. He stirred when I braked for a corner, and the dog stirred too, snuggling closer. Still dreaming, the boy laid an arm across his inseparable companion.

We were on our way to a little brook that cascades from a series of forested, glacier-carved basins. The brook meanders through meadows filled with stirrup-deep wheatgrass, then empties into the main river four or five miles upstream from where the highway exits Glacier and elbows hard against the Middle Fork of the Flathead River.

Besides its driver, the boy, and his dog, the truck carried three of the most reliable horses from the herd I was building for a new venture. The truck also hauled saddles, camp gear, and enough groceries to see our little party through our journey.

This was the eight-year-old's first overnight horseback adventure. His object was to hook some of the pan-sized cutthroat trout that overpopulated our target stream. My object was to begin making a man out of the boy.

The idea for this father/son adventure began with a similar journey I'd taken with the boy's sister the previous year. Its real purpose was rooted in a power struggle with his mother over the boy's fate. Though I knew all the right words to prod a balky mule along a perilous switchback trail, I couldn't seem to find words to trigger his mother into releasing the kid from his debilitating childhood to enter a man's world. Lord knows, if I let her have her way, she'd baby him clear up until he was nine. Or maybe even ten.

Marc danced excitedly about after the announcement of the pending journey. He sobered a little when he discovered Mom wasn't going, dubious perhaps about undertaking a *man's* adventure. But when I told him to chase out in the horse pasture and corral a bunch of grasshoppers for fishbait, the lad and his dog galloped off.

Kids at eight ordinarily have trouble catching up to a grasshopper, and cheerleading dogs seldom contribute any real help. Marc appeared to have all the usual problems, scampering around, jumping at the hoppers and coming up looking disgusted. But when he came in around dark and I asked if he had enough for bait, he nodded.

Had he put them in a safe container?

He nodded again.

Had he poked air holes in the lid so the hoppers wouldn't smother?

He trotted back out to do it.

The boy's mother sent us out with her usual rib-sticking breakfast. It was just as the skyline struggled to free itself from the shadowy grasp of darkness. Jane chewed her nails as she thought about her baby taking his first faltering steps toward manhood, but she bore up with little more than a hug to mollify her fears.

Her baby was sleepy. Maybe an eight-year-old can't slip as easily into the four a.m. habit an outdoorsman considers essential to maximize enjoyment of wilderness adventure. He climbed into the truck cab while I loaded horses, saddles and packs. His eyelids had already begun to droop when I asked about his fishbait. So he clambered from the truck, disappearing into the early-morning gloom. When he reappeared, he packed a dilapidated, round, two-pound oatmeal box that had five or six knife slits in its ragged cardboard top.

"Marc!" I said. "You can't carry grasshoppers on a tough packtrip in an oatmeal box!"

He yawned. "Why?"

"Why? Because every time you take the lid off to get one, the others will jump out. Then you'll go chasing half a dozen and the one you got in your hand will sneak off. And even if you catch some of the ones that get loose, you'll let more out when you try to put them back. Besides that, boy, the box is too flimsy to stand up to the battering it'd take on a mountain packtrip. And double besides, how do you expect me to pack a round, two-pound cardboard oatmeal box on a horse?"

It was getting on toward daylight and I saw tears welling in eyes that would make an executioner weep. He shifted self-consciously from one foot to another, holding that oatmeal box like a starving waif clutching a loaf of bread. He looked defeated—like he'd failed his first test of manhood.

The dog cowered behind the boy's feet, lip curled and growling up at me. To add to Marc's misery, the boy's mother peeked out the kitchen window.

I sighed, then reached down, took the box, and gently pushed Marc toward the truck. Then I picked up some bailing twine and lashed the box's flimsy top in place while the boy and his dog boarded the truck like prisoners bound for Devil's Island.

We unloaded the truck and saddled our horses at the

trailhead around seven a.m. The ride into Elk Creek was leisurely. I had considerable trouble with that blankety-blank oatmeal box, but we still arrived at our destination well before noon.

I sent Marc out to gather firewood while I unpacked and unsaddled the ponies, then turned them out to graze. The boy's mind was more on fishing than on a decent wood supply, and I had to call him back from the creek twice. Finally, while fastening the hobbles to the last horse, I took pity on the little tyke and told him to fetch his fishpole.

The lad bounced in excitement as I finished tying fishhook to leader. When I asked about his bait, he brought the oatmeal box on the run. With father/son rapport building amid pleasing surroundings and no interference, I once more explained that a two-pound oatmeal box was hardly the thing to carry grasshoppers on a long fishing trip. "A big oatmeal box like this can sure hold a lot of grasshoppers, but it's just not husky enough to stand up to the knocking around it's bound to get on a big packtrip."

His head bobbed again and again at his father's sage advice. Even the dog paid rapt attention, head cocked to one side, tongue lolling from an open-mouthed grin.

"Now a can," I continued, "with a secure lid is better, or even a jar." I untied the cord and gently raised the boxtop, ready to grab at a horde of grasshoppers swarming at the opening in a frenzy to escape.

I raised the lid a bit more. Then more. Finally I could peer inside the big box at six (I counted them) grasshoppers lounging comfortably on the bottom. I slapped the lid shut and bellowed, "Marc!"

The boy's mouth dropped open like a beached flounder's and his dog slunk behind a nearby log.

"How many grasshoppers did you put in this box yesterday?"

"Six," he replied, staring up in anxious wonder.

"Six! Marc, you can't catch a mess of fish with only six lousy grasshoppers!" Tears welled, but I pretended not to notice. "What in the world do you figure to use for bait after these six puny, measly few grasshoppers are gone?"

He mumbled, "I don't know." The tears spilled over and trickled down his bewildered face, but he never took his eyes from mine. I was the one who finally broke contact, shaking my head.

I raised the box-top and shook a grasshopper into my hand. Marc watched in silence while I baited his hook. At last I handed him the pole, patted him on the shoulder, and told him to catch us some supper. As he ran off to the creek, I wearily turned to the nearby meadow to look for more grasshoppers. The dog soon tired of water sports and came to help.

<hr>

"Star light, star bright, first star I see tonight. I wish I may, wish I might, have the wish I wish tonight."

A cheery fire crackled between us. Our horses had been grained and staked out to deep grass. We'd eaten a supper of my specialty: wild trout so tasty that Betty Crocker would be green with envy.

The boy picked around the burned edges and only mentioned twice that his mother would have cooked the fish differently. Finally the dishes were washed and put away, and I relaxed atop my sleeping bag with hands clasped behind my head. The light dimmed in the west and the first star poked out in a darkening sky.

"Boy, isn't this the life, Marc?"

The lad was noncommittal, content to crouch by the fire and pet his dog. I had to prod him into rolling out his sleeping bag. After doing so, he looked about at the inky night and dragged the bag over next to mine.

I chuckled. Where he planned to sleep was on rough, uneven ground—I'm not sure if he got the connection when I told him it'd be like trying to sleep on top of a woodpile. So I showed him another spot that was an excellent choice—level ground, deep grass, no stones.

The little guy pulled his bag over where I pointed, but he looked like he was being sent to reform school. He spent a long time smoothing that bag by the dancing firelight. And as we crawled into our bedrolls, he looked

longingly at that magnetic spot near my bag.

The fire flickered low. My eyelids had just begun to droop when a small voice piped into the night: "Dad, what about bears?"

I chuckled. "Don't worry, Marc. Bears are more scared

Tom Saubert's rendition of Marc's first packtrip

of us than we are of them. Besides, I can handle any old bear that dares show his head around here."

The fire burned down to coals. Marc had been still and silent so long I supposed he was asleep. The stars were out by the millions now, the crisp way they can only be in the northern Rockies. The Big Dipper, the North Star, the Milky Way. As I searched for the Little Dipper, a bat fluttered past overhead.

"What's that?" Marc blurted.

"It's just a bat, Marc."

My eyes grew heavier and heavier. Then Marc said from somewhere deep inside his sleeping bag, "Is that the kind that sucks your blood?"

"No! Dang it, Marc, knock it off and go to sleep."

Some time passed, and then came a tiny voice from the darkness, "Dad, my eyes won't go shut."

What do you do with a child on his first journey into the wilderness unknown? One who's afraid of unseen monsters? One who wouldn't mind at all having a mother around to baby him?

I did what you'd do—what any father worth his salt would do. I got up, rebuilt the fire, and invited my son to drag his bag over next to mine.

Even the dog seemed to like the new arrangement better. ■

Chapter 10

Hemmed by Limits

Gradually our differences over life's goals evolved into aloofness between Jane and me. She was wounded that the husband she had bet on when no one else saw value in him—with whom she'd struggled so hard and sacrificed so much—appeared to disdain society's accepted standards of success. I was determined not to be hemmed in by those same standards. Love and respect kept us together; stubbornness and idealism kept us apart.

It was a recipe for disaster. Had it not been for our children (who proved wiser than we were), for friends who liked us in spite of our weaknesses, and for our own obstinate belief that commitments made are commitments kept, our marriage might have crashed. For awhile we went our separate ways: Jane with women's clubs, church, and school events; I with macho friends who also harkened to the songs of the natural world.

Two such friends were neighbors. Outside of people from my work, those two neighbor families were nearly the only folks with whom Jane and I both socialized. Fortunately, Stan Ove's and Lyle Ausk's wives became Jane's friends. Each couple had children near our kids' age, and the children played together. The two families' arrival in the neighborhood may have been a factor in helping us cope with our marital relationship and some of life's other hurdles.

The year was 1970. Lyle had never before visited the Bob Marshall Wilderness. He made his first trip in as a charter member of the "Montana Short-Name Society," three neighbors living in a rural area south of Columbia Falls. I'm not sure who dubbed the Cheek-Ausk-Ove team the "Short-Name Society," but it stuck.

Stan and I invited Lyle to join us during a Labor Day weekend while we packed into a remote section of the wilderness and set up a hunting camp. Disliking the steep, grueling trail we'd used to reach the region the year before, Stan and I decided on another route. It proved to be a poor choice.

Lyle, with no horses of his own at the time, borrowed an overage, over-fat, over-lazy animal that wasn't exactly a bargain, even though he cost nothing. We'd traveled but a couple of miles when Stan observed, "A stick of dynamite under his tail might make him move." We paused for lunch thirteen trail miles in. Lyle asked, "How much farther?"

Neither Stan nor I knew. We'd not been into camp via this particular trail and could only estimate. The "halfway"

Perhaps more cheerful times would come.

we told Lyle seemed to discourage him. We ate swiftly, then hurried on.

The Forest Service trail turned muddy and rocky, and we frequently had to stop our string and scout out a path around windthrown trees. Sometimes we were forced to use an axe or crosscut saw to make our way through the forest. It was slow, heavy work and our energy was being drained away through the tool handles.

When we first sighted the distant cliffs, Lyle said, "It can't be far now."

Stan caught my eye. At last we'd reached familiar country. But neither of us had the heart to tell Lyle the route we had yet to follow snaked up and over those cliffs, following a little-used game trail.

An hour later our little cavalcade broke out into a tiny meadow below the cliffs. A waterfall cascaded down from above. It was indeed a sylvan setting. Lyle craned his neck, searching for our campsite. Stan and I rode right on through the opening, heading for the cliff. Lyle called for us to wait.

When he and his horse, Old Red, joined us, he asked, "Where are you going?"

I pointed at the cliff with my chin.

"You're joking!"

Stan shook his head.

"Is there a way?"

"We found one last year."

Lyle sighed. "I don't know if this horse can make it."

My only reply was to cluck at my saddle pony and ride away, pulling two packhorses. Stan followed. Lyle had no choice but to keep us in sight.

A few minutes later we started clambering in earnest. Finally we dismounted and cut loose the packstring from one another so they could better scramble for a hundred yards up a steep sloping ledge. The trail was little more than a goat path, with the cliff face to the left, yawning chasm to the right. *Get the ponies moving and there's but one way for them to go—hope to God nothing goes wrong with their packs!* I clambered ahead to catch and hold them after they'd passed the danger spot. *Okay, start 'em up. And for God's sake, get out of their way or get trampled in the rush.*

As first one horse, then another disappeared over the ledge above, Lyle's face fell. Soon he and Old Red were the only two left below. Finally he and Red made it, joining the rest of the party where the windswept ledge widened. "How much farther?" he croaked, leaning over with hands on knees, gasping.

We had but two miles left before reaching our campsite. There was another half-mile climb ahead of us, but from here on it was a shoo-in. For some perverse reason I merely grunted, "I hope we make it before dark."

When I glanced back, Lyle was telling Stan he wasn't sure his old horse could make it.

Our campsite was at the point where a tiny stream of toothchilling spring water sank into the ground amid the rocks of a dry streambed. The stream came out of a cliff only a few feet above the camp and, to all appearances, the broad ledge where we headed was devoid of decent water.

The next time we stopped to blow our ponies, I turned to Stan and glumly said, "I hope there's water in that creekbed at camp."

My friend was startled. "Why wouldn't there be?"

I winked. "Well, it's been an awful dry year...."

Stan's white teeth flashed. "Yeah. We've never been here in a really dry year."

"What happens if there's no water?" Lyle said, taking the bait.

I shrugged and Stan clucked at his saddlehorse.

As we topped the low ridge that put us on the broad ledge we sought, I reined my pony in and pointed at a muddy pool of water below. The pool had been there each year since I had first hiked this bench some years before, and it was always muddy. But I made a stage performance out of my announcement: "My God, Stan! That pond's never been muddy before."

He muttered loudly enough for Lyle to hear, "Don't look good for us, does it?"

Lyle stared at the pool, stricken. "What do we do if we

can't find water?"

Stan and I shrugged.

For their part, our horses were eager to get on to camp. They were on their home turf now, where feed was plentiful and they were free to roam. Lyle knew none of this, of course. Nor did his horse. And it was clear that Old Red was, indeed, badly jaded.

We rode into a slight depression where tiny trickles of clear water had run during previous years. But as luck had it, the trickles really *had* dried up during this driest of summers. Stan and I made the most of the dead rivulets until our crestfallen companion must have thought real gullywashers flowed there during normal times.

We ignored his plaintive queries about what would we do if our camp was dry. He said he was thirsty and his horse tuckered. Stan and I were thirsty, too. But we knew something he didn't: that the coldest, purest water in all the world was just three hundred yards ahead. So I made a production out of letting my shoulders slump.

Stan shouted ahead, "I'll bet the camp is dry."

I shouted back, "What'll we do?"

Lyle echoed the refrain.

I squared around in the saddle just as my lead horse clattered into the dry creek bed near camp. Just before I came into sight of the first deep clear pool, I reigned in Old Yeller and turned to my partners with a stricken look. "My God, Stan, there really is no water!"

Lyle stared in horror at that barren, rocky streambed. My horses blocked both Lyle and Stan from a view of the sparkling pools ahead. Stan's voice was soft. "What will we do, Roland?"

"My horse can't go any farther," Lyle blurted.

"We can't stay here," Stan said.

I stared up at a distant pass. "Let's get ahold of ourselves, fellows. We know we can't stay here. We've *got* to go on."

Stan murmured, "I don't want to face it, but you're right."

Lyle looked wildly at first one, then the other. Then an inner strength took over just as evening shadows stole across the wild land. "How far is it to water, Roland?" he asked in a subdued tone.

"About four or five miles."

"Which way?"

I pointed to the pass. "We'll have to climb up through that notch. Then it's two, three miles down the other side."

Lyle studied the pass for several seconds. Then he reached forward and patted his old sorrel horse on the neck. His voice sounded like that of a man being led to the hangman's noose: "I don't believe Old Red can make it, and I'm not sure about me, either. But we'll try."

I spun forward in the saddle and reined Old Yeller toward the pass. "Giddyap."

Our string went about ten feet before splashing into the clear, fast-flowing little stream. As our horses bent to drink, a voice rose from behind:

"I think I've been had …" ∎

Chapter 11

Heroes Are Made, not Born

J ohn, what was the toughest bronc you ever rode?"

The old cowboy braided a rawhide hackamore, working the moistened cowhide strips with a deftness that belied his stove-up fingers. "Cannonball," he said without hesitation.

John Bullock had converted an old chickenhouse into a leather shop. He'd shoveled out six inches of dried chicken manure and nailed planking over the dirt floor. Then he attempted to knock most of several decades worth of accumulated dust from the rafters and rough-sawn inside walls, even hosing them down. The building squatted back in a grove of spruce and firs. The stove cooled off an hour before, and a chill seeped into the drafty room. Shadows stole toward the tiny house. Four of John's five children played king of the mountain atop a remnant snowbank.

"Where?" I asked.

"Cheyenne, in '38. She was a little mouse-gray. And could she buck!"

Minutes passed as I waited patiently for the old man to continue. Finally I prompted: "What happened?"

"Caught me coming out of the chute and knocked me off balance."

Again I asked—after minutes passed: "And?"

"I didn't make three jumps before I grabbed dirt with both hands. She bucked back o'er the top o' me."

"So, what was the result?"

"Three broke ribs and two broke arms."

The reticent cowboy's silence was again a long one. Finally he cut the stillness with, "I got so's I could ride the first time in Fort Worth, come the spring of '39."

I shifted on my stool as he murmured, "Guess what horse I drawed?"

"Cannonball?"

"Yup."

"What happened that time, John?"

"A broke leg, a broke arm, and two broke ribs."

John paused in his braiding and knotted the ends of his rawhide strands together to keep them from raveling. Darkness fell as he finished. Outside, the children—two still in diapers—shouted and laughed and darted in and out of light streaming from the windows of their home. John laid his work aside and stared at the scene.

At last I asked, "Did you ever draw Cannonball again?"

He sighed. "Nope. And I wouldn't have rode her iff'n I had."

Sweat dripped from the big, mud-splattered buckskin horse standing spraddle-legged in the center of the pole corral. The animal's nostrils pulsated as he gasped for air. The sweat ran in tiny trickles from beneath an equally mud-splattered saddle hanging from one side of the heaving creature. At last the horse moved, turning to stare wild-eyed at the man lying in a crumpled heap thirty feet away.

Horses are vital to any northern Rockies horseback guide operation; especially vital where the land's still the way God made it. Men and women working that kind of country are at least as dependent upon quality horseflesh as any old-time cowboy, and much more so than the modern variety.

And by the spring of 1970, I had the beginning of a secret dream I'd thus far shared with no one....

Early cowboys, so I'm told, loved a horse that would buck, turn on a dime, and run cat-footed over cobblestones. If so, I find little to qualify that same cowboy's horse as the perfect steed for traversing sometimes perilous mountainside trails.

Outfitters working the mountain country I roam look for strong animals with heavy legs for scrambling over fallen lodgepole and through alder brush. They should be tall enough to keep your saddlebags from ploughing water during stream crossings and have enough heft to carry a fat rider all day. A mountain horse should also travel swiftly at a walk, scramble well instead of win horse races, and have a temperament that won't blow up if a horsefly takes a nip out of his hinder.

In short, the way a person *wins* during mountain wilderness adventure is by returning home to tell about it.

Buck was six years old when I bought him and his five-year-old half-brother Joker. Both animals were sired by a registered thoroughbred stallion named Smoke Jumper. Smoke Jumper was foaled at the since abandoned U.S. Forest Service Remount Station at Perma, Montana, in 1952, during the government's noble experiment in improving the quality of their horse and mule strings by mixing in top-quality bloodlines from outside. Smoke Jumper's papers show he was traded at six months of age to Roy Brock of Eureka, Montana, for "two good saddle horses."

Both Joker's and Buck's mothers were grade mares of good conformation and spirit. I bought both of the horses for two hundred dollars. That was a good buy, even in those halcyon days before inflation ran away with the country— except for one thing: neither Buck nor Joker had ever had a saddle on. I saw the two horses as turning into key components of my secret plan for more adventure.

Buck stood 15-1 hands high (61 inches at the withers) and weighed in at twelve hundred pounds. He was buck-skin-colored, of course, and had what I thought was a steady disposition. The big horse really did like people. Both he and his brother were broken to lead when I bought them, and could be caught anywhere with only a piece of twine.

I began breaking the new ponies immediately, starting them with a headstall, smooth snaffle bit, and long driving reins, working them in a corral, teaching them the rudiments of reining, "giddyap" and "whoa." During the same period, each horse was packsaddled dozens of times. After I was satisfied with their progress with the long reins, I lashed a couple of old automobile tires to their packsaddles and turned them loose to buck. Neither did much more than crowhop a couple of times.

Thinking I must be the best horse breaker south of the Yukon, I jerked off Joker's packsaddle and threw on my heavy Visalia riding saddle, cinched it, and eased up to straddle the pony.

A half-hour later I was well satisfied with Joker's progress. He walked hesitantly at first, then quickly gained balance and confidence until we'd circled the corral several times. And although he did rein a little rough, he never once offered to hump up or get spooky.

Buck, still tied to a corral post, yet wearing his packsaddle loaded with tires, followed his brother's progress with considerable interest, nickering softly if Joker wandered farther than he thought proper. A few minutes later I eased into my saddle again—this time on Buck. He stood quietly during the saddling process, interrupting it only to sniff first the pad, then the saddle, then me. And he laid his head against my hip and nuzzled as I drew up the cinch.

Buck, too, carried me around the familiar corral with no trouble. In fact, if anything, the big buckskin was much better during his first ride than was Joker, stepping out more willingly and reining easier—as if he enjoyed the activity. I wondered if anyone had ever broken out two such fine spirited ponies in such a brief time, with so little effort.

Jane came from the house to watch. "They seem to be working out," she said. "But tell me again why we need two more horses?"

I laughed. In a moment, ego overwhelmed common sense and I asked her to drop the gate bars so I could take the well-performing Buck into the pasture.

The horse balked at the gate. For the two weeks he'd dwelled here, he'd never been out of this corral. Oh, he'd stared wistfully over the gate at the lush pasture beyond, but all the food and water he could want was always present in this, *his* corral. Besides, his life-long buddy Joker was here, too. Now this damfool riding him wanted him to leave his corral comfort for the unknown. And leave Joker.

Buck took one hesitant step forward, then another. The animal's muscles were bunched between my legs like tight rubber bands holding a ball of coiled rattlesnakes. I rode as if the big pony floated over eggshells.

The pasture Buck and I headed into is small—about six acres. Directly abutting this particular pasture on the west is a piece of land owned by other folks. They kept a few horses and one donkey. The donkey was standing at the dividing fence as Buck and I rode into the pasture.

The horse tried to turn back a couple of times, but I held a tight rein and kept him moving away from the corral. I enjoyed bending the horse's will to mine. Up to that time, I hadn't any great shucks of experience breaking horses, and I enjoyed putting into practice the things I'd read and heard.

Buck settled down, so I gave him a little more rein as we headed for the back fence. The big pony spotted the jackass and stopped abruptly, rolling his eyes first at me, then at the donkey. I nudged his ribs with my boot heels and he took a faltering step, then another. Joker whinnied from the distant corral, and the donkey strained over the fence to touch noses with my hesitant horse, now merely a few feet away.

Again Buck stopped. As if on cue, the donkey extended his neck and brayed.

The rubber bands holding the rattlesnakes snapped as the big horse broke into thousands of pieces, each heading a different direction. When I came to my senses, the startled donkey darted into the forest behind, while Buck galloped back to his corral. Jane ran from the gate where she'd been watching, shading her eyes against the sinking sun.

I rolled over and pushed to my hands and knees, glaring after the donkey, muttered a couple of obscenities at the retreating horse, added another about a worried wife who wouldn't let the world's greatest horse-breaker die in peace.

I met the woman halfway to the corral, brushed off her concern and hobbled after the first double-rotted, bloody-hearted nag ever to blow away my dreams of bronc-stomping greatness.

Buck was standing by Joker as I limped into the corral. He nuzzled me and nickered softly. I jerked up his trailing bridle reins, glared at him, then swung into the saddle and jerked him toward the gate. Jane shook her head, bit a lip, and said something as we rode through. But so intent was I on getting that damned horse up to that damned back fence in damned quick time that I'll be damned if I know what it was.

The donkey was again leaning over the fence as a faltering Buck approached. This time I was ready. My feet were tucked firmly into the stirrups and I held a good tight rein. In addition, my free hand squeezed a death-lock on the saddlehorn.

That time I bounced twice when I hit the ground.

Buck again nuzzled me when I limped into the corral.

The donkey was gone when Buck and I approached the fence for the third time—perhaps because of the tree limb I had heaved at him. As a result, my pony and I finally round-tripped intact. But unknown to me, on that day a precedent was set—Buck learned to buck before I learned to ride.

I usually returned from work around five in the afternoon, poured a cup of coffee from the ever-ready pot, and sat at the kitchen table to drink while reflecting on the day. Jane sometimes joined me to discuss matters of concern. After a second cup, I'd push back my chair and tackle jobs around the house, or read a book, or write a letter. Now, with Buck, my routine changed.

I'd still drink the coffee. And I'd still talk with my wife—

usually absent-mindedly. And I'd still push from the table to put on old clothes saved for tough jobs. Then I'd walk to the corral and catch and saddle Buck.

It was great sport—for the horse.

He'd trot to my side each time I stepped into the corral carrying a halter. He'd nuzzle me fondly while I saddled him. Even in those early horsebreaking days, the big buckskin was always eager to take a bridle, reaching out with an open mouth. Soon we were ready for our day's sport.

Buck would stand calmly while I turned the stirrup and lifted my toe into it. Then, when I grasped the horn with my right hand, he'd brace himself and I'd swing into the saddle. I'd always settle myself gingerly and tuck the right toe into the off-side stirrup. I'd always cluck my tongue once and Buck would always step right out like a well-trained trail horse should. Most of the time, we'd make a full circle around that corral—sometimes two—before he came unglued.

When he set his mind to bucking, the results were inevitable: I landed in a busted heap somewhere in that corral's dust. I'd pick myself up and brush my clothes and glare balefully at that damned horse. He'd stare back with wide-eyed innocence. And if I never stomped over and grabbed his bridle reins quickly enough, he'd sidle hesitantly up to nuzzle me. That was when, in a fit of pique, I might grab my hat and slap him with it to keep the damned pony from becoming too familiar.

The funny thing about this daily charade was, after that first time with the donkey, the big buckskin never threw me but once each day. After he had his daily game of flinging me like a spitball flicked with a thumbnail, I could climb back on and ride him peacefully in or out of the corral for an hour or a day.

But he always unloaded me first. That's how I knew it was nothing more than sport for him: throwing me first, then carrying me wherever I wanted to go.

God, it got tiresome. It got so's I hated for my workday to end. I took to dawdling longer and longer over my coffee, listening attentively to everything Jane wanted to say.

Sometimes I asked leading questions about what Mrs. Haskell, or Sumner, or Brown had done or planned to do.

The family made it harder. Jane kept asking how Buck's breaking was progressing, even though she'd long since stopped watching. Cheri, blossoming now into teen-age womanhood, never, ever gave up on me, and would usually come from the house to cheer me to dismal defeat. And nine-year-old Marc seldom failed to be sitting astride a corral rail, or perched on the barn roof when I picked myself from the dust of my latest debacle.

My efforts to break Buck became a neighborhood event. One day I came home from work to find Marc and several of his young friends playing in our yard. I smiled absent-mindedly at them, went into the house and poured my coffee, then sat down and tried to engage Jane in a conversation so I wouldn't have to think about how I was losing the war in our corral. But she was busy, so I sipped coffee alone. In a few minutes, the kids were all on our back porch, peeking in the kitchen window, whispering among themselves. Then Marc cracked open the door and asked, "Are you going to ride today, Dad?"

I grunted like he'd kicked me. "Yeah, I guess so."

The door slammed and I could hear the boys whispering excitedly to each other. Then the door cracked open again. "When you going to ride today, Dad?"

I broke off eye contact first, sensing that Marc thought I was weakening. Was I to disgrace my very own son in front of all his friends? "Just as soon as I finish this coffee, Marc. And change my clothes."

The door slammed again, and even more excited whispering came from the porch. I stared into my coffee cup and cup's bottom stared back. So I shrugged, slammed down the cup, shoved back the chair until it collided with the cupboard, and stomped from the room.

Jane still pretended to be busy.

There seemed to be a kid perched on every fencepost around that corral when I finally walked out to do battle with Buck. "You charging admission?" I asked. And when my boy shook his head, I muttered, "Maybe you should."

I took extra care brushing and saddling the big pony. As a result, he must have become impatient because he fed me a mouthful of corral dirt without the usual docile turn around the corral.

Even at that, the kids must have got their money's worth because they clapped and whistled and hooted for the entire duration of the short ride. Then they turned silent as I wiped my mouth with a handkerchief and hobbled over to ride Buck.

In the parlance of the trade, the buckskin was known as a sunfisher. He would go up and twist while he was in the air, and sometimes twist again on the way down. He bucked low and mean. As soon as he hit the ground, he was twisting up and off in another direction. There was no way I could ride him. And I guess it's fair to tell you a couple of folks who supplied bucking horses to rodeos heard about him and offered good money to take Buck off my hands. By then I'd passed the point of no return—that double-rotted horse was going to bend to my will or I'd die in the process.

Because he was a sunfisher, the saddle was seldom under me when I left it, even though I might still have both feet in the stirrups. Actually, with his sideways twist, I usually hit the ground easy. One particular time, the saddle was fluttering around somewhere in the sky above and I could see I wasn't going to make it this time either. And when I shook my feet loose, rolling to hit the ground, dirt was only six inches from the end of my nose.

Finally it rained and rained—just what I was waiting for! I rushed into the house, dumped the coffee Jane had waiting for me, ignored her attempts to be polite, and jumped into some old clothes.

As I hurried to the gate with a halter in my hand, Buck stood in a far corral corner, watching with what I thought might be indignant reproach. The horse didn't resist, however, when I slipped the halter over his head and led him to my saddle. But he seemed more aloof than usual when I saddled and bridled him, disdaining to even sniff my glove or nuzzle the small of my back as I bent beneath for the cinch. Was he sensing the coming showdown? Did he think such a face-off was unfair in that muddy corral, where he had slippery footing?

I swung into the saddle, took a death grip on the horn, and started Buck around the corral. Around and around he walked. He was as peaceable as a milkwagon nag. Once, twice, three times. I reined the horse to a stop and he cocked his head to stare innocently back. I clucked at him again and he walked off as if he was a well-trained trail horse. "Damn you," I muttered, driving my heels hard into his flanks. Let the fireworks begin. I was ready.

The muddy footing worked to my advantage. Up. Down. Twist. Turn. But that ever-smart bronc could only pussyfoot in the mud. Still, though I was locked into place, the big horse was rattling my teeth with every leap. He grew more desperate. But try as he might, Buck couldn't get enough momentum to shake me loose, let alone get me to holler uncle. But the pony wasn't quitting either. Mud and water flew. My hat was gone, lost on the first couple of jumps. My head, shoulders, hands, legs, and feet were splattered with mud, but it didn't matter—I was sticking like a burr. I was riding the sonofagun!

Up and down. Up and down and around. I couldn't believe he could still be doing it! My legs and arms and back and teeth hurt. My grip loosened. Up and down and around and up and down. My fingers slid from the horn and I no longer even tried to pull his head up with reins. Up and down and around. Up and around and down. I was off to one side of the saddle now, and my head lay slightly below the level of the seat.

Then Buck stopped.

I couldn't believe that either. He stood spraddle-legged, panting, in the center of a corral whose ground looked like someone had just rototilled it. I was gasping as hard as the horse, but as I pulled myself upright in the saddle the thought struck—*I've won!* I tucked my toes farther into the stirrups and took another grip on the horn with raw and blistered fingers and I gathered wind into my lungs and let out a spine-tingling *"YIPPEEEE!"*

And somebody touched a match to the powder keg!

Buck went up and Buck went down and around and up and down and back the other way. Sweat and mud and snot and blood flew. And, at the last, so did Roland.

I slid on my nose through mud and manure for five feet.

Tom Saubert's artistic rendition of Buck breaking me in the home corral, while neighbor kids enjoy the entertainment

Then I lay crumpled in a heap, gathering my senses before rolling painfully over and sitting up.

A small voice piped from the barn roof: "Boy! You almost rode him that time, Dad!"

I raised my head to glare up at my son, then turned to look at the mud-splattered, heaving horse. Buck returned my glare with studied, wide-eyed innocence.

———※———

I didn't ride that horse for over a year after our Armageddon in the mud. There were two reasons. The first was that my innards were so shook I was unable to ride *any* horse for over two months. Hell, I could hardly *walk*. Neither could I eat for two days—which was just as well because nothing could have passed through my knotted intestines anyway. Fortunately, nothing was broken. No bones anyway.

But my pride was shattered.

The second reason I didn't ride the horse until more than a year had passed is because I was so dog-knobbed, double-rotted mad at that illegitimate cross between a rack-afrack and a dodohead that I couldn't spit straight. I'm stubborn, I know. That's the Scots blood cropping up. But God also gave me two brains to rub one against the other. And that was the day when I learned for lead-pipe certain the minute my nose commenced plowing corral mud that there was no way I could ever ride that damned horse if he didn't want me to.

As I sat there in the mud and stared resignedly back at Buck, I said across the corral, "All right, you sonofabitch, from now on you're a packhorse. And you'll carry some hellish loads—I'll guarantee that!"

Buck was a great packhorse, too, just as he's been great at any task he ever thought we wanted him to do—even bucking games in the corral. He carried the worst loads we mustered that summer and fall, and into the next summer. From clumsy wooden packboxes to heavy elk quarters picked up from the bottom of some deep-timbered canyons—he carried them all.

But along with the malice he aroused in me, there was a grudging admiration for a superhorse with a will as strong as mine. ■

Chapter 12

Into the Abyss

Jane couldn't miss the notice lying on the kitchen table, where I'd purposely left it. It was stamped **1970** in the upper left corner.

"Roland, what's this?"

I slipped out of the barn boots and shrugged off my coat. "My outfitter and guide's license."

"I beg your pardon?"

"It's a license from Montana's Fish & Game Department for me to guide hunters on horseback packtrips into the Bob Marshall Wilderness."

"But—but why would they send it to you?"

"Because I applied for it. Because I went to the Forest Service and got approval for a campsite in the Bob Marshall. Because I met all Fish & Game requirements for equipment, passed the test, and paid the fifty-dollar fee."

She sat down abruptly. "Why would you...." Then she said, "How long has this been going on?"

I laid my palms flat on the table and leaned forward. "The process began several months ago. Now I'm a licensed guide who can take hunters."

She bit her lip, but her voice was subdued: "What does this mean?" When I didn't respond immediately, her voice went up three octaves. "Roland, I want to know what this means!"

I turned my back to her. "Nothing right now. It's too late to schedule hunters for this season. Besides, I'll need another horse or two. But it means next year I'll guide hunters on my vacation." I spun to eye her. "This is part of a plan, Jane. It's a way to make our investment in horses and camping equipment pay for itself."

"*Your* investment!"

"Right. My investment. But the point is I now have a license. And a place to camp. There's rumor the Forest Service is going to put a cap on the number of outfitters permitted to guide in the wilderness. By acting now I've made the cut."

"So you'll quit your job at Plum Creek, just like you left your job at …"

"No, dammit. I'm not quitting my job. Can't you hear, woman? I said I was going to guide on my vacation. It's a part-time job. That's all."

She shook her head as if to clear it. "We used to discuss these things together."

I sighed and pulled out a chair across the table from the woman I loved. "Jane, that was before we began arguing about everything; before we fought over every damned niggly little thing one or the other wanted to do. That sort of takes away my will to talk about even the big things."

That triggered her to fight back the only way she knew: "You don't care about us, do you?"

I focused on a spot beyond her head. "Yes, I do. But I'm not at all enamored with the way our marriage is going. You claim I've changed from the man you married, and I believe you're trying to turn me into something I've never been and never will be. Who's right? I don't know. But," I pushed back my chair and headed for the door, "the question, Jane, isn't so much where we've been, as where we're going. Maybe we'd both best think on that one."

The decision to seek the license and permits necessary to lead wilderness packtrips was not a mere whim, though it may have appeared so to my wife. In fact, the seed had been planted as much as seven years before, when an Oregon hunting buddy learned we planned to move to Montana and suggested I should someday consider guiding others to fishing and hunting adventure. Though I'd dismissed Mark's idea as poppycock at the time, the seed gradually germinated and took root under my ever-burgeoning lust for the outdoors.

Though the time still wasn't ripe as far as my job and young family were concerned, when word of the Forest Service's proposed cap on outfitter permits trickled in on the wind, I decided I must act. Had I waited, the chance of ever raising the necessary capital to buy out an existing permittee would be slim.

And in truth, had I not acted when I did, our lives would've certainly turned out very differently.

As it was, the license and permits provided nothing more than an opportunity to develop a guiding business. Success, as always, rested entirely upon the shoulders of the entrepreneur. We were not only under financed but woefully weak in business acumen. And considering that the partnership I named the Skyline Outfit included the handicap of one less-than-enthusiastic participant, few business start-ups appeared so ill-fated. Outsiders failed to take us seriously. Very few expected the business to succeed, and none thought it would flourish.

Call it the hand of providence, or consider it shrewd management or blind staggering luck, but I made two decisions that first year that played prominent roles in future success: we mortgaged our home in order to buy eighty acres of pastureland for the additional horses we needed, and I truly did intend to pursue guiding only as a source of supplemental income.

Even with my regular Plum Creek paychecks, we struggled. The major reason was my infantile idea that all I had to do was hang out a shingle as a guide and the world would beat a path to our door. That concept looked all the more ludicrous when hunting season 1971 rolled around and we had but *one* paying guest—and that man able to hunt but four days. But by great good fortune my single client, Oregon lumber broker Carl Henning, included a tip generous enough to enable me to buy sufficient hay to winter the horse he rode. It was Plum Creek who supplied the paychecks I used to purchase feed for the rest of the herd.

Carl Henning also contributed another element to my getting started in a guiding career: he opened a charming door to the diverse range of people seeking the type of adventure we offered—a diversity characteristic of such folks, as I later discovered.

During the years prior to my hanging out that guide shingle, I wasn't at all sure I wanted anything to do with the rich people who could afford to pay me for my guiding expertise. I was, so I reasoned, plebian and proud of it. I had the *American* franchise where all citizens are equal, no matter their economic, managerial, or social status. My attitude might be summed up by the tale of a wealthy Englishman who ventured West by rail, rented a buckboard, and drove into the ranch yard of his Sussex uncle's New Mexico cattle spread. Spying a stove-up old cowboy limping across the yard, the Englishman jerked his buggy horse to a stop and said, "I say, my good man. Would you be kind enough to show me to your master?" The old cowboy spat a stream of tobacco juice into the dust, tilted his greasy wide-brimmed hat to the back of his head, glared up at the English pilgrim and growled, "The sonofabitch hain't been borned yet!"

My fears were groundless, however. Carl's story was fascinating. Born of Jewish parents in Germany in 1927, Carl and his family fled for their lives in 1937; the boy escaped with an aunt to China, the only country that would grant the fugitives a visa. They wound up in Shanghai only days before the Japanese marched in.

The boy used his time to study languages. When he came into our camp, Carl spoke five: German, French, English, Chinese, and Japanese. He witnessed atrocities by Japanese occupation forces, yet somehow eluded their nets.

In 1945, Carl Henning joined the United States Army as a means to escape to America. It was discovered that the new recruit spoke fluent German and he was posted to Germany as an interpreter. While there, the young man was able to trace his parents to Switzerland and they were reunited.

While in China, Carl learned Korean karate. When he came to Montana as the first guest of my Skyline Outfit, Carl Henning was a fourth-grade black belt in the five-step martial art—one of a mere handful of Occidentals to progress so high. The man demonstrated that he wasn't funning us when he picked up a two-inch-thick slab of limestone rock from a creek bank and broke it with a blow from the side of his hand. It was a performance guaranteed to get our attention.

My guiding country.

The learning wasn't all one-sided —Carl learned, too. His first lesson was when one of my guides, on his way to the trailhead, turned a truck carrying eight horses on its side just two miles from our home.

When the phone call came about the accident, Carl and I had not yet left home. "Entertain the man any way you can," I told Jane, leaping into my pickup. "I'll be back when I can."

None of the horses were injured, nor was the metal-sided truck beyond repair. But we had hell to pay after we'd righted the vehicle, pounded out the dents, and got it running again, especially in getting the ponies to walk aboard. And it was after midnight before I rejoined Carl and Jane.

"This reminds me," Henning said, "of Robert Ruark's stories about his African white hunters and how they guided day after day, then repaired trucks and Land Rovers night after night. What men they were!"

Whatever else might be made of this first fiasco-shot guiding adventure, it provided graphic insight that a new era was dawning for me. But such an inauspicious beginning!

Aside from her obvious anxiety for both me and our horses, Jane's only comment when I returned home with the battered truck was, "I didn't say I told you so, did I?"

Besides buying the pastureland and making the decision to keep my day job, there were two 1971 developments that were to have long-term ramifications:

I came home from my first guiding attempt with a fascinating story to weave around countless evening campfires.

And I came home riding Buck—my all-time greatest saddlehorse. ∎

Chapter 13

Stitching the Pieces

O nly an idiot would've tried riding that buckskin whirl-
wind in the middle of the wildest mountain reaches
in America. Besides being far from civilization and life support, I was also alone—just me and that damned horse.

After packing our only guest back to civilization, I had
headed back to camp, pulling Buck and another packhorse
loaded with grain. Our little cavalcade was half the distance to camp, traveling an easy stretch of trail, when I
twisted in the saddle to study the packhorses and their
loads. My eyes lingered on Buck, on his catfooted walk and
the way the animal's muscles flowed. I shook my head.
What a great saddlehorse he could have been!

I gazed around at the tiny glade through which my little
string plodded and again glanced back at Buck. "Naw,
Roland, you wouldn't dare." But the thought wouldn't
leave. "After all," I muttered, "it *was* in the corral and pasture where the damn fool did all his bucking. And he *did*
think it was a game."

I swung from the saddle and tied up the string, stripped
Buck's packs and packsaddle, and threw my riding saddle
on him. Then I swung gingerly atop the big buckskin,
thinking all the while that this may be the dumbest thing
I'd ever done; I'm alone, miles from another soul, about to
get plastered to a tree by a horse I can in no way hope to
ride.

So I swallowed and clucked at the big pony.

Buck rolled his eyes back at me, and his ears began working like those of a jackrabbit stalked by a litter of coyote pups. Then the big horse stepped out proud and strong and sure. We came to bogs and downed trees and cliffside trails, and the horse never once faltered. It was there that we turned into a team, Buck and me.

Roland leading a string of horses and riders on Buck—his all-time favorite saddle pony.

Never, I think, has there been another such intelligent horse as Buck. He led packstrings for thousands of miles over some of the roughest trails in America, and he always did it just right—always at the correct speed for us to make the best possible time without wearing down or playing out, or soring the backs or legs or muscles of the horses behind. It made no difference whether our journey was three miles or thirty-three, whether our trail was across mountaintop rockslides or along gentle river bottoms, Buck's inner speedometer was always set to the proper speed.

My legs ultimately straddled that big buckskin for over twenty thousand miles. Buck and I once traveled fifty-five miles on a mercy mission—with me walking and running as much as I could, him either trotting untethered behind or carrying me down the trail at a trot or a lope. That was another thing about Buck—he always rose to any occasion.

I could catch the buckskin anywhere, at any time, for anything. He was a four-mile-per-hour walking horse down a mountain trail—which is about as fast as can be sustained, despite what some folks might tell you. But he would slow down to whatever speed I might prefer if I wished to carry on a conversation with the rider behind, or move packhorses at a slower speed.

Even as he aged, I dared not take liberties with the big pony when first climbing on him each spring. He passed sixteen before he quit testing my riding acumen when he first came off new grass. But by then the big horse was only bucking to prove a point and was careful to see I never again had to grab dirt.

Buck would follow me anywhere without a lead rope, even while pulling a string. And I guess if I wanted him to do it, he would've jumped off a cliff.

One year, when the horse was twenty years old, we had to move our party across a swollen stream and the athletic old pony swam the current sixteen times as he and I crossed back and forth to lead one guest, then another, to safety through the surging waters.

I've had other fine horses since the buckskin came to

dwell with me. But I'll never again have an equine friend and partner with whom I've worked so hard and suffered so much.

Buck and I earned each other.

It was some months before that September day when Roy Babcock stopped by my safety-department office at Plum Creek to say he'd heard that I'd begun taking hunters into the Bob Marshall.

"That might be stretching it, Roy. I have my license and campsite. And last year I took my first hunter. But to say I'm a full-fledged outfitter—well, I might have some growing left to do."

"And how did your one hunter fare last year?"

I shrugged and held out my hands, palms up. "He didn't even get to see an elk. But he only had four days. Sometimes it takes longer to fulfill a dream."

Roy and I belonged to the same local sportsmen's club. He knew that for several years, my personal elk hunting success had been phenomenal. He asked, "Are you filled for this coming season?"

"Huh-uh. At this point I don't even have anyone interested. I'm too dumb to figure any advertising or promotion into the start up."

The businessman shook his head at my naivete, then said, "I have these friends from back home who called, wanting me to recommend an outfitter. Are you the one?"

"I'll do my best."

My best included making out a menu, a grocery list, and doing the shopping—Jane still refused to have anything to do with the endeavor. She did leave her kitchen long enough to cast a practiced eye on the groceries I scattered over the lawn while stowing them into packboxes. When she saw the four cases of beer, she blew a cork. "All you're going to do is go in there and drink!"

I twisted from where I knelt to look up at her. "Jane, how many of us are going on this trip?"

"What does that have to do with anything?"

"Lots. There are eight. We'll be gone for ten days. There are ninety-six cans of beer in those four cases. That means we can have one beer per day each. And on two of those days, we can have two beers. Now does that sound like we're headed for a big blowout?"

She wheeled and stomped into the house.

The Wausau, Wisconsin hunters and I circled warily, like stiff-legged dogs meeting on a country lane. No hackles were raised, but each man's metaphoric tail was up and barely waving. There were four of them, all professional men. It was midafternoon, the day before their opening-of-hunting-season adventure into the Bob Marshall Wilderness. I was bent over a canvas-wrapped pack, cargoing for the trip, when they drove into the yard. I knotted the rope, then stood, waiting for them to switch off their vehicle's engine.

This was my first full hunting group and, though I'd taken a single stranger into my camp the year before, I still had no real idea of what to expect. Initial caution seemed prudent.

Jim, the one I'd had several phone conversations with, was first from their transport. The others—Glenn, Bob, and Jerry—followed. Introductions were made. Glenn and Jerry wandered off to look over horses in the corral while Jim and Bob watched as I continued mantying packs.

As the sun slid into the west, my hunters and I sat on packs, ready for our before-daylight departure. "Tell me, Roland, what are our chances for taking a bull elk?" Jim asked.

There it was, the question every guide dislikes because it depends so much on circumstances beyond his control: weather, rut, luck, and physical conditioning and ability of the hunters. I sipped my coffee and said, "I believe bulls are more active during the rut when there's a waning moon. The moon is full on the sixteenth—the second night of your hunt. I'm predicting you'll do better later on, say toward the end of the hunt. But who knows?"

Bob pulled a letter from his pocket that I'd written the guys earlier. "I see one of your guides, Dennis Swift, is originally from Wisconsin. How is it you hired him. Is it because we're from Wisconsin?"

I shook my head. "Denny is a friend and neighbor. Lives only a mile from here. We've taken several personal trips into the wilderness together. I asked if he'd care to guide for me. He said yes—that's all. He's a forester for a different lumber company than the one I work for. He'll be on his vacation, same as me. Denny's father, by the way, was a noted conservationist. His name was Ernie. He ..."

Bob jerked. "Ernie? Ernie Swift? He was head of our Wisconsin Department of Natural Resources. Went on from there to head the National Wildlife Federation. I sat on a couple of conservation boards with Ernie Swift!"

This was more information than I had on my taciturn guide's background; more than my friend had ever shared. But the unexpected disclosure set a favorable tone for our adventure. And it was a good thing because, while stars were still out the next morning, about halfway to road's end, one of my heavily loaded stock trucks blew two tires on one side.

The only thing we could do was unload the eight horses, tie them to roadside trees, then drive on with the rest of our cavalcade to the trailhead. There we unloaded the other half of our string, saddled the riding stock, and sent Denny and our hunters on to camp while Lyle, Carl, and I returned with the surviving truck for the rest of our pack-stock. As a consequence, our packstring was hours behind the hunters, finally arriving at camp so late nobody gave a damn where the little hand on the clock pointed.

When one hangs his shingle out as a guide, neither frailty nor sympathy is permitted. Thus I was up almost before we hit the sack to light the cooktent lantern and build a fire in the cookstove. And while Carl flipped flap-jacks and scorched slabs of ham, Denny, Lyle, and I wrangled and saddled horses for the coming day.

Hunting proved tough, and though these were good men who hunted long and hard, the elk weren't cooperating. The Wisconsinites were an upbeat bunch, however, full of fun and hijinks. And they needed every bit of good humor they could muster because my camp management lacked polish—like when their sleeping tent blew down twice during the ten-day hunt.

Our camp perched on a broad cliff ledge that was ravaged at odd times, day or night, by the wind gods. Because of the high elevation, shallow soil, and ill-tempered winds, trees grew scraggly and hardly at all. On the entire plateau, there was no tree of a length suitable for ridgepoles for our 16-foot canvas wall tents.

In years gone by, while hunting the country with a couple of friends, we called the high ledge "the wind funnel." In those pre-outfitting days I managed to locate a usable sapling for our single ten-by-twelve tent. But to find two longer ones for tents that were six feet longer—no way. We wound up taking two of the longest trees, overlapping their tops, and lashing them together with binder twine. That such high-altitude trees might have an eight-inch base and a two-inch top only served to make the entire support structures for the big tents rickety. Of course, the first forceful breeze roaring down the wind funnel would collapse anything that appeared more like a sampan junk than the Great Wall of China.

Luckily, both disasters occurred while we were out hunting and the sleeping tent was unoccupied. The first time we rode up to the flattened tent at twilight, Glenn looked especially stricken. "If that bottle in my duffel bag is broken …"

The bottle wasn't broken, and five days later, when we returned to camp and again found the tent lying on the ground, it made no difference because the bottle was empty.

Our hunters nailed their first elk on day seven. And it was while on the way back to camp, our little cavalcade bumped into a band of elk in a sidehill meadow. Bob and

Jim both took their animals.

"You were certainly right about the hunting being better later in the trip," Bob said as he speared a third piece of liver at the supper table.

Later, we sat in contented silence on the woodpile outside the tent. Jim cleared his throat and said, "You know, Roland, we've talked about this among ourselves and you know what our conclusion is?"

"As if I could?" I murmured.

He grinned. "We think we could look all over Wisconsin and not find four more compatible guys than you and Denny, Carl, and Lyle. We think that's remarkable and want you to know it."

I nodded. "Your group has exploded some of my myths, too, Jim. Tell the truth, when I got into this racket I didn't know if I'd be able to put up with the rich S.O.B.'s I'd be serving. If you guys are any indication of the people I'll get, I'll be looking forward to a whole bunch of good times." ■

Chapter 14

Rending a Family

I came out of that 1972 hunting camp with more than merely an understanding that people who would tackle the kind of wilderness adventure I offered were folks I'd be proud to lead. During several late-night conversations, Denny, Lyle, and I made a compact to fight the direction National Forest Wilderness management was taking.

For decades, the U.S. Forest Service had been in a rush to develop every last vestige of land they managed. Rumblings of discontent from local throats swelled to a nationwide tsunami as the widespread destruction of the public's forests became more and more apparent. Gradually, people-power forced the agency to backpedal toward their former custodial role. And as a result, the men in green, reflecting normal human behavioral patterns, swung from destroyers of wildlands to zealous protectors. From a management philosophy that advocated clearcut logging right up to wilderness boundaries, and aircraft landings so routine as to allow delivery of tomorrow's papers to backcountry cabins, the agency became so enthusiastic in returning their landscapes to nature that they began removing wilderness signs, abandoning trails, and allowing stock and foot bridges across dangerous streams to deteriorate. Even more foreboding was their drift toward eliminating horses and mules on the remaining trails, removing their own fine old cabins, and threatening to require permits for public entry.

There was a term for the new twist in Forest Service Wilderness management—"purism"—and many people believed it was applied to put the squeeze on critics of forest management. Our bad luck was that the architect of U.S. Forest Service's wilderness purism had recently headquartered in the agency's Northern Region, and he had apparently selected the Bob Marshall Wilderness for pilot implementation.

Thus far, only lone voices had been raised to challenge the agency's drift toward turning wilderness into control plots largely off limits to the American public. It was during those late-night campfire discussions in a Bob Marshall hunting camp that we three agreed: only *organized* resistance could succeed in blunting the thrust of wilderness purism.

On January 17, 1973, a public meeting was called at a school gymnasium in Columbia Falls, Montana. Jane, who had been a quiet observer while Denny, Lyle, and I did the preliminary legwork for the meeting, volunteered to act as temporary secretary. I moderated. From that meeting, forty-three people became charter members of a group they called Back Country Horsemen. I had the honor of being elected their first president.

Soon that first group had swelled to two hundred, and chapters were springing up around the Treasure State and beyond. The thrust of wilderness purism began to wilt as more and more citizens understood the end result of management so restrictive as to deny them opportunity to experience the wilderness.

※

I think of 1973 as a watershed year in other ways, too. It was the year a lovely Australian lass came to live with us as a foreign exchange student. And it was the year my wife began taking her own wobbly steps toward falling in love with the same outdoor wonderland I was embracing with such ardor.

Valerie Chambers' parents raised pineapples just outside of humid Brisbane. She had never seen snow or real
mountains. Our family took her on a horseback packtrip
into Glacier Park's Belly River country so she could experience both. Within a week, she'd stared open-mouthed at
towering sharp-topped mountains, watched her first grizzly bear, and discovered how excruciatingly cold water
seeping from snowbanks could be.

It was but six miles into Belly River Ranger Station and
Jane, though she disliked riding horses, elected, for the
first time in several years, for a combination of reasons, to
join in. For one thing, our kids, Cheri and Marc, had both
gone on overnighters with Dad and enjoyed it. Then Jane's
lady friends from the neighborhood appeared to envy her
the opportunity she seemingly disdained. When the young
Australian came into our life and was so enthusiastic for
adventure, the combination kicked Jane over the edge.

She enjoyed the short journey and the splendid surroundings. Too, nothing is as important to my wife as her
family, and she reveled in being part of their adventure.

The kids had no more than returned home when they
began agitating for a longer, more strenuous packtrip. "We
want to go with you into your hunting camp," Cheri said.

"Please," Valerie added.

Eleven-year-old Marc stood just behind the two girls,
eavesdropping. "You wanting in on this, too, Marc?"

He nodded.

Jane's voice wafted in from the kitchen. "Me, too."

This presented a dilemma. The journey to hunting
camp was nearly thirty miles and terribly grueling. Jane
was the only one with any experience on that trail, and I
could hardly believe that she would be ready to try it again.
The kids I wasn't worried about—they were young and
would get over it. It was Jane. I saw this as an opportunity
to expose the lady to the kind of adventures that were bur-
rowing deeply into my soul. If she once had the chance to
spend time in a comfortable hunting camp ... well, there
was no telling what might be the result. Still, with opportunity came danger—if it wasn't handled delicately, Jane

could be turned off forever.

I now knew the country and trails intimately, and the quality of our horses was much better than when Jane joined me in her first wilderness odyssey. The problem wasn't so much the grueling horseback ride as the combination of that and the tortuous drive to the roadhead. Then there was the necessity of setting up the camp upon arrival. So I caucused our family.

"Here's what we'll do," I told them. "I'll go in a few days earlier and set up the camp, then come home and get you. We'll drive to the end of the road the evening before and camp at the trailhead. Then we'll get up early and start on the trail as soon as possible. With camp already set up, we'll have it easier on the other end, too. What do you think?"

The kids bounced up and down with eagerness. And Jane? She seemed to expect nothing less than for me to do whatever it took to expedite her family's outing.

It was a piece of cake. The trip in took, as I expected, ten hours. But by making a bushwhack camp at road's end, we were on the trail an hour or so after daylight and pulled into the comfortably established hunting camp by late afternoon—light years ahead of Jane's first horseback debacle.

Within minutes of our arrival, Cheri and Valerie were swimming in the creek, Marc was fishing, the horses kicked and snorted as they galloped out to pasture, and Jane hummed while organizing the cooktent to her satisfaction. I turned out to be the one who sat dejectedly on a hay bale, sipping on a beer, trying to get enough energy to unwrap the rest of the packs and stow hay and grain in the feed tent.

There's mystery why people who love each other—especially when each feels in the right—have so much trouble saying they're sorry. One evening Jane and I sat outside the cooktent in companionable silence. Marc walked up the trail toward camp, feet dragging, shoulders slumped, hands behind his back.

"What's wrong, Marc," Jane asked.

"The girls took my fishing pole."

I laughed and Jane clucked sympathetically.

Then the boy's face split into a grin and he brought his hands out to show an eight-inch cutthroat. "So I just went fishing with my hands."

I gave the lad my pocket knife so he could clean the fish. After he'd trotted away, Jane said, "They'll be grown soon."

When I said nothing she added, "What then?"

"They'll probably get married, maybe go elsewhere to raise families."

"That's not what I mean. I'm talking about us."

"Us?"

"Yes, what about us?"

I shifted on my block of wood to stare at the mountain. "I don't get your drift."

"Yes you do. What will we do then? When the children are gone, is what I'm talking about. You're seldom home. These days I'm almost a widow. I just wonder what I can expect from the future."

A silence fell. At last I said, "Life can only be what we make of it, Jane. After the kids leave, we'll have none but each other. Kids are always destined to leave home. In the end, same as at the beginning, you're all I've got—and ever expected to have. And that should be the same for you. I hope you'll think on that while you're worrying over what you'll do after the kids are gone."

She turned her head to stare up at my same mountain. The words may have been the same, but they held no anger: "You're not the man I married."

"And you've said that before. I am what I am. If I'm no longer good enough, I'd reckon that's a decision you'll have to make."

She came to her feet, dusted off the seat of her jeans, then started away. At ten feet, the lady stopped and, with her back still turned, said, "Roland, I'm scared."

⁂

Ken Averill joined my Skyline Outfit in 1973.

Kenny worked for the same lumber company where I was employed. His brother Les owned the biggest "dude" outfit in northwest Montana, and Kenny had worked as a hunting guide for Les's outfit for many years. He was a top-notch horseman and a fair packer. Though he was sixty-one years old when first joining my outfit, the guy was a spry sixty-one, able to outwalk, outride, outdrink, and outtalk men half his age. It was the talking that most often got him in trouble.

Kenny jumped at the chance to guide for me on his vacation. He rode into camp over Labor Day weekend in order to get a feel for the country, then returned during mid-October when we brought in a family group from Iowa and Minnesota.

They were a fine bunch of young men, less than half Kenny's age. But the old mountain goat had the flatlanders hollering uncle by day three. Then came the big snow.

I rode out to get hay. When I returned a day later, Kenny met me with nosebags full of grain as I pulled into camp. "I may as well tell you," the old man said as I swung from my saddlehorse, "before them other guys tell it their way."

I lashed my pony to the hitchrack and turned to drop packs from the weary string of packponies. "Tell me what, Kenny?"

"I, uh, sort of got lost during the snowstorm."

"What's the big deal about that? I've been turned around in a blizzard myself. Haven't you ever got mixed up in a snowstorm before?"

"Not *three* times," he said.

"What? What do you mean, three times?"

Here's the story the way Kenny told it: One of the lads downed an elk up on the High Plateau just ahead of the storm. After Gene, his guide, had cleaned and skinned the animal, then marked where it lay with flagging ribbon, they had to cut and run for camp to beat darkness and the storm.

The next day, with snow still falling like God was empty-ing celestial feather beds, Kenny and the cook headed from camp leading two packhorses. Their plan was to meet Gene and three of the hunters who'd already gone ahead. Kenny and Tony would trail the packhorses up the Long Ridge, to where it bumped against the High Plateau.

Mark, one of the young hunters whose knees had gone out trying to keep up with Kenny, planned to walk a few yards from camp and watch a tiny meadow where a couple of game trails crossed. The hunter had just brushed snow from a log and taken a perch when Kenny and Tony and their packhorses loomed out of the snow. Mark waved, Kenny waved, Tony waved, and the cavalcade disappeared.

Twenty minutes later, Kenny and Tony and their packhorses plodded by Mark's stand again.

In Kenny's defense, I'll say the trail up the Long Ridge is confusing, winding through a flat stocked with big spruce trees. In addition, we purposely obscured the entry point to the trail so chance passers-by wouldn't easily discover it. Then, too, it was snowing an inch an hour of heavy, wet stuff.

Kenny paused in surprise when he spotted Mark, then waved and turned to retrace his steps.

Thirty minutes later, here came Kenny and Tony and the now fidgeting packhorses. Kenny paused to wave again at the amused hunter just as Tony pushed to the front. "I'm taking over the lead," he snarled. And the cavalcade disappeared for the third time into the snow.

"So that's the story, eh?" I said, jerking the last packsaddle from the final pony of my string.

"That's not all," he replied, slipping the empty nosebag from the horse's ears, "although the rest maybe wasn't so much my fault."

I leaned back, elbows against the hitchrail. "Okay, Kenny, let's have the rest of it."

The rest of the story is that after Kenny and Tony finally arrived where the elk lay, and after the butchered animal was loaded and the party began their mountain descent, Kenny started drifting off the ridge trail, heading down into an impassable canyon.

"Kenny, you're going wrong," Gene said.

"No I ain't."

"Kenny, dammit, you're going wrong."

"If I'm going wrong," the old man said, "I'll eat horse-shit."

So Gene shrugged and followed the old man's lead. The route steepened. Soon his steps faltered. At last Kenny turned and grinned sheepishly at Gene. Then he turned to the cook. "How do you normally fix horse turds?" he asked.

Things were deteriorating for me at Plum Creek. It was fated. Anyone with one eye and half a rear could read the signs, and my wife was certainly no dummy. The mega-corporation who owned the company brought in new management and though my department was directly unaffected, it was apparent that my best future lay in playing office politics. I declined. There seemed but one honorable course—to leave the company.

Besides, I had other horizons to conquer.

As said, it was fated. Bookings for the 1974 season came in fast and furious. Before February ended, I had sufficient hunters clamoring for trips to fill our camp throughout September and October.

"Jane, I'm going to leave Plum Creek." I expected a scene. Instead, there was only resignation.

"How will we live?"

"I believe we can turn the outfitting business into a profit."

"Why don't I believe you?"

"I've got to try."

She sighed. "Of course you do. Do you think I can't see where you are going? The children and I will try not to get in your way."

"Don't make this any harder than it already is."

"Who is it hardest on, Roland? Tell me that, please." ■

Chapter 15

Prescription for Disaster

I left Plum Creek on the first day of September, 1974. There was no crepe paper or ribbons, no party hats, no whistles, no fanfare, no tears. There wasn't even much sentiment. I left a bunch of friends, a difficult job I'd done well, and an adequate steady-as-clockwork paycheck. I left to take on the far greater challenge of outfitting and guiding others to adventure amid some of the wildest lands in the northern Rockies—a profession whose demands had broken the will and pocketbook of better-qualified men and women.

From the vantage of hindsight, I was vain, stupid, and arrogant to think I could succeed where so many had failed. I had no lodge as a base of operations to tap into wider market opportunities. I worked from no private ranch to provide a stable recreational resource not subservient to whimsical hiccups of government employees who resented *any* private enterprise making a profit from activities on public land.

To add to my problems, I made some disastrous management decisions. The first was insisting on leading only small parties to insure a higher quality of experience for my guests and myself. The second was insisting that each of our trips be demanding, deep penetration adventures into the middle of the Bob Marshall. As a consequence, trips I led were expensive and labor-intensive in terms of horses and my human support team. Even a second-semester business-school dropout could have predicted disaster.

The year was running out for our exchange-student "daughter." Valerie begged to be taken on one last horseback packtrip before boarding the airplane for her Australian home. We made it a family outing—a short journey into "the Bob" in mid-June. By then Jane was becoming accustomed to the horseback regimen. Cheri was developing into an accomplished rider, and Marc was taking to the outdoors like a fish to water.

Then we waved good-by to Val and turned toward the rest of our life. That life was the second time I'd uprooted Jane from a comfortable environment amid familiar surroundings to drag her into the unknown.

From Jane's point of view, she was saddled with a lunatic husband who insisted on pursuing a lunatic endeavor. But to give the lady her due, each time I decided to give rein to a dream, the woman who was my first dream in life—no matter her trepidation and dissent—did her share to help make my dream *our* success.

With but a day between hunts, Jane became my purchasing agent and logistics organizer. It was Jane who contracted farriers, arranged for vehicle maintenance, and lined out supplies for packing.

Our first party in '74 was the rollicking Gassner bunch from Wausau, Wisconsin, who'd been with us in '72. Bob and Jim brought a couple of new friends. Francis appeared to be the least fit of the four, and at the trailhead I selected an old reliable mare as a saddlehorse that would take care of her rider. Despite her name, Pepper was indeed careful, picking her way over the long and arduous trails. But to my annoyance, Francis wanted something, uh, peppier. It was dusk on day four, while I selected the next day's mounts, that Francis asked if I had something with a little more spirit for him to ride?

"Are you sure you can handle a pony with more spirit?"

He smiled. "Oh, I don't know—I do okay with the fifty-six quarterhorses I have in my barns back home."

I stared. He wasn't joking. "Kenny!" I shouted to the wrangler working the corral. "Catch Joe for Francis to ride tomorrow."

Tomorrow was when Francis took an unusual trophy—a big mule deer buck with antlers yet in velvet. Getting that mule-deer cape back to civilization in condition for Francis to have it mounted was one of the toughest packing jobs we ever accomplished.

Another watershed came for me with our second party—which included two ladies. I suppose to some, I was a macho male chauvinistic pig. But damn! The trips I led were tough. I saw how, for five years, that long trail had destroyed the will for adventure in Jane. So I equivocated when Frank Dufek of Ann Arbor, Michigan, called and said there would be three in their party for sure—one a woman. And when he added that "there may be another woman before their September hunt," I protested.

"This is a tough trip, Frank. You need to know that up front. I don't know if a woman could handle it."

"Don't worry about Lena. I know that lady. She can take it. I just don't know about the other one yet."

All sorts of images flitted through my mind as I squeezed the phone. Clearly, two fellows and one of their wives were working hard to convince the other wife—against her will—that she should take on this grueling adventure. No doubt the second woman was overweight, out of shape, and mentally unprepared. It sounded like a recipe for disaster. But when one hangs out that shingle as a guide, how selective can he be?

It turned out that neither woman wished to hunt. All they wanted to do was go along for the adventure. They promised not to intrude on our hunts, and at the last I threw in the towel in order to rake in the revenue.

What an idiot! It wasn't at all like I thought—the lady in question wasn't a hold-out on the adventure. The real issue was whether she would consent to marry Frank. He planned to go on a Montana elk hunt. If they were to marry, the adventure would be their *honeymoon*! Her answer to the big question would also provide the answer to a whole bunch of Frank's little questions.

Her answer was yes.

I was not so sanguine. Great God! A mere blushing bride of an outfitter myself, and already I'm running into world-class problems. "On your honeymoon! Frank, you can't do this to me. I've only got one big sleeping tent for our hunters. It's got a stove in it, but this is rustic camping at best. Aw, hell, there's been no need for privacy before. Please don't do this to me."

Buck and "my" mountain

He laughed. "Surely you can think of something. Hang a blanket down the middle of your tent. Mike and Lena are my aunt and uncle, for crying out loud. They practically raised me. They're nice people who will mind their own business. And Linda is a wonderful girl who's looking forward to the trip. We both are. Don't worry so much."

So I really worked at giving this group the preparatory information they needed to cope with the demanding journey to camp: detailed clothing and equipment suggestions, what to expect from their horses and tips on handling their ponies, something on the country they would be traveling through, and inside info on the support crew I'd have with them.

Frank and Linda Dufek were in their mid-twenties and obviously very much in love. They were also physically fit and eager for adventure. Mike and Lena Schneider were of an earlier generation, but came from hardy rural stock. The entire party was a delight to have in camp and afield. In fact, it's probable that during all my years as an outfitter I never led a group more appreciative of their adventure. And along the way, a macho myth I'd harbored since childhood exploded.

"Jane," I said upon returning the honeymooners to civilization, "the women were something else. No way could a man have lapped up adventure more than those two gals."

She rolled her eyes in a put-down as eloquent as anything Gloria Steinem could produce. "And you think men have some sort of prior right?"

I grinned. "Right now I don't think anything. Except I wish you could've been there. It might have opened your eyes, too."

One day, while the other guide led Frank and Mike into some upriver spruce bottoms, I took the ladies to view the Chinese Wall. They loved every minute. After we'd returned and they relaxed in the cooktent, I overheard our cook ask Lena, "Really now, wasn't that trip all the way to camp tough on you."

Lena was so short—not even five feet tall—that most of the time we'd lead her horse to a big rock or a log to enable her to mount. She took a few seconds to answer. "Oh," she said at last, "he prepared us well."

I could have hugged her.

I could have hugged her again the last night before we packed back to civilization. Her husband Mike and I were locked into a chess game. The cook and the guide watched while, in the sleeping tent, Frank and Linda murmured sweet nothings.

The moon was full. It was sky-clear and the early October air fairly crackled outside the heated tents. At last the chess match ended and I looked around. "Where's Lena?"

I said.

The guide shrugged, and Bob the cook said, "I don't know. She wandered out of the tent quite a while ago."

Mike waved. "Don't worry about Lena," he said. "She can take care of herself."

It was almost an hour before the woman returned. She hurried to stand shivering by the stove while I sighed in relief.

"Where you been, Lena?" her husband asked.

"Out sitting on my mountain in the moonlight."

Our camp was indeed in a beautiful location, at the foot of a gigantic avalanche path feeding from a picturesque mountain that towered over camp. Climb the avalanche chute a short distance and the entire valley spread before you. I imagined it to be exceptionally beautiful in the moonlight. But at twenty degrees!

Besides, it wasn't *her* mountain—it was *my* mountain.

Talk about two faces of Eve—our next party could hardly have been more different.

They were from this narrow little mountain valley in extreme western North Carolina. Their names were Whitey and Blackie and Sheriff and Burke. They were young and tough and Smokey Mountaineers to the core.

In the years to follow, twenty-eight of those brothers, cousins, uncles, sons, fathers, and friends of the West family were to make annual fall migrations to hunt elk in the middle of the Bob Marshall Wilderness. They came for fourteen years straight. One of the West brothers, Robert, came nine years in a row, ten overall. Whitey made four hunts, Roger four. Burke, a cousin, also came four times. They came for September bugling and tried November's bitter cold. And over the years, they sampled most dates between. And it's entirely possible that, if I offered hunting trips in August and January, somebody from that North Carolina valley would've also tried those.

They were young and hardy—working men all, clearing contractors and building contractors and farmers and loggers and shopkeepers. They scheduled with us because an uncle of theirs worked at a lumber mill with Denny Swift. Their uncle knew that Denny had guided for me during a couple of his vacations. And the uncle knew anyone tough enough to make our trip would get his money's worth and then some.

They called me "Mr. Guide Man." It was, "How much farther, Mr. Guide Man?" Or, "Mr. Guide Man, these have got to be the toughest horses I ever saw." Or, "I swear, Mr. Guide Man, you're tryin' to kill me." And that was *before* we even got to camp their first year. Right from the start, they had my number—all of them. I'm not necessarily a serious guy, but those fellows kept me off balance with their ribald good humor, practical jokes, and all-in-the-family highstakes evening poker games. "Come on and set in, Mr. Guide Man," they'd say.

I'd laugh. "No thanks, boys, I've got every vice known to man save one—gambling. I don't gamble."

"You brought us along, didn't you," Whitey said. "If that's not a gamble, I never seen one."

That first year, after we finally arrived at camp, one of 'em said, "Tell the truth, Mr. Guide Man, I don't care if I never set on another horse. You ain't goin' to make us ride them horses tomorrow, are you?"

I shook my head. "After carrying you in here, Blackie, those horses deserve a day off. We'll hunt on foot tomorrow."

But when they came in after following Kenny or Gene or Rich up and down the Rocky Mountains, Blackie sang a different tune. "I swear, Mr. Guide Man, you must be savin' them horses for better folks. That old man you got guiding for you purt' near killed me today. If I don't get a horse to ride tomorrow, you might as well use my sleeping bag for a body bag and carry me out face down over your saddle."

When I grinned and said nothing, Blackie added, "I swear, I thought them horses was tough. But that old man you got is tough as whang leather."

The Wests hunted hard. They also played hard, laughed

hard, talked long, and made out like my crew and I were all part of their family. And when we packed out at the end of their hunt, they talked of coming back soon.

The West boys pulled out of our home place just as another longrunning crew pulled in. It was anchored by Rufus Gehris, the Pennsylvania-Dutch owner of a Boyertown shoe factory.

I told the Rufus story in my book, *The Phantom Ghost of Harriet Lou,* in the chapter titled: "Great Heart and a Mile of Guts." The tale was of how the little Dutchman was a physical wreck, but had the will to live despite his frailty; how the man suffered getting to and from our hunting camp; and how incredibly beautiful he thought the country was. Rufus hunted with us, always on our last high-country hunt of the season, for seven straight years. Each year, he brought a companion: Ted Modlens, Ken Gaugler, Pete Ganovsky, and others. Those tough old Pennsylvania buzzards were, without exception, inspirations to be around.

In retrospect, I was sandbagged that first season of full-time outfitting. Each of the four groups scheduling with us was composed of the finest folks God ever sculpted. From the south, the north, and the east; from the Great Lakes to the Great Smokies; from hex signs to moonshine, shoo-fly pie to sugar-cured ham—no outfitter ever lived to entertain more wonderful people.

The quality of those 1974 guests set the bar of my expectations unusually high, a standard that, in retrospect, was met surprisingly often throughout subsequent years. The downside to having one hundred percent happy, gracious guests was that I was still unprepared to meet the other kind. There was still some learning to do on the way to a degree in *Adventure Guiding-101.* ∎

Chapter 16

Pondering the Plunge

I've been haunted all of my married life by the specter of my parents' rupture during their middle years. I know their genes lie within: the stubborn willfulness of my mother, the paradoxical quick temper and inherent kindness of my father; a dedicated work ethic from both; dad's hunger for knowledge and mom's urge to social success. During solitary journeys along countless trail miles, I thought about the cause and effect of their bickering, and finally, their parting. I tried to relate those lessons to my present life and the erratic course of Jane's and my life together.

Was I being fair to her by dragging the woman unwillingly into a way of life with only a fuzzy picture at the end? Where were we headed? Jane was right, the kids, both teenagers, would soon be gone. What then? One need not have a Harvard Ph.D to know she must be anguished over her prospects.

Following that line of reasoning, of course, seemed to lead ultimately to the conclusion that I must yield to her wishes, bury my dreams, and seek unfulfilling work with a clockwork paycheck (withholdings deducted). That I could not do.

Though the fourteen folks I led in 1974 were all of the highest caliber, and though I enjoyed the thrill of their companionship in the big lonesome, and loved the demanding physical regimen, clean air, pure water, and fabulous vistas, I received a quick reality check—there was no way guide fees from a mere fourteen people would maintain our family, let alone in the three-square-meal manner to which we'd become accustomed.

Here's the way my arithmetic went:

> *1.* Fixed expenses for an outfitting and guiding service were considerable, whether we even turned wheel or hoof. There was a bunch of rolling stock—trucks, pickup, passenger van, stock and tack trailers—and their initial investment, insurance, and licensing were there whether or not we scheduled a single person. Likewise the horses: they ate year 'round, whether they carried a soul into a wilderness or stood in a barnlot.

> *2.* The investment in horse tack was as much as our investment in horses—the dozen riding saddles and ten packsaddles, the halters and bridles and saddlepads. In addition there were the tents, stoves, cookware, and never-ending wear on ropes and canvas (we bought both by the roll).

> *3.* Actual trip expenses were significant: food, gas and oil, grain for the ponies.

> *4.* Jane and the kids had an annoying habit of wanting at least *something* in their bellies.

The way I figured it during that mid-seventies Christmas season, fixed expenses—investment, depreciation, licenses, permits, liability insurance—required $30,000 per year to maintain. Then came direct costs and our need to show a profit. After the smoke cleared, my pencil came down on the far side of $50,000 of income as necessary for our little Skyline Outfit to survive.

Now that our problem was clearly defined, the only question was *how* to generate that volume? Clearly the best way would be to find *one* person willing to pay fifty grand for the privilege of having me guide him through the Wilderness. I shrewdly deduced, however, that it was unlikely we'd ever find anyone willing to pay more than the going rate for my services, so I cast about for a better idea.

A second alternative was to guide fifty people at one thousand each. But any expansion of client numbers would require more horses, more equipment, more labor. It was the same old business conundrum faced by every entrepreneur from traveling cave salesmen to Deep Space Nine rocketeers. Fortunately, in those chicken-or-egg early years of my outfitting and guiding odyssey, our credit line was still intact.

I applied for and received an okay to establish a late-season hunting camp at a much lower elevation, thus expanding the outfit's hunting opportunities. With the second camp in use during November, I was able to serve an added twelve elk and deer hunters. In addition, I expanded into summer trips: horseback journeys through the Bob Marshall's high country and horseback-in, river float-out fishing trips down the remote South Fork of the Flathead River. I also toyed with the idea of leading a spring bear hunt by horseback.

It was only then that I began thinking about advertising. What if fifty people fail to beat a path to our door come next summer and fall? What do other outfitters do?

"Isn't this the sort of analysis people do *before* they take a plunge like we did?" Jane asked one evening as I pored over advertising options.

I didn't bother to look up. "Nobody ever took me for a rocket scientist."

"What does that have to do with anything?"

"It means I'm a bunch more interested in what's ahead than what's behind."

She threw a couple of envelopes onto the pile of magazine and sport-show advertising brochures that lay scattered about the table. "While you're planning our future, you might plan how we're going to pay these bills."

Neither sport-show or magazine advertising looked good enough to me. Both were expensive, unaffordable to a business whose CEO was finding operating income as elusive as a garden snake in a grease pit. Instead, as is all too often my modus operandi, I chose an unconventional promotional scheme. I loaded up the "yellow banana"— our family sedan—and headed east on a slide-show tour.

"When will we see you again?" Jane asked, standing at the door.

"Hopefully when I have some good news to report."

"Isn't being away from your family all summer and fall enough? Must you be gone all winter, too?"

"We've got to eat, honey."

"We were doing quite well before you took us into this crazy scheme."

I was gone five weeks doing Lions, Kiwanis, and Rotary

Our first float fishing party camped at Big Salmon Lake.

Club programs in Minnesota, Wisconsin, and Michigan. Sometimes I'd give a breakfast meeting in Waupun, a luncheon meeting in Fond du Lac, and an evening meeting in Marshfield, all in the same day. Sometimes I stayed with friends. Most times I stayed in a motel. Occasionally I slept in the car.

But I came home with enough deposits to pay our taxes and get Cheri's braces fixed.

With the wolf so close to our door and the first guests still some months in the distance, I set out to find honest work. A job with the state forestry department on tree-thinning projects carried us through spring and early summer.

By the first of August I was doing some preparatory packing for our first big horseback-in, river float-out fishing trip. There were six in the party, including a 12-year-old who proved to be an adept flyfisherman. They called themselves the "Saginaw Fin & Bottle Club" and they were the equals in gracious good humor of any of the folks we'd previously led on hunting excursions. In addition, they were fishing fools, plying the waters from daylight to dark, day after day.

"Don't your arms ever wear out?" I asked Jim Dye and his red-haired son as they mechanically fed line to their waving flyrods as we drifted through a river canyon.

"Hey," Jim said. "I work fifty-one weeks out of the year and fish the other. This is the other."

We'd begun at Big Salmon Lake, then packed our gear down to the river at Salmon Forks to begin the float portion of the journey. Jim and Tim finally ran low on their hand-tied flies on the last day. I asked the master fly angler what fly worked best.

He never paused his rhythmic pumping. "Anything," he said. "Anything at all."

Just before the float ended, Jim said something I've never forgotten. "You know, Roland, our group of guys goes someplace different every year. We've run bigger whitewater on the Colorado, caught bigger fish in British Columbia. We've been on lakes just as beautiful as Big

Salmon and rivers flowing through country just as picturesque as the Bob Marshall. We've had fine guides, fun adventures."

Then he paused to gaze at distant mountains before adding, "But we've never before had it all on the same trip."

From the end of that August float until mid-September, I was busy setting up camps and packing supplies for the coming season. The first hunt included yet another brother from the North Carolina family—Roger West. Roger, a thin, wiry blade, quickly wormed his way into our hearts and under my skin, making it plain from the outset that he didn't like the long ride to camp and cared only moderately for elk hunting.

The Carolinian's day might begin with him answering the call to breakfast wearing pajamas and house slippers and packing a back issue of the *Wall Street Journal*. While everyone else ate hurriedly, swigging copious quantities of strong coffee, Roger would dawdle. While others laced boots and donned coats and hats, the young man eyed them all with amused good humor, making effortless wise-cracks that would send us all guffawing from the tent.

"Aren't you planning to hunt today, Roger?" I might ask.

"Naw, I believe I'll just rest up from yesterday."

So I'd tell the wrangler to unsaddle Roger's horse and turn him out with the rest of the grazing herd.

The evening before our return to civilization, the Smokey Mountaineer busied himself with a pencil and paper. "What are you working on, Roger?" Larry asked.

"I'm just figuring out that it'll take me longer to ride out of this godforsaken place and drive to town than it will to fly from Montana to Atlanta, then drive on home. Can't you boys arrange for air pickup in the middle of this wilderness?"

"Are you so anxious to get away from this terrible place?" I asked, while pouring cake batter.

"You purt near killed me, son. I think it's time I got out where I can heal up."

I laughed and handed him the stirring spoon to lick. "You haven't hunted for the last three days, Roger. If you're not healed by now, you never will."

"I was just trying to rest up for tomorrow's ride."

The guy was funnier than a Charlie Chaplin movie. Roger West was also well-read and intelligent. But patience was not among his virtues. Instead, impulse turned the hands on his clock. "We won't see him again," I told Jane after she returned home from dropping Roger at the airport.

That's why it was such a surprise when the Carolina bunch trooped in the following year with Roger in tow.

⋯⋯⋯

From New Jersey and Wisconsin, California and Minnesota, Pennsylvania and Montana, Oregon and Iowa and Michigan—they came. From all points on the compass they came. But we had only six more hunters in '75 than we did in '74.

Those people followed a pattern, however. Even though there weren't many of 'em, we were the guide service of choice for the nicest people in the world. The float trip proved that a summer operation could be possible. And we opened our late-season camp on the upper Spotted Bear River to slight hype and little promise. But perhaps the best indicator of the profit-making potential of our business was the fact that financial disaster was barely averted by subdividing a portion of our pastureland and selling a couple of lots.

⁕

The little Pennsylvania shoemaker, Rufus Gehris, returned with another fine elderly gentleman, only to have us blindsided by a big dump of snow. Rufus watched from a strategic high point while his friend and I stalked migrating elk through a huge open basin, until we at last overhauled a respectable bull who paused for lunch.

But the snow continued to build, much to Rufus's aesthetic delight. "It's so beautiful, Roland."

"Only if you don't have to live and work in it for a month and a half," I said.

"It looks like a Christmas card."

When we left that high country for the season, we broke camp and took the tents and equipment out with us. The problem was we were short of horses. So Kenny Averill and I packed our riding saddles and walked to the halfway camp, holding onto horsetails and floundering through sixteen inches of snow. Rufus and his trusty saddlehorse for most of a decade—Blondie—broke trail, with the little Dutchman knocking snow from tree branches on our way through the laden forest. He looked like a snow ghost himself, but the Pennsylvanian wore an ear-splitting grin and seemed to consider the storm and challenge as merely part of one of the greatest adventures he'd ever experienced.

After returning home, Rufus wrote a letter about the great trip he'd had. In it he had this paragraph:

> This year's trip differs in no way from that of a marriage. It is not too hard to get into a marriage, but oh boy! is it hard to get out of. We sure paid the

price, especially you and Kenny. How you guys held up I'll never know, walking all that distance in snow. How I wish I was in that good shape—but let's not think of that. I just simply enjoyed it no end.

⚜

There was much less snow at the lower camp where Kenny and I dropped packs from our riding saddles and climbed wearily into the saddle to complete our exodus to civilization.

But all was not roses. Yes, we had our tents erected at the lower camp. But our woodpile was only sufficient for a few days instead of three weeks, and we had altogether too little hay and grain stockpiled in a camp where supplemental feed for the ponies was a must. I'd tried to take too much onto my own shoulders and was simply unable to accomplish all tasks. In addition, I was running out of energy and wearing thin, mostly down to bone and gristle.

But my luck still held—our next party was an outstanding one. My great good fortune came about in this manner:

Bud Sayre was a best friend of Jane's and my Oregon neighbors, Buck and Arlene Fritts. (Buck and Arlene were the couple who showed up on our Montana doorstep on a whim, then stayed and helped us build an addition to our home). Bud wanted to dabble in Montana elk hunting, so Buck brought him to the Flathead and made the introduction.

Bud and Lacy Sayre became fixtures in our camps for many years. They were hands down the most experienced elk hunters we were ever privileged to serve. Bud's sidekick, Poke Spalinger, and son-in-law, Bert Jones, completed this savvy crew of ex-loggers and railroad engineers.

As soon as Bud and Poke saw we were short of wood, they took my crosscut saw and felled a couple of dead spruce, then bucked them into blocks and rolled them to camp.

These guys' idea of my guiding them was to take them into good elk country by horseback, then get the hell out of their way. The elk were there, right enough, but so was ever-deepening snow. Much of the high country wound up closed to us, despite the best efforts of our horses and me to get them there.

Still, they got into elk. Bull elk. Saw them. Got some shots. It was during this hunt that an exhausted Bud pulled up puffing in thigh-deep snow. Yet another band of elk had made fools of us. I cursed, but the taciturn railroader passed along a bit of wry advice calculated to turn every elk hunter's crank:

"The bulls are here, Roland. The bulls are here."

Burt Coleman and his party had hunted with us at the high camp in '73. But on their way back to civilization the party had also watched distant Spotted Bear River bulls. So the canny Iowans and Minnesotans opted to fill our last-week-of-November trip.

Jane, bless her, sent in roast turkey and all the trimmings for a special Thanksgiving dinner. But with the expansion into late season, my outfitting business not only conflicted with the Thanksgiving holiday with my family, I also missed our November 27th wedding anniversary. ■

Chapter 17

Who's Playing the Game

I'd begun writing a newsletter to past and future Skyline Outfit guests in 1972. In 1976 we increased the frequency of our *Just Over The Skyline* newsletter to twice per year and had it commercially printed. Jane, assuming growing responsibility in the effort to make her lunatic successful in his lunatic adventure, took over the burden of its mailing.

One of those first higher-class versions included a few rules (22 to be exact) to govern operations of the Skyline Outfit's hunting camps. They were not, of course, meant to be taken seriously. In the introduction:

> … We've found these rules to be indispensable for the smooth operations of the camp and to maintain the well-being of our many fine guests. We're adding those rules to this copy of JUST OVER THE SKYLINE so that you may show your friends and neighbors how a REAL hunting camp should be run.

Hunting Camp Rules

1. Spike boots and spurs should be removed at night before climbing on your air mattress.

2. Dogs are not allowed up at the dinner table, but

can set off to one side and look hungry. No more than one dog allowed to be kept on one sleeping bag at night.

3. Candles, warm water, and other luxuries are charged extra. Also towels and soap.

4. Dishes are washed daily when kept within reach. Insect powder for sale at the bar.

5. Craps, Chuck Luck, Stud Horse Poker and Black Jack games are run by the management.

6. Special rates to "Gospel Grinders" and professional gamblers.

7. Every known fluid (except water) is for sale at the bar.

8. A deposit must be made before soap, candles, coffee cups, or drinking glasses can be carried outside the main tent. When the party is leaving, a rebate will be made on all soap, candles, or parts of candles not ate.

9. Twelve or more persons must sleep in one tent when requested by management.

10. Baths are furnished down at the creek, but bathers must remember the deposit rule for soap and candles took down.

11. No complaints regarding the quality or quantity of meals will be allowed. Assaults on the cook is discouraged.

12. Quarrelsome or boisterous persons, also those who shoot off, without being provoked, guns or other explosive devices in the tents, and all boarders who get killed, will not be allowed to remain on the premises.

13. When guests find themselves or their luggage thrown out in the rain, they may consider they have received notice to quit.

14. *It's best not to consider your valuables safe—nothing is safe around here.*

15. *The proprietor will not be held accountable for anything.*

16. *The bar will be open day and night, but helping yourself is prohibited. The proprietor will ration all liquids. No mixed drinks will be served except in case of death in the family.*

17. *Only regularly scheduled guests will be allowed the privilege of sleeping on the bar tent floor.*

18. *Guests are forbidden to strike matches, spit on the tent, or annoy the proprietor in any way.*

19. *Meals served in the sleeping tent will not be guaranteed in any way. Everybody else is hungry, too, and not above temptation.*

20. *To attract attention of proprietor, wrangler, cook, or guides, shoot three times. Two shots for deck of cards, one for ice water, and so on.*

21. *All guests are required to rise at 6 a.m. This is imperative as the sheets are needed for tablecloths.*

22. *No cheques cashed for anybody. Payment must be made in cash, gold dust, or blue chips. Everything is cash in advance. Tariff subject to change without notice.*

I headed east on another program tour in mid-January. This time I was gone for two months. The results were depressing, and though we had a few deposits, there wasn't enough money to see us through until our cash flow picked up during hunting season. With fewer hunters booked for the '76 season than we had served in '75, there simply was not enough for survival.

"Jane there's only one way. I'm going to have to borrow

more money against our home."

"No!"

"Honey, there's no other way ..."

"I don't care. I'm not signing. If I won't sign, you can't mortgage the roof over our head."

I said nothing, so she said, "Sell some more land."

"That land's the life blood for our horses. We sell that and we're out of business. We don't sell it and we're out of business. Either way, we're dead in the water."

"Then sell the outfitting business. It's doing nothing but dragging us down anyway."

I picked up an empty cup and stared into it, then slapped it back to the table. "What do we have to sell? A few horses. A little tack. A couple of worn-out stock trucks, and a dream. Without turning it into a profit, who will buy?"

"Getting mad will get us nowhere," she said.

We mortgaged our home in April for twenty-five thousand. Jane signed. Meanwhile, I'd been bidding on Forest Service thinning contracts. And in May, Cheri and I, along with my friend Jack Watts, began work on the first thinning tract to be "let" that spring. Since I had no summer trips scheduled, we worked throughout the summer—until I left to set up the two hunting camps.

We began the first hunt with standby volunteer guides, Larry Gleason and Lyle Ausk, and cook Carl McLauchlin. The West family—this time three of the brothers, Whitey, Robert, and Roger, accompanied by their tough cousin Burke—elected to try the high camp once again. Veteran crew, veteran hunters; what more could an outfitter wish?

I sent Carl on ahead with the hunters while Larry, Lyle, and I saddled and loaded the packstring. Eleven hours later, we pulled into camp to find it vacant.

"What the hell is going on?" I growled. "They had to be ahead of us."

As soon as we dropped the packs, I returned to the main trail to see if our bunch had missed the trail fork and headed on downriver. There were no fresh tracks in the dusty trail beyond where our string had turned off. No, we'd simply failed to notice where they'd gone wrong. Wherever it was, it *must* be miles away.

The light was beginning to fade by the time I returned to camp. Our own horses were exhausted. There was no chance of returning to look for lost hunters at night.

Meanwhile, far behind, our lost hunters and their hapless guide toiled up to the mountain pass that opened to the basin of our camp. What had happened was they'd been laughing and joking when they came to their key trail junction, and Carl led them on up the Spotted Bear River for four miles before discovering his error. Four miles up and four miles back meant eight additional miles tacked onto an excruciating, saddle-wearing, twenty-seven mile, eleven-hour journey from road's end.

We had all the food. Since it was the day *before* hunting season opened, the Carolinians carried only empty rifles, having packed all their ammunition in duffel bags—also on the packstring.

It was well after dark when our cavalcade of cook, hunters, and horses plodded to the top of the pass. Two of the horses lay down on the way up and had to be goaded to continue. But at last, with but four miles to go—all of it downhill—the weary, blister-butted hunters fell from their saddles to stagger on, leading their jaded mounts.

There were several flaws in that plan. First of all, human nightvision is woefully inferior to that of most horses. Too, by then the ponies knew where they were—knew camp was only an hour away. At trail's end they knew there would be grain and they'd be loosed to roam. From the pass on, while their riders were stumbling amid the inky night, groping for the trail, the horses surged ahead, eager to get down the hill and join their buddies.

"Goddamn!" Roger muttered as his horse stepped on his heels for the third time. "If I had any shells for this damn gun I'd shoot this damn horse." The slender Carolinian who, the year before, so hated the long journey bumped into Carl's pony in the dark. "And if I had any more damn shells," he muttered, "I'd shoot this damn guide."

They made an hour ride a two-hour stumble down a mountain. At last they arrived at the final trail junction into camp—a path we had deliberately obscured so outsiders could not easily find their way into our hunting country. Every one of these men except Robert had been here before, but with the black of night cloaking their way, each scratched his head in exasperation.

"Goddamn!" Roger said. "Where's that guide man. How come he ain't out here to lead us to camp?"

"Hell," Carl said, "they're all asleep by now. They ate a big supper and their bellies are full and they went sound asleep. We're going to have to find the way by ourselves."

"The least they could do," Robert said, "was hang a lantern in a tree."

Carl had it right—we were sound asleep. We also had our saddlebags packed with extra food and the alarm set for three a.m., planning to hit the trail long before daylight, heading in three directions.

"Goddamn!" Roger said. "If I had any shells, I'd wake 'em up. I'd mow down every tree on that hillside so they could see to get out here and take us to camp."

It was after midnight when they finally straggled in. They found the trail when somebody's saddlehorse jerked free and trotted across the dry creek bed, disappearing into the trees on the other side. "That's it!" Carl said. "That's got to be the way to camp."

I met Roger as he staggered toward the sleeping tent, saddlebags across his shoulder. "I'll tell you one damn thing, Mr. Guide Man. You're a-taking me out of here tomorrow." He paused while the import of what he'd just said washed over him. "No you ain't neither. I'm sleeping tomorrow."

When I merely grunted, he added, "But the next day, you're taking me outta here!"

Roger did sleep the next day, appearing in the cooktent about the time the rest of the party was ready to hit the brush for elk. He sprawled on a bench at the kitchen table, unfolding a copy of the *Wall Street Journal*. "Y'all have a good time. Hear?" he called to our backs. "I'll just hang around here and see the cook doesn't lose his way tryin' to find the outhouse."

Robert and I hit for the upper basin. We stopped for lunch on a rock ledge, high above a lovely meadow. Sharp peaks thrust up in every direction. "I swear, this is the most beautiful country I ever saw," he muttered, leaning back against a rock outcrop and taking a bite from his sandwich. "I can see why my brothers fell in love with it."

Elk were scarce, though. Burke took a respectable mule deer buck and Whitey nailed a black bear in another drainage. But elk?

"Too hot," I told them. It was true, the weather was blistering. Late in the hunt, Robert and I relaxed against the same rock outcrop where we'd eaten lunch during our first hunting day. "Mr. Guide Man," he said, "I sure did want to shoot something on this trip."

I nodded. What could I say?

"Yep, I sure did want to shoot something."

When I continued my silence, he said, "Why don't you make a break for it?"

❧

Lessons in life were easy to come by from these rollicking North Carolinians. With them, poker was a big thing. Though the game didn't often interfere with their hunting, supper wasn't always easy, what with the big games that seemed always in progress at the cooktent table.

Obviously, the way these guys scattered money around between them, they had a bunch more than I did. I once saw a *fifteen* hundred-dollar *raise*. Robert called. Roger wasn't bluffing. Gradually I came to understand they were merely trading dollars among the family. When I understood that, it was easy to see we weren't much different, them and me. They just had a few more zeroes tacked onto their bank account.

"Come on and get in the game, Mr. Guide Man," Robert said one evening after we'd finished dishes and they'd cleared the table for yet another poker sweepstakes.

I laughed. "I've got every vice known to man, boys—I

told Whitey that two years ago—except gambling. I don't gamble."

"Is *that* why you took up guiding?" Roger said. "You wanted a sure thing?"

I watched for a while, then the ten-dollar bill I had tucked into a shirtpocket notebook took to itching. I carried the ten for emergency money to buy enough gas to get home—if I could first get out to the road. I knew it wouldn't play in this game, but *What the hell?* and I pitched the ten on the table.

There were squeals of delight and a place was cleared for me. My ten dollars wasn't even enough to play out the hand, so they split the pot and Robert won my ten dollars. He chortled with glee as he tucked the ten-spot into his wallet.

"You want this tenner back," he chuckled, "you're goin' to have to bring twenty next year."

As I've already made abundantly clear, as a businessman I'm playing with something less than a full deck. But an idiot I'm not. If I could book a trip for just twenty dollars, it was the least expensive promotion we ever did. "Okay, you can count on it," I said. "I'll bring twenty next year. You just be sure and be here."

Throughout the following winter, I scrawled notes to Robert: "Dear Robert, Jane has been asking about that ten—she sorta set her eyes on it until you took it from me."

Or, "Dear Robert, Jane can't hardly sleep at night what with the kids crying 'cause they're hungry."

Or, "Dear Robert, Do you still have my ten? Don't you go spending it before I get a chance to get it back."

We had no one scheduled for the high camp for the next hunt, so I utilized the time by packing horsefeed to the low camp and spent a couple of days bucking blocks of firewood until the woodpile overflowed.

At one point, Jane met me at road's end to resupply. She'd been pressed into service, and was reluctant (and perhaps a little frightened) to drive a hundred and fifty miles of forest road alone. But on her return, a grizzly bear crossed the road in front of her, and fed on berries across a broad river bottom. She watched the bear for an hour, until dark. And when at last I returned home, it was she who had the story to tell. Within our family, it was a role reversal of some significance.

***

Finally it fell late October and I hosted the first party to make me wish I'd never taken up guiding.

The hunt was scheduled by a father, his son, and son-in-law. Few of my hunters ever had better chances at both great herds of elk and lots of trophy mule-deer bucks. But the father was an overbearing man who was positive he knew everything worth knowing and wasn't at all shy about advising anyone within earshot of his vastly superior intelligence.

The son took a respectable bull elk and mule-deer buck. The son-in-law shot at a bull we never caught before he disappeared beyond the Sun River Game Preserve boundary. Then we stumbled onto what might have been the biggest concentration of elk we ever spotted during my years as a hunting guide. There were over fifty head, with several large bulls. Some were grazing, but most lounged in a big, grass-filled sidehill meadow.

I tried to get the party strategically stationed before approaching the herd, but the father took off running toward the animals. On the way, he bumped into a dandy mule-deer buck and missed a two-hundred-yard running shot at the animal. At the gunshot, the elk decamped for Minneapolis, passing through their escape routes out of the basin before our other hunters could get into position.

The father held us responsible. Fortunately, the fourth hunter in our group was a former Air Force colonel who told the overbearing lout what a S.O.B. he was.

Finally, I could no longer tolerate being around the arrogant father and devised what turned out to be an excellent plan for coping with the man: I assigned Kenny to guide him.

Kenny, while an excellent guide, did not hear well. In addition, he was always happy, believing only the best of people. They got along fine because Kenny heard little of what his hunter said and did little the man demanded they do.

One problem cropped up, however—the hunter wanted to ride his horse off-trail, cross-country. And he insisted on foraying off on his own. "He'll kill a horse or himself," Kenny said.

"Himself I wouldn't mind," I said. "Give him Domino."

Domino was a black and white paint mare who was at least as dumb as her soon-to-be rider thought himself brilliant. She went where she wanted, when she wanted, and then only if it had little work attached to it. No amount of coaxing or beating would drive the horse to do anything that didn't have others of her kind associated with it. The problem of the man demanding to ride his horse into dangerous situations was solved.

Then it was time to return home. The guy raved to Jane about what a great trip they'd had, asked her to air-freight the meat to his Pennsylvania home (despite the fact that he flew his own airplane to Montana), wrote us a check for the remainder of their hunt, and disappeared into the sunset—then stopped payment on his check.

In those days I had so much confidence in our hunts that I didn't ask for final payment until we'd completed a trip. What saved us was that the guy had pulled this trick so often his bank tired of the sport and let his check to us go through.

During a later investigation of the guy, I discovered he'd come to our hunt directly from one in Idaho. While talking to the Idaho outfitter, I learned that this Pennsylvania lawyer had jerked him around, too.

To be fair about barristers, however, I must add that I led two other attorneys to wilderness adventure and they proved to be okay guys. Thus, in my limited experience, attorneys are, as a group, about two-thirds good, one-third bad—an average I've since found to be ballpark-true about the profession as a whole. ■

Chapter 18

Tanglefoot Terror

The auctioneer paused to wipe his face with a big white handkerchief and take a quick sip of water. Then he picked up the microphone and in a low, confiding voice said, "Boys, a hunnerd and ninety-five is way too cheap for a seven-year-old Tennessee walker mare!"

And the chanting began again, moving the price quickly to $225. The mare moved quickly and smoothly around the ring. The young lady riding the horse knew what she was doing, reining the mare to-and-fro, putting the animal through her paces. The lady was a pro.

Again the auctioneer paused in his chant to say, "The mare is way too cheap," and to give the crowd a better chance to watch the horse's fluid motion. For her part, the sorrel mare's patience had boiled dry. She stopped abruptly at one end of the arena, ears flared. The lady rider either didn't see the set of the animal's ears or failed to interpret them correctly as she jammed spurs home. The mare's ears went back tight against her head.

"Two-thirty. Do I hear two-thirty?"

The rider again rat-a-tatted her spurs and tried to rein the mare around. Suddenly the animal reared upright on hind legs, nose to the rafters. Off in the crowd, a woman screamed and several men shouted in alarm. The mare stood aloft for a moment, then dropped down to all fours.

The rider was game. With color draining from her face, she tried again to turn the mare. Again the animal reared.

"Two thirty once ..."

In a detached sort of way I saw the scene. I lifted my hand chest-high and waggled it once. The sharp-eyed auctioneer caught it, stared my way for a moment, and said, "Sold for two hunnerd and thirty dollars to—what's the name?"

⚬⚬⚬

I made a mistake, buying that sorrel mare. It looked to me, sitting in the stands at the Kalispell horse sale, like the mare was kid-spoiled. Rearing like that, I thought, was a trick she'd developed to scare kids into letting her have her way, and I thought I could break her of the habit.

The $230 price tag, even in the mid-70s, was a bargain. The mare was a pleasure to sit when she walked out. She was short-coupled for a Tennessee walker, but had good long legs and was heavy quartered. More to the point, the animal had a tremendous ground eating stride. She was smooth. Riding her was like floating on a cloud.

She was also crazy.

If anything happened that she didn't like, she balked. If her rider tried to force her, she reared. The first time she did it with me was at the home place when I tried to ride her away from the other horses. She balked. I popped her with the bridle reins and she did a little stationary shuffle. I popped her again and she reared.

In my opinion, there's no more dangerous trait for a horse to have than the habit of rearing to get rid of a rider. When those front feet leave the ground, it takes a swift and agile rider to dismount before horse and rider are in danger of crashing backwards with horse atop human. All the advantage lies with the horse. If the rider dismounts when the animal first rises, then, with mission accomplished, the horse simply drops to all fours and wins the fray. If the rider stays on until the horse is up, then with saddle vertical, he cannot move without perhaps pulling the horse over, and he chances being crushed. At that point, the only alternative is to throw one's self as far forward as possible, grasping the pony around the neck, trying to add forward weight to the animal.

The best way to break the inclination to rear is to pull the horse over on its back. It takes a long set of bridle reins and superb physical agility, coupled with great timing. You must swing quickly from the saddle at precisely the last moment as the animal is still going up and you can still bail without pulling the steed down on you. As quickly as you hit the ground, you must leap behind the horse, and while the creature is at the top of its rearing pull it on over in a crashing heap—without being in the way to cushion the fall.

Most horses fear going over backwards, pulling them over a couple of times is usually enough to break them of the habit. Not the sorrel mare—an apparent veteran of these games. So sensitive was she to the feel of the rider, as soon as she felt him shift in the saddle to dismount she stopped her rearing motion and fell forward to all fours. The first time I bailed, I was embarrassed to find the mare back on the ground before I had both feet under me. But if I stayed in the saddle, the mare reached for the sky. And she proved too adept for me ever to manage to jerk her over.

She had developed another aspect of her rearing trait that was as deadly as a striking snake—unlike other horses, she didn't appear to *care* if she went over. Going on her back was her last line of defense and I finally concluded the trick had never failed to rid her of a rider.

When a heavy horse crashes down on top of you, it's bad stuff. There are probably more serious injuries—and deaths—from a horse falling on a person than from any other horse-related accident. It's especially dangerous when a saddlehorn acts as a spear with twelve hundred pounds of thrust behind it.

I was fortunate that first time by throwing myself sideways, avoiding a horn that smacked into the ground with the whack of a stamp-mill press. My left leg was pinned momentarily, but was protected by cantle and horn. Luckily, with iron-shod feet flailing, the mare rolled away from me. As she rolled, my leg and foot were mashed, but I was immediately freed as she came to her feet.

The ground was soft, and nothing appeared broken. I had the hell scared out of me, though, and as I rubbed life back into my leg I knew it was war. I limped into our shop and cut a club from an old baseball bat, then donned spurs. Back in the saddle, I reined the mare away from the other horses. She balked. I spurred.

I was ready as she started up, and I swung the club at a spot between her ears—the second way a horse can be broken of rearing.

Apparently the sorrel mare had been there before, because even as she reared, she watched me from the corners of her eyes. As I swung my club, she jerked her head left. The club just tickled an ear as it went by, but the miss caused me to lunge, almost falling from the saddle.

I muttered a curse and settled back into the saddle, ready to swing again as the mare did a fast-foot shuffle in preparation for another go at me. Again I missed. But my effort was not in vain, as the act of dodging her head broke the animal's rhythm and caused her to drop to the ground.

Under the goad of my spurs, she prepared to lift off again. Each previous time she had dodged left, so this time I swung for her left ear. She dodged right and I missed again—missed the horse, that is. I hit myself in the left knee. God, did it hurt! I took a moment to rub the knee and reflect, then took a shorter grip on the club and prepared for a shorter swing, focusing between her ears. Then I buried my spurs.

Up she came, screaming in rage! Her ears were laid back and out like target sights. I couldn't miss. But the short stroke had little force behind it. The mare kept going up and I grabbed around her neck in a paroxysm of fear. But the light blow *had* disrupted her momentum, and she fell forward.

She went up again. I swung harder. Dodge. Miss. Up again. Dodge. Hit an ear. Up again. Dodge. Miss. Then it was over. The mare walked out into the pasture as if that pasture was precisely where she'd always wanted go, striding from the other horses with her easy, flowing gait. She reined well and turned in any direction I wished. No doubt about it—she was the world's most well-trained pony.

The mare paused, however, when later we moved through the corral and past the other horses. Her ears began to flare, and I got ready for action. But a moment's reflection was all the animal needed, and we traveled around and around that pasture without further problem.

Later I learned from an observant guide just how well developed the sorrel mare's habits were. Kenny was riding alongside when the mare blew up and began rearing. He said that as she went up she squatted with her hind legs so her tail was never far from the ground. That's why, unlike most horses, she didn't care if she went over—from that height it was unlikely she could be hurt.

Not so the rider. Her specialized technique meant he had even less time to get clear of the saddle.

After our pasture confrontation, I'd hoped the mare's bad habits were a thing of the past. But I soon found out differently. Some days were great, and she'd perform flawlessly. On her good behavior, I've never sat a more pleasurable horse—such easy grace, like floating astride a feather.

But there was her other side. If she found something she didn't like, she became balky. If I tried to bend her will, she'd rear. A club became standard equipment whenever my saddle went on the sorrel mare.

The things that made her explode might be simple. Perhaps I wanted her to turn down a country lane she'd never walked before. She detested wading through water. And sometimes she blew for no other reason than my checking her so as not to get too far ahead of other riders.

The places she picked for a contest of wills were not always filled with pasture grass. Sometimes it was a hard roadbed or a steep mountain trail. Conditions weren't always right, either, with a packstring trailing behind, or guests up ahead. We went at it several times that summer and early fall, me and the sorrel mare, but she always wound up doing my bidding. Still, I had this gnawing feeling that it was merely a matter of time before she won one. Knowing what could happen if she did, I grew wary of her and only rode the animal sparingly. Instead we packed her, loading her with big and awkward loads.

She reared a time or two with packs. She even went over backwards with a load on her back, but she did that only once, discovering to her discomfort that it was she who rolled away moaning. To further compound her problem, she was roped to the packhorse ahead and that animal resented her stupidity enough to deliver a few well-aimed kicks while she struggled on the ground.

❦

Finally that 1976 guiding season wound down, and it was the 19th of November, the beginning of our last hunt. I'd overworked my favorite saddlehorse, so Buck was home resting in the pasture and I straddled the sorrel mare. Behind me toiled five packhorses. My two hunters brought up the rear. The weather had been well below freezing for a week, and when our little cavalcade pulled up to the first stream crossing, ice crusted it most of the way across.

The evening before, I'd slipped and fallen, wrenching my back. Within minutes the back had stiffened so badly I couldn't bend. Since there were only two hunters and few horses necessary for this last hunt, and since there were but ten hours of daylight at our latitude at that time of year, I thought I could handle the chores alone: packing, guiding, cooking, wrangling. But now?

Fortunately, I'd wrenched the back after most of the heavy prep work was done. Jane came, just as it was growing dark, to help me finish mantying packs and loading them onto the truck.

"Roland, what are you going to do tomorrow?"

"Lead the packtrip, honey. There's nobody else. I've got to go in and do what I've been paid to do."

"Look at you try to walk. You can't." When I said nothing, she added, "You're a fool!"

The alarm went off at four a.m. It was hard to roll out of bed, and when I did, I couldn't bend. Jane helped me pull on my boots, then laced them. When Mark and Burt walked into the house, they took one look and asked how I could continue.

I told them I thought I could ride a horse or walk, whichever way we needed to hunt. But I couldn't bend, and it was going to be impossible for me to lift anything heavy until I worked the stiffness out of my back.

Both hunters had been with me twice before, and they were superb, saying they would help wherever possible if I would just tell them what to do. And they did. At road's end, they unloaded our heavy packs from the truck while I caught ponies from the corral. Then they threw saddles on the horses while I cinched them. Finally, they lifted the packs and held them in position while I threw the necessary

The sorrel mare (Tanglefoot) and Buck, with guide Rich Mattson. We've loaded our saddles with shed elk antlers. It's a spring photo, taken in May

hitches to lash packs to saddles.

After the packhorses were strung together, I found I could not mount the sorrel mare without help. At last, we were ready. I'd chosen the sorrel mare because of her easy fluid gait. I only prayed she'd wouldn't act up.

As we approached the first frozen stream, the mare hesitated. After battling her all summer, I could read the telltale signs. A temper tantrum was pending; the frozen creek was to provide the excuse. In my condition, I doubted I could handle her. So as she approached the ice and lowered her head to sniff, I let out a sudden yell and buried my spurs in her flanks. It caught her by surprise and she bolted forward into the tiny stream and out the other side, packhorses streaming behind.

I'd weathered the first obstacle. But there was a much larger creek six miles ahead. Just as I feared, the larger creek was also nearly frozen. The only thing I had going for this crossing was the fact that we always watered the string here, and the ponies should be thirsty. An open lead was ice-free in the middle, but the mare lowered her head to sniff before she even approached the stream. And she began shuffling her feet—a sure sign of impending trouble.

As she faltered, I drove my spurs into her flanks. She stopped. I spurred her again and she reared.

There was no way. I was hardly able to dismount, let alone do acrobatics with the fool mare. To compound the problem, I'd discarded the leather-thonged saddle club earlier in the fall, after giving up on the ding-a-ling pony.

The mare came down on all fours and stood eyeing the frozen stream. The more experienced packhorses fanned out, crowding ahead, wanting water. Again I urged the sorrel mare ahead. She began her shuffle, and I snapped the reins to call a truce.

Burt and Mark sat their horses, eyes wide. "What can we do?" Burt called.

I shook my head and reached for the only club I had close to hand—the single-bit cruiser axe hanging from my saddle. The axe head was sheathed with stout leather, so there was no danger of doing serious damage to the mare. I choked up on the handle and held its leather covered blunt side poised above her ears, then drove home the spurs.

Up she went, screaming in rage. I swung. She dodged. I missed. She fell forward. Again I spurred. Again she reared. Again I swung. Again she dodged. Again I missed. Again and again and again. Finally I connected with a half-swing. And another.

A brief fight flared between a couple of impatient packhorses, wanting water. Meanwhile, the deadly battle between the sorrel mare and me continued. Up she reared. I swung again, and a red welt appeared between her ears.

My back was killing me from the punishment I took, but I remember feeling a grim satisfaction that I'd finally scored a solid lick. I swung again as she reared, and once more felt a solid blow jolt along my arm. As quickly as it began, it was over. The mare waded out into the stream as if nothing had happened and stuck her nose into the water.

I guided her up the ice-free lead and brought the five thirsty packhorses to water, then reined her around to wave my axe and shout to the hunters, "You guys ride your horses into the creek so they can drink."

Mark jumped as if I'd broken a trance. "I'll do anything you say," he cried, eyeing my axe and urging his horse forward.

After four days, I was able to bend without too much pain. Mark and Burt had really been swell to help lift down the packs and unmanty them during that first day at camp. They carried water and helped in myriad other ways, allowing me to muddle through.

Finally it was Thanksgiving Day. I moved well by then and thought I'd be in top shape by the time the rest of the week passed and we packed out. I was riding ahead of Mark and Burt as we wended our way up a semi-open ridge, through deep snow. The sorrel mare had not given me one bit of trouble since our Armageddon at the frozen stream. But now she stopped. I prodded her.

The horse reared without warning. We were climbing a mountainside, and gravity was in her favor. Before I could react, we were going over! I tried to roll away, but only partially made it when the twelve-hundred-pound horse crashed down on me. The saddlehorn glanced off my left hip, and I was conscious of a sharp pain in my lower back. Then the horse scrambled to get up, feet flailing, rolling across where I lay sprawled.

When my eyes flickered open, Burt knelt by my side while Mark held the horses off to one side. "Roland! Roland, are you all right?" I don't know whether there's truth to the tale that a man's life flashes before his eyes just before his death. But I know for a fact that it occurs when the issue hangs in doubt. What of Jane? The children? So much left to do. So many mountains left to conquer. *Please, God, don't let it happen.*

"Don't try to move me," I said. "Just let me lay here a moment." It was peaceful. I was so tired—it'd been a long season. For some reason I thought of how our bathroom scales had weighed me in at 162 pounds just before this trip began—down from my regular 190.

It took several minutes before I recovered my wits. Then I said, "Let me see."

"Wait a minute," Burt said. "Maybe we ought to …"

I raised my right leg and flexed it. Then the left. Unless you've been there, you'll never know how relieved a man can be when he knows he could have a broken back but finds it's only bruised.

The deep snow saved my life. In avoiding the saddle-horn, I'd landed with a football-sized rock under my lower back. There was just enough snow to cushion me when the sorrel mare smashed down on top.

⚜

Eventually we came to an understanding—that sorrel mare and I. She spent most of her career in a packstring. Eventually, my understanding of equine mentality progressed until I could recognize her signs of growing anger and think of ways to blunt it—though I never learned to trust her until she neared twenty.

It's true the damned horse almost killed me. And there's no doubt that I made a mistake when I raised the bid on her to $230 dollars. But then I remember the Minneapolis printer's apprentice, Mark, eyeing my axe fearfully and saying, "I'll do anything you say!"

And I grin and cannot find it in my heart to resent the sorrel mare quite so much. ∎

Chapter 19

Bridging the Gap

Jane and I had married so young, neither of us knew much about the outside world. We were barely pubescent and certainly provincial, raised by old-fashioned parents of Southern lineage. I'd groped my way to a more cosmopolitan awareness, propelled in part by my work for Plum Creek, then by my profession as a hunting and fishing guide. But Jane, I thought, still hovered just beyond the bounds of entry into a wider sphere, trapped by narrow interests and the demands of near-single parenthood while I pursued dreams and ambition. Our daughter was to marry, however, and our son Marc was nearly fifteen. Perhaps Jane was ready to venture into the outside world.

My plan to promote our business through a service-club speaking circuit was proving less profitable than I'd envisioned and finally I threw in the towel and opted to pursue the sport-show circuit. Perhaps this would be an opportunity to involve my wife.

Jane was, after all, an attractive woman. She'd been sufficiently involved, albeit reluctantly, in the outfitting and guiding business so she could talk about our adventures with some authority. I put it to her: "Would you like to go to a sport show with me?"

She accepted with alacrity.

I'd not previously been on display. With our guiding business sinking for want of clients, Jane and I took out exhibit space at a January sport show—a ten-foot booth in a far corner of Houston's Astro Hall.

Because we knew no better at the time, our booth was designed pretty much like that of every other unimaginative Rocky Mountain horse outfitter guiding for fishing and hunting. There were a few elk and deer racks and a fish or two. A continuous carousel slide show was projected on a back-of-the-booth screen, and a scrapbook lay on the counter for casual page-turners to thumb through.

In addition, we had thousands of shoddy letter-size, threefold, black and white brochures I'd designed myself to hand out to the thousands of innocents waving C-notes we thought would throng our booth, begging to be led through a northern Rockies wilderness.

That's not the way it happened.

The doors to the show had supposedly opened two hours before the first visitor sauntered by our remote back-corner location. The guy looked to be in his mid-fifties. He had his hands in his pockets and was whistling tunelessly in an effort to quell boredom. He paused to read the hand-lettered sign hanging from the back of our booth—I'd sweated blood over that sign. The guy walked to our counter.

"Montana," the man said.

"Yep," was my reply. Apparently he expected more, so I racked my brain for something intelligent to add.

"You know," the man said, "I was in the army with a guy from Montana."

"That so?"

"Yeah. In Normandy. We didn't hit the beach, but come in right after."

He continued to stand across the counter, neither watching the slides nor leafing through the scrapbook. The way he continued to stare at our booth's back-curtain sign, I wondered if he expected his army buddy to emerge from somewhere within.

"His name was Johnson," he said. "Or Johnston—I don't remember which."

In a state filled with descendants of Scandinavian emigrants, Johnson (or Johnston) was the most common name listed in phone books. I sighed. Still the guy seemed rooted. In order to ease my embarrassment I said, "What was his first name?"

A mouth corner turned up in a wry smile. "Gosh darn, I can't remember."

A full minute went by before I asked, "Well, what town was he from?"

"I don't remember that, either. It's been thirty years, you know."

Another minute went by. Two. Three. Then he said, "You don't know him, do you?"

"Not an auspicious beginning, is it?" Jane said after the guy finally walked away.

A few other people trickled along our booth's aisle, but not many. None seemed interested in Montana, the northern Rockies, the Bob Marshall Wilderness, elk, mule deer, or float-fishing trips down a wild and pristine river.

The one bright spot during that ordeal streamed from a door directly across the aisle from where we stood. I was writing a letter, lost in thought, when something or someone flicked by the booth, then another. I glanced up. It was girls running past—a seemingly endless line. They were scantily clad maidens. *Beautiful scantily clad maidens.* They spilled from the door across the way, then ran down the aisle like football players trotting down a stadium runway, heading for the playing field.

No, not at all like football players, I decided!

I glanced surreptitiously at Jane. She stared back, eyes dancing. "Go ahead and look," she said. "You're beyond hurting them."

Later we learned the Dallas Cheerleaders were in town to do thrice-daily floor shows in the Astro Hall. After gleaning that fundamental truth, the only thing left was to learn the precise floorshow schedule, then straighten my tie and smooth the cowlick just before the girls' dressing-room door swung open.

⚜

Hang around long enough and even somebody trying to blend with the woodwork will stand out.

"Have you noticed that guy in the light blue coat?" Jane asked, jerking her thumb toward a man who lounged near the corner of our booth, staring across the aisle.

Average height. Average weight. Tastefully dressed, nothing gaudy. No gold earrings, either. "What about him?"

"He's been hanging around for a while. I asked him if I could help, but he said no. I think he was here earlier in the week, too."

Just then, a well-dressed couple sauntered to the booth, the woman's spike heels clicking on the concrete. The man asked about elk hunting, and as I went into what by now had developed into routine, I noticed the man in the blue coat edging nearer.

After a time, the spike-heeled woman shifted in boredom and her escort took the hint. As they turned to leave, I asked the man in the blue coat if I could help. But he was already turning away.

Two hours later he reappeared. He strode right to the counter where I shuffled what I now recognized as poor-quality brochures. "Yes?" I said.

"I'd like to schedule a hunting trip," the man said.

Believing the guy's statement was a request for information about our hunts, I began: "First off, we don't take any easy trips—all of them are ..."

I trailed off as the man pulled a checkbook from an inside pocket of his blue coat and asked, "How much do I make the deposit check for?"

It took a moment to gather my wits. By then he had the checkbook open and a pen poised. For the first time, our eyes met. His twinkled. "Don't you even want to *hear* about the kinds of hunts we do before you make out that check?" I said.

"I already know. I've been standing around listening to

you talk to other people—I was here earlier in the week, too. I'm impressed with you people and believe you're offering just the kind of elk hunts I've dreamed about for years. You seem honest. You make no claims except that you'll work very hard to get a hunter on an elk. You've always told everyone the same story. Now I'd like to schedule a trip with you."

That's how Alex Tully, pipefitter from a Texas City oil refinery scheduled with us—the first of his five hunts. I shook my head to clear the cobwebs. "What a neat way to do your homework!"

He smiled. "And how much is the check?"

❦

A week-long sport show (nine days, actually) is grueling for those tending the booths as well as for folks visiting the show for information. There were literally hundreds of choices, from Caribbean cruises to Canadian caribou, from Colorado dude ranches to Cancun beaches. Walking the aisles at the Houston Boat, Sport, and Travel Show, I shook my head at the creativity of many of the displays. Ours was among the poorer ones.

Despite the low quality of our display and despite what I felt was a lousy location, we did talk to some interested— and interesting—people, even scheduled a few.

Then the show ended and Jane boarded a plane for home while I pointed the "yellow banana" east for yet another six-week program tour, including a talk in Athens to the Forestry Department of the University of Georgia. Athens is, of course, but a short distance from the North Carolina valley from which many of our guests hailed.

Robert West took me on a tour of the valley. We stopped at the saw shop owned by his brother Roger. After shaking hands around, Robert said, "C'mon, Roger, let's go out to Montana hunting again." "Hell no." Roger replied, recollection of the previous season's debacle still firm in his mind. "I ain't never goin' to Montana again."

Robert laughed. "Aw c'mon. It ain't but a thousand dollars."

"A thousand dollars?" Roger said, dragging it out in his high pitched mountaineer's drawl. "A thousand dollars? Hell, I'll give him a thousand dollars if I don't have to go!"

Robert put his hunting party together without Roger, and they chose the last trip of the season, gambling that elk would be migrating through, on their way to winter range.

So I pointed the yellow banana on to Pennsylvania and a series of service-club programs. And finally, just before the Ides of March—after being grounded by blizzards in Michigan and North Dakota—I made my way home.

"We may not have to take out a third mortgage on our home," I told Jane, handing her enough deposit checks to carry us until hunting season began. "But we still haven't found the key to developing summer interest."

"What about selling?" she said, waving the checks. "You said you can't sell the outfitting business until you can prove it successful—isn't this proof? Isn't now the time to sell?"

I laughed. "Just when we're getting it going? Don't be daft, woman."

I did a few "drop camps" during the summer—packed small parties into remote areas of the wilderness and dropped them off. Some hiked out on their own, others had me return for them at a prearranged time. Though there's little profit and less fun packing for drop camps, the work did pay for my horses' feed and conditioned the animals for the coming hunting season. With a jam-packed schedule, hunting season 1977 had all the earmarks of being a doozy. I didn't know the half. ∎

Chapter 20

Poker with Scared Money

They were a bedraggled lot riding in. The guide, Ed, lashed his saddlehorse and packhorse to the hitchrack, then turned to help the two trailing riders dismount. Something should have nagged me about that because both hunters were young and strong and full of vinegar. Now, however, their faces were drawn and haggard and bore the shadow of a two-day stubble.

"How'd you boys do?" I called, heading after nosebags for the ponies. I paused at their lack of response, and turned back to Ed. "Any elk?"

"Saw some on the way back."

I glanced at my watch. It was early afternoon. "How come you're not chasing them?"

The guide dropped a pack and turned to the snarl of ropes holding another to the pony's back. "Nobody felt like it." The young man's usually cheerful, upbeat banter seemed subdued.

A few moments later I pushed through the flap of the feed tent, carrying nosebags full of grain for Ed's horses. Norm was just striding to the tent compound, saddlebags across his shoulder and his .300 Weatherby in his hand. As he brushed past, he said, "Don't be too hard on the kid. He didn't mean it."

I turned to stare after him in surprise, but the lanky

Midwesterner disappeared into his sleeping tent without another word.

Al, the older of the two, trailed his Wisconsin neighbor by a few feet. The stubbed-off father of three seemed more shrunken as he wobbled toward the tent. "Al, what's going on?" I asked.

He shook his head. But as he went by, he muttered, "He didn't mean to do it."

I carried the nosebags on out to the shuffling, stomping, nickering ponies. Ed stripped saddles, carrying them to the nearby rack. Then he started rubbing down the horses. While the guide and I both rubbed the same horse, I said in a low voice, "What's wrong with Al and Norm? Why'd they tell me not to be too hard on you?"

He straightened, peering at me over the pony's back. Again there was no smile. "I was going to talk to you as soon as I got through here."

"About what?"

"About the lost hunters."

"About *what* lost hunters? Who?"

"Al and Norm—they got turned around and spent the night out. I found 'em just before dark, but couldn't get to them. There was this big cliff, see? And they had a fire going so I could see they were all right. And ..."

I waved my guide to a log, then sat down beside him. "Maybe you ought to start at the beginning."

<hr>

Ed had, the day before, led his two hunters to a spike camp—a small tent set up in an isolated basin far from our main camp. They planned to spend the afternoon and evening hunting on that first day, then follow up with a morning hunt before returning to the main base.

It was wild and isolated country: a towering ridge whose crest had, for miles, been scalloped by glaciers into tiny hanging basins. Vast forests crowded right to basin meadows and ridgecrest tundra. It was steep country. The ridge, though rounded and sculpted on its upper reaches, plunged over three thousand feet to swift clearwater streams crowding both mountain flanks.

The three men followed the Forest Service trail to a point where they overlooked the basin where the spike tent was located; then Ed, in his eagerness to help his hunters to success, suggested that while he led the ponies down to their new camp, unpacked, unsaddled and watered them, Al and Norm could hunt down into the basin beyond and swing around the mountain's flank to camp. The men were eager to do it.

The flaw was that what appeared so easy from the ridgetop looked less likely after the men entered the deep forest. The land steepened and turned rocky. They slipped and skidded and clambered right past the little ravine they needed to follow upstream to camp, continuing on around the mountain heading God knows where. Meanwhile, Ed had the horses out to graze and his hunters' gear neatly arranged in their tent. At last he left a note at camp and hiked down the mountain looking for his hunters. He returned to camp twice in the hope the others had straggled in. Finally it began to grow dark.

Meanwhile, Norm and Al had entered their third basin without finding camp and were growing weary.

"We're not going to make it out before dark," Al said at last. "What we'd better do is stop and gather wood for a night fire."

At last, as the sun faded into crimson to sink beyond the distant horizon, the men leaned against the bole of a big spruce tree, a merry fire crackling at their feet. "Wish I had that apple core I threw out for the squirrels a few hours ago," Al said.

Norm fumbled in his jacket pocket. "I've got two lifesavers," he said. "Which do you want for supper? The lemon or the peppermint?"

"The lemon."

Meanwhile, Ed grew frantic. Though a veteran woodsman, this was his first season as a guide. These were his first hunters. They were lost! He lighted the lantern, loaded a knapsack with food, picked up his rifle, and headed into the night.

On the trail, two miles from camp, he fired a signal shot. To his relief there came a distant reply. He started into the forest. Several hundred yards later he stumbled out to the edge of a precipice and waved his lantern. A thousand feet below and hundreds of yards in the distance, a campfire winked. Again, he fired his rifle. Voice contact was made.

"D-o-o-n't tr-y-y it," came the distant shout. "Cli-i-i-ffs be-etwe-e-en. To-o-o ri-i-sky."

There was nothing for the guide or hunters to do except wait for daylight. At the end of his tale, Ed flashed his endearing grin. "It was the longest night I ever spent." He spread his hands. "But I suppose it was nothing compared to those guys down there, lost in the middle of one of the biggest wildernesses in America."

⚬═══⚬

This, hunting season was our busiest-ever, and team-work was essential. Jane was pressed into service; she had groceries for humans and horses set out and ready. With but one day between those early trips, we spent that day working from daylight to dark mantying our incoming hunters' gear, horses' hay and grain, and packing food boxes in preparation for the following day's four a.m. departure.

The second trip included three fine gentlemen from Houston and our son, fifteen-year-old Marc. In order to squeeze in more paying guests during hunting season, we switched to the low camp for an eight-day hunt. There was no layover day between. I was young then, however, and determined to make Skyline Outfit into a success. So I just worked harder and faster.

Then we again headed for the high camp with veteran hunters Rufus Gehris, Ken Gaugler, and Alex Tully, and a newcomer, another Pennsylvanian, Harold Lohmiller.

It was a fine adventure. Rufus, one of the most deserving hunters I ever led, at last took his long dreamed-of bull (recounted in my book, *The Phantom Ghost of Harriet Lou*).

The weather continued mild. Our hunters were enjoying a modestly successful season, and full-time guide Ed Ernst was proving to be an unusually fine workman. Another month and this grueling hunting season would be over.

Jane flipped on the porch light so I could see to finish making up packs. Our incoming hunters had turned in for the night, and there were just the two of us remaining. I straightened to survey the helter-skelter packhorse loads lying on our lawn. "I'll get the pickup and load them in a minute."

She handed me a cup of coffee. "I'll get the pickup. You sit down and drink this."

I sniffed. There was more than just coffee in the mug.

We sat together on a hay bale. "The kids?" I asked. "Everything still okay? School? Job?"

She nodded. "Cheri still plans to marry in the spring. You will be there for that one, won't you?"

"I'll be there. What about Marc?"

Her smile lit up the yard light. "You ought to know. You see more of him in the backcountry than I do in town."

I chuckled. "He's going to make a good hunter."

A comfortable silence fell. Then Jane said, "I'm much more worried about you than about the kids. You need a week to sleep, a month to rest."

"In a month. Then we'll both rest."

"Roland, this work is too much. I used to think it would be our undoing. But the way it's going, you won't last long enough for us to fall apart. Sell the outfitting business before it kills you."

We returned to the lower camp with the Sayre outfit— the fine Oregon bunch. This time the outfit included Buck Fritts, my long ago Webfoot State neighbor who helped us move to the Rockies, then showed up on our doorstep to help frame and roof our Montana home.

"You know," I told Buck as Jane handed us each a beer after the pre-trip work was done, you have a pleasing way of walking into our lives when we need you the most."

Buck grinned. "Not this time, young guy. This time I need you more than you know. They retired me off the railroad because I can't see my hand in front of my face. And I'm getting contusions of the lower arsenal. But Bud's been telling me how great your camp and your elk hunting

is, so I decided to come see for myself."

"Buck, it'll be the best trip we've ever had."

My friend slapped me on the back, spilling my beer. "I know that, Roland. It's already the best trip I ever had."

We brought three fine bulls out from that hunt. Unfortunately, none of them was Buck's, though we tried as hard as we could.

The West bunch from North Carolina in the deep-snow year of 1977. Left to right: Robert, Burke, Whitey, and Bud.

Elk were definitely on the move, though. Every day a new band traveled through. "Why aren't they pausing?" I asked Bud and Lacy. "The weather's nice. They should hang up someplace where they have plenty of food and wait for the next storm to move in before heading on to winter range."

Our next party was another bunch of Wisconsin white-tail hunters. Elk still moved through the country without pause. And as it turned out, we spent most of the remaining hunts trying to overhaul migrating elk.

"Why? Why?" I asked, bewildered by a migration pattern I'd never seen. The answer came as we packed back to civilization—a savage blizzard with driving snow and plummeting temperatures.

It took a hearty group to buck the deepening snow and zero cold of an early winter. Fortunately, the three Michiganders and two Montanans knew what cold-weather hunting was like. Hunting, though, was growing chancier under the onslaught of bitter weather. The former steady pattern of migrating elk was drying up as God turned His weather tap to suit celestial vibes.

At last our final party of the season arrived: the West boys from North Carolina.

"Roland," Robert said, stepping from their airport rental car, "I brought that ten Janie has been cryin' over ever since you lost it. Are you goin' to bring twenty to get it back?"

"Got it in my inside shirt pocket, Robert. Right next to my heart."

We went in with the thermometer hovering at ten below. These guys were tough Smokey Mountaineers, but this trip was a test even for a tough Montana outfitter. Here are excerpts from my diary:

> The thermometer dropped to twenty below the first night. For two-three days it stayed cold and stormed hard. Snow built to two feet around camp and deeper in the high country. We shoveled snow constantly from the tents. Lord, it was cold. Our eggs froze. So did the tomatoes, potatoes, and all the canned goods. The beer even froze, which should be an indicator of the seriousness of the situation. The whiskey turned cloudy.
>
> We tried to hunt, but couldn't find any critters. Most of the tracks we saw were under the trees, where they were sheltered from the piling snow. I guess the animals are smarter than we are and are sticking pretty tight to their equivalent of our warm tents.
>
> After a few days the weather began moderating and it warmed up fifty-two degrees and started raining. Then we fought water as the solidly frozen ground shed the water onto our tent floors. Then it was shovel, shovel, shovel to get snow away from the tents. Wish I'd brought more shovels.
>
> We still tried to hunt and drowned out, froze out,

and got cranky. Then the rain again turned to snow.

The bitter weather did make for one thing—plenty of time to play poker. And those Carolinians lost no time getting started, crowding around the cooktent table to begin the game while I unpacked groceries and their guides cared for the horses.

"C'mon Mr. Guide Man," Robert said. "You'll never get your money back if you don't get into the game."

I smiled. "Too busy right now, Robert. You guys go ahead without me." After that it was easy to beg off because they were hungry and I had to cook supper. After supper it was, "Sorry, boys. I can't get in now because I have to clean up the kitchen."

My *real* plan was to avoid playing as long as possible. You see, I knew I'd lose the twenty—planned to lose it, as a matter of fact. Me play poker? That's a joke. I knew nothing about the game. With these guys, cards were a way of life. The way I saw it, my twenty dollars was nothing more than a promotional tool to use—and lose—in order to add another dimension for my guests. Therefore, the longer I avoided losing it, the more their anticipation was whetted.

Finally the lights dimmed and we went to our sleeping bags.

It seemed as though my head had just hit the pillow when the alarm jangled in my ear. God, it was cold. I kindled a fire in the cookstove, then went to move the five-gallon bucket of water we'd left atop it the night before. It was frozen solid!

Outside the cooktent, the thermometer we had hanging in a tree read twenty below zero. The crisp air bit my nostrils and penetrated through my clothing. How could we even hunt?

The guides, Ted, Rich, and Ed, stumbled out to check the thermometer, then returned to their tent for more clothes. The saddles were frozen stiff. So were the saddlepads. When the boys brought the horses to the hitchrack for their grain, they stood with backs hunched against the bitter cold. Saddlepads and saddles had to be laid atop the ponies and loose-cinched until body heat from the animals thawed the leather enough to allow them to mold into place.

My hunters eyed their outfitter suspiciously when they straggled in for breakfast. "Are we a-goin' out today, Mr. Guide Man? Are you shore? Ain't no elk movin' in this kind of weather."

To their credit—and ours—we tried. But the deep snow and bitter cold drove us back to our tents by midafternoon. The poker game started again.

"C'mon, Mr. Guide Man. We want some more of yore easy money."

I looked around. The tents were toasty warm. The horses were cared for. It was still two hours until I must begin supper. Robert taunted, "What's the matter, Mr. Guide Man, feared o' losin' yore money?"

I pulled out the twenty and, to much whooping and shouting, pitched it on the table. They swept off a space for their Guide Man and I sat down.

Whitey eyed his kin and said, "Boys, let's make it a two-dollar limit in order to be fair to Roland." It was agreed. They dealt. Wonder of wonders, I won. I looked at the pot pushed toward me and chortled, "Now I'll be able to play two or three hands."

Then I won again.

Three hands later, I won again. Now I looked at the pile of money at my place at the table and began to sweat. I didn't want to win money from these guys. All I wanted to do was *play* a little while because that's what *they* wanted me to do. But win from them? No. So I began taking chances, trying to lose. If I bet on a pair of treys, the guy who raised me was bluffing a pair of deuces. I drew to inside straights—and hit them. When at last I pushed from the table to begin supper, I had a hundred and twelve of their dollars.

"You can't quit now," Robert said. "You're the big winner."

So I pitched my money to one of my guides, saying, "Go ahead and play for me, Ted."

It was a bad choice. The ex-navy submariner had spent his poker-playing apprenticeship in countless shipboard blanket-games. He played three hands and won $56 for me.

Despite all my efforts to lose, I came out of that camp with $312 more in bills pinned to a shirtpocket than I took in.

But the big lesson I learned that year wasn't how to win at poker, but how to win at life. The oddity in the lesson came—where else? From a poker game.

It was "jacks or better for openers." I opened on a pair of kings. Whitey stayed. So did his son Bud. Burke threw in. Robert raised the limit. The betters all matched him. I drew three cards, as did Whitey and Bud. Robert took nothing. I bet modestly. Whitey threw his cards onto the pot. Bud stayed. Robert raised the limit. I looked across the table at the man, then down at the backs of his cards. Then I showed my openers and pitched my cards in. Bud did likewise.

Robert laid his cards face up, one at a time: a trey of clubs, six of spades, seven of diamonds, ten of clubs, jack of hearts.

"But ... but you had nothing!" I said as he raked in the pot. "I had you beat easy."

He chortled. "You shore did, Mr. Guide Man." Then he eyed his nephew. "And I'll bet old Bud had me beat, too."

Bud, red-faced, nodded.

"Let me tell you something, boys. You cain't play poker with 'scared' money."

I stared at the man for the longest time. "What's the matter with you, Mr. Guide Man?" Robert asked at last.

I sighed. "You just passed along a metaphor for life, didn't you Robert?"

"I surely did. And don't you *ever* forget it." ■

Chapter 21

Jane's Arrival

The 1977 hunting season had been a particularly grueling one. In order to squeeze in more hunters during the season, I'd put together several eight-day trips—all back to back without a layover day between. I worked sixteen-, eighteen-, sometimes twenty-hour days throughout September, October, and November without a day off, spending just nine nights at home. In addition, the weather during November sapped us. And my working weight, normally 190, fell again to 160 pounds.

"You have shadows on your face," Jane said as Ed and I unloaded the last of our equipment. It was the first day of December.

I rubbed the stubble on my jaw, then gathered her into my arms. "It's over," I murmured, eyes closed, tears squeezing out. "At last it's over."

"Sell," she said.

"We've almost turned the corner."

"Sell," she said.

"Next year we'll be able to hire more full-time help instead of depending on volunteers."

"Sell," she said. "Now, before it's too late."

"No. I'm not ready."

She squeezed. "You feel like a shadow, too. There's no meat left on your bones."

There were lessons to be learned from that 1977 season, yet so little time to apply them. We had yet to find the key to unlock summer business. The sport show at Houston's Astro Hall hadn't brought us a stampede of Texans, nor was the early promise from service club circuits manifesting itself.

Jane was right, of course—I could not continue at the pace I'd set in 1977. I had already admitted to myself that we'd tried to serve too many hunters during a limited season. So we went back to the ten-day hunting schedule for 1978.

"At least we made some money during '77," I said, laying aside my paintbrush. "Not enough yet, but we're on the right track."

"That's comforting," my wife said, as we worked to design a more attractive display booth for the coming season. "At least I'll have money to spend when you're in the ground."

What we really needed was to further develop our client base, especially with regard to summer activities. So we added two sport shows to our itinerary, one in Edmonton in early March and one in Los Angeles the first of April. I also considered expanding our trip options with a black-bear hunt in the spring.

In addition, Minnesotan Del Lietzau lobbied hard for us to get into wintertime mountain-lion hunting. Jane bitterly opposed the cougar idea.

"I won't feed dogs while you're gone," she said. "Twenty-five horses is enough."

"Won't or don't want to?"

"I *won't!*"

But the lady did look thoughtful when Del mentioned how welcome a few additional dollars might be during our winter season. "It wouldn't cost that much to get into it, either." he said. "A thousand for the dogs, two thousand for a snowmobile, maybe another thousand for equipment."

"I don't know enough about winter survival," I told him,

"or winter travel."

He laughed—Del and his wife and Jane and I discussed the lion idea during an overnight crosscountry ski trip into Glacier Park. We were standing in lion tracks at the time. "You don't know about winter survival? Don't tell me you've forgotten those late-November hunts into the Bob when it was blizzarding out and the temperature down to twenty below."

Another friend said I'd be missing a bet if I didn't consider guiding for mountain-lion hunters. The man headed a wolverine study in the Flathead's South Fork. He spent his winters out amid the peaks, live-trapping, tagging, radio collaring, and tracking wolverines. Howard Hash had a master's degree in wildlife biology, and he worked directly under Dr. Maurice Hornocker, the world's foremost authority on mountain lions. His recommendation to get into the sport was not to be sneered at.

We tried it. A friend, Richard Smith, brought his hounds up from Salmon, Idaho, and Del Lietzau came from Minnesota to join us. Del took a huge male cougar that stalked a deer herd up the Flathead's North Fork. I didn't like it.

The ten minute chase was exciting. And Jane's hindquarter roast from the lion was delicious. But I hated riding around all day in a pickup truck while looking for tracks in the snow.

* * *

After leaving Los Angeles and our final show of the season, Jane and I toured the country, driving through Texas and the Atlantic Seaboard, into Pennsylvania and back through Michigan and Wisconsin, Minnesota, and North Dakota, visiting friends and giving occasional service-club programs.

Instead of the 34 hunters scheduled for the previous fall, we wound up with 25 for the autumn of '78. But upon our return from the East, I led my first spring bear hunt in May, and we had two summer horseback trips for August as well as a September horseback in / river-float out fishing excursion. So our expanded summer season more than made up for the drop in fall hunters.

And the extended schedule over six months instead of two and a half made my work easier.

Bill Kreitzer was a vice-president of an oil exploration company. When he and his partner flew from Houston to climb on a horse and travel deep into the wilderness in pursuit of a black bear, it made the first time I'd had guests arrive via private jet.

They proved to be wonderful guys. When we returned to civilization and Jane and I drove them to the airport to meet their company plane, Bill invited us aboard while the aircraft was being refueled. Everything was first-class, I could see that right off. The copilot mixed cocktails and set out a plate of prepared hors d'oeuvres. This was luxury! Soon the tanned and handsome pilot boarded the plane to report all was ready for the takeoff. Bill gazed appraisingly at Jane and me. "Close the door," he told the captain. "We'll take them to Houston with us."

Jane's eyes widened. I shook my head. "Can't."

Bill said, "Why not? You don't have another trip going out right away. You can visit in our home, meet my wife, catch a commercial flight back when you're ready."

"Marc. Marc is home alone."

"That's your son?"

I nodded.

Jane said, "He *is* sixteen years old, Roland."

"Old enough to take care of himself for two or three days," Bill added.

It was all so sudden. The captain and copilot smiled and waited for an answer, glancing from one passenger to another.

"You can call your son after we're airborne," Bill said. "Tell him you'll be a day or two coming home."

I pushed to my feet, holding out one hand to Jane, taking Bill's hand with the other and pumping it. "Thanks, though, for your offer, friend. I'm sure we'll regret not doing it."

I was right. I draped an arm over Jane's shoulder as we watched the Learjet climb into the distance. "I'm sorry, honey."

She caressed my hand. "Me, too."

⚜

The signs were hard to ignore. My wife was pushing toward becoming a first-class outdoor woman. She launched into Dutch oven cooking with a zest, and developed real mastery of the culinary art around a campfire. In her saddlebags, she carried books on mushrooms, wildflowers, and birds.

She still feared the power of horses, though, and preferred walking over riding. She turned into a prodigious hiker, and when I led our next summer horseback "gypsy" trip through the Bob, guess who went along as cook and chief flunky?

It was an idyllic adventure with two wonderful people: Bob Wylie, who'd hunted twice with us, and his wife Grace. It was Jane who eased any fears Grace had about the rigors of the venture. After all, if this dainty outfitter's wife can do it, why can't I?

The weather cooperated, with balmy, sunshiny days and crisp, cool, star-studded nights. There were deer in camp and elk in the mountains. One day we rode to Jane's and my secret place—the one we call "God's High Table"—for a picnic. Grace carried an easel and paints in her saddlebags, and the rest of the party sprawled in the grass and watched in awe as she re-created the gorgeous mountain scene spreading before us.

After a while I yawned, stood, and pulled a gold pan from my saddlebags, and moved to a nearby stream to dip some gravel into the pan, then began swirling it. As Bob headed my way, I surreptitiously spilled some gold flakes into the pan.

"You're not going to find gold here, Roland," the civil engineer said. "This rock is all sedimentary in origin."

"Probably not," I replied, dipping and swirling, dipping

and swirling. Then, "WHAT'S THAT?"

Bob followed my finger to a tiny fleck of yellow. "My God!" he breathed.

I dipped and swirled again, then again. More flecks of yellow. Bob's nose was almost in the pan. "Grace!" he shouted. The women hurried over. Bob looked up at me, at my grin. "You salted it," he said. "And I fell for it."

<hr />

Our next party was more challenging—a family from New Jersey. The father was a chemical engineer. Both children were in their teens. The mother, though a courageous woman willing to try anything her husband and children wished to do, was frightened of horses, heights, and imagined horrors, not necessarily in that order. To add to their difficulties, the family had ignored the suggested clothing list that we routinely provide clients and brought only light jackets and no raingear.

You guessed it—the weather turned sour, raining for three days before turning to wet, soggy snow. Still, the father and I hiked to the Chinese Wall and the Wall Creek Cliffs while Jane and our son Marc entertained the rest of the family nearer camp.

At the end of their week, our trail to the low country skirted a perilous pea-gravel slope above a high cliff. I've always considered that hundred-and-fifty-yard stretch to be the most dangerous trail on this circuit, so I routinely ask our guests to dismount and walk past the peril.

I led our party, pulling the packstring. I'd warned the group about the trail, so they weren't surprised when I paused at the pea-gravel and told everyone to dismount. Then I led off, striding steadily along the narrow path, only occasionally glancing down at where gravel kicked loose fell into space. The packstring, for their part, seemed unconcerned.

I glanced back at the father and the two teenagers. They walked without hesitation, leading their saddlehorses. Jane and the mother had yet to appear.

We reached the far side and entered the alpine forest.

After I'd led the string past danger and left sufficient room for other horses and riders to reach safety, we paused.

Still no Jane, nor the other lady. We waited five minutes. Ten. Then the father said, "It's the kids' mother. She's paranoid about height."

I looked at him aghast. I lashed my string to trees and started back across the pea-gravel scree. Then here came the ladies' horses picking their way along the trail. Apparently the women had turned them loose.

Now I really worried. Then I saw Jane. She was leading the woman step by step across the scree. The other lady was blindfolded!

Later Jane told me the woman was too frightened to attempt the path while she could see it. So my wife did the only sensible thing she could, tying her kerchief around the lady's eyes, then guiding her across the danger spot, all the time whispering encouragement.

It's fair to say I swelled with pride at the way my wife rose to an occasion I might well have mishandled.

⁂

Our last summer trip of the year came in September— a group of orthodontists and their wives. The men had gone to dental school together, the couples had all been friends, gone their separate ways, but maintained their friendships. It was, to say the least, educational for me.

One very attractive lady had just had a baby before their journey. When she swung onto her horse for the first time, one of her friends, Ann, screamed, "Ohh! Ohh! There go the stitches!" I was at the new mother's side, adjusting stirrups. I turned red, beginning at my collar and spreading upwards until the bald spot on top looked like a crossroad blinker light. But the lady whose leg I held at the time laughed as hard as all the rest of her party.

⁂

The World Series was in progress during our last high country hunt. And Robert West was driving me nuts wanting to know the outcome. "Who you reckon won, Roland?" he'd say. "The Yankees or the Dodgers?"

Over and over again, day after day: "I shore wisht I knew who won the Series, Roland."

Finally I told him, "Rich will be in on Friday with a load of Hay. He'll be able to tell you."

"Shore nuff? Boy, I cain't hardly wait."

Rich pulled in just at twilight. Robert had been outside the tents waiting for two hours. Before my packer could even dismount, Robert called, "Rich! Rich! Who won the World Series?"

The young packer swung down and lashed his lead horse to the hitchrail, then turned. "Who's playing?" he asked.

<hr/>

1978 was also the first year Jane actually spent time in hunting camp. It was during one of the hunts at our lower camp. We had only two hunters, and I told Jane that the guides Rich and Bret could easily handle guiding chores if she wanted to join us. She did—and had the misfortune to choose a trip when the powers that be sent down a bunch of snow. Jane was undaunted.

One day, because our hunters had yet to see game, I suggested we might help the luckless guests by riding up a distant ridge to search for elk or their tracks. When Jane and I prepared to mount, she said, "Where's your gun?"

"What do I need a gun for?"

"What if we see some elk?"

"Do you expect me to shoot one?"

"I do. We eat meat, you know."

The last thing I wanted to do was shoot an elk, then have to butcher it, return to camp for packhorses, and pack it out. Still, I didn't want to look small in my wife's eyes, so I snapped my rifle scabbard to the saddle rings and swung up.

It was a wonderful day. Atop the ridge, the snow was maybe eighteen inches deep. The day was a crisp, clear fifteen degrees, but we were bundled so well the cold didn't bother us. Besides, I had this warming feeling that the woman was beginning to think she hadn't married a loser after all.

We paused at a spectacular viewspot for lunch, and I built a bonfire. Jane sat in the snow and hugged her knees for perhaps an hour, then returned to the fire to kneel at my side. She trailed her fingers along my jawline. "Beautiful, isn't it?" I said.

Jane fishing at Dean Falls on the Spotted Bear River in the Fall of 1978. She was just beginning to show how tough she could be. The world's greatest grouse dog is at her side.

"It is that."

"You realize we're miles and miles from the nearest other person?"

"I once thought that was scary."

"Not now?"

"Not now."

The hours slipped away, and soon it was time to return. Our horses' tracks through the ridgetop snow remained the only mar to the dazzling blanket. Then Jane, riding ahead, spotted an elk.

He stood about 400 yards away, beneath a wolf tree, a lone bushy fir that provided shelter and warmth. The elk was a small bull. Just below his feet, the sidehill plunged into a deep canyon. "Aw, Jane, I don't want to shoot it."

"Why? You have a license."

I sighed and slipped my .30-06 from its scabbard, then swung from my horse, handing her my pony's halter rope. Carefully laying the rifle barrel across a stout tree limb, I took aim, deliberately holding high, wanting to either anchor the bull or miss clean. I missed. The bull broke from his cover in a rush, plunging into the canyon.

I said, "Now I must walk out to that tree and see if I really did miss."

"Do you want me to go with you?"

"No need. It'll only take a few minutes."

But when I returned it was to tell her, "There are lots of other tracks heading into that canyon."

She said nothing so I added, "The ideal thing would be to follow them, hunt through to the Soldier Creek Trail, then hike it back to camp. But it's tough country. No way could a horse make it."

"How far would it be to camp that way?"

Probably eight to ten miles."

"If you're not anxious to shoot an elk, why would you undertake a hike like that in deep snow?"

"To find out where the elk went. Perhaps help our hunters."

"So you'd like for me to take these two horses on back to camp?"

I smiled up at her, patted her on the knee. "Can you do it?"

Her answer was to cluck at her saddlehorse. I watched until the woman and our two horses were swallowed by the mountain and its forest. She would have a six-mile ride through deep snow, following a trail she'd been on for the first time that morning. Lord was I proud!

Jane was at camp when I straggled in around dark. Her horses were in the corral, a pie made, and supper near perfection.

<hr />

Jane and I planned to return home before the trip ended in order to prepare for our next hunt. The rain drummed down on the morning of our departure, and the wind howled through the treetops.

Our late-season camp was sheltered in the valley bottom, amid a grove of huge spruce trees, so we had no idea of the extent of the windstorm. I was leading five packhorses and Jane brought up the rear. We'd not gone far before we began to encounter toppled trees across our trail. We picked our way around most, but some had to be laboriously chopped from the path.

The wind was intense on the glacial benches, where the trail snaked up from the river bottom. We could hear trees falling in the distance. A couple of times we heard them crash to the ground behind us. I knew it was foolish to travel in this kind of windstorm, but we were so deep into the forest now that one place was as good as another.

Then Jane screamed!

I could hear the roots popping, even hear the swoosh! of branches as the tree swept down. But where? I twisted in the saddle to see where Jane pointed. Then the treetop swatted the ground only five feet to one side, followed by the ground-jarring thump of the trunk striking with death-dealing force. Then the rodeo began.

By the time I had the horses under control, Jane sat her saddlehorse at my side. "All I could see was it coming right for you."

"It was close."

Another tree fell in the distance.

"What are we going to do, Roland?"

I reached over and gripped her shoulder. "We're going to ride like hell for road's end. After we get there, we're going to climb in the truck and drive like hell for home. And after we get *there* I'm going to take a shower—maybe with you." ■

Chapter 22

Love at a Price

We had a couple of days to ourselves after the windstorm, discovering anew how deep was our fancy for each other. Then it was back to work. For the first time, I didn't wish to head back into the mountains; I wanted to be with the woman I loved. We had to eat, however, and the only way to satisfy that persistent urge was through my guiding others to adventure.

Fortunately, the separation was made more palatable by the spirit and good nature of our four hunters: Jack Wallis and Wayne Dierks of Little Rock, and Minnesota's Joe Rogers and Dick Bol.

Jack, back for his second hunt, used his unique blend of humorous one-liners ("Cheek, you're so ugly I'll bet your mother had to borrow a baby to take to church.") to keep the camp in stitches throughout their ten days. But it was Joe, a Minnesota lumber broker and country-music guitarist and singer with several successful recordings, who delivered a lesson not to be forgotten.

Late one evening, after the others had drifted to their sleeping bags, Joe and I sat in quiet communion at the cooktent table drinking the last bitter dregs from the coffee pot.

I studied the man who was twenty years my elder, wondering if this is what my brother would have looked like had his bomber made it home from England: longish gray hair, a deeply lined face, laugh crinkles at the eyes and mouth corners. Damned if he didn't project the image of an aging country-music artist—Roy Acuff maybe, or an older Johnny Cash.

"Tell me about yourself, Joe," I said. "How did you get into country music?"

The man shrugged. "I like it."

"But you write the lyrics and put them to music. Did you train for that?"

He shook his head, then wet a finger and wiped a coffee stain from his mug. I smiled at the unusual act from such a cultured and debonair guy. "Well, where did you attend college? What's your degree in?"

He snorted. "I didn't attend college. My degree is in hard knocks." He gripped his mug with both hands, bringing it halfway to his lips, staring into its darkness. "I've only gone through the eighth grade."

Hot dog! A kindred soul. A man who actually did what I'm trying to do—succeed in spite of a lack of education. "Really! Well isn't that something. I never graduated from high school either."

Joe glanced up from his cup, eyes narrowed. He threw off his coffee dregs and said, "And you're proud?"

What could I say? What *should* I say.

The man continued: "You've just told me more about yourself in thirty seconds than you've done during the last six days."

"I don't understand …"

"You've just told me you're too damned lazy to get an education, son." I started to protest, but he waved a hand. "Anyone who really wants an education can get one in today's world. Isn't that true?"

I looked at the toes of my boots, no longer so cocky.

"I'll bet you had the chance—maybe more than one— and turned it down, right?" When I shook my head, he thundered, "ISN'T THAT RIGHT?"

"My father wanted me to go to college," I mumbled, "Offered to help me through."

Joe nodded, then shuffled to the stove and refilled his cup. "I thought so. You're too bright not to have had the chance. But you have no guts. Or else you're too lazy to take it."

Joe had returned to his Minneapolis home before I remembered that I'd not bothered to ask why *he* only attended school through the eighth grade. But the upshot of that conversation was that Rogers was the last person to whom I ever bragged about not having an education.

⌘

Our last guests of the season also hailed from Minnesota. Greg Melges owned a sporting-goods store in Spicer, west of Minneapolis. Vern Thorstad was a successful businessman and the Mayor of Maynard, also west of the Twin Cities.

"Another wedding anniversary," my wife said, eyes welling as I prepared to swing into the saddle. Jane was to take our pickup truck home, then meet us the day after hunting season with enough hay to hold the ponies until I could go back in and pull camp.

"And this one is on Saturday," I said squeezing her shoulder. "But we'll be out on Monday, the 29th. Then I'll make it up to you."

She stepped back, fingers trailing down my ribs, then falling away. "You're turning gaunt again. But with only two hunters and Jack and Rich to help, maybe you'll be able to rest a little this time."

I didn't rest, though. We'd not done well for elk on the hunt before, and to do poorly twice in a row would be unthinkable. We left camp before daylight and returned after dark, day after day. Deepening snows blocked us from some of the high country, however, and the elk seemed engaged in their old elusive magic.

"They're here," I told my hunter, pointing at tracks in the snow. Twice we stumbled on small bands of cows on the move. But we failed to come upon any bulls.

Greg had brought two pairs of snowshoes in a new design, and we gave them a try. With the shoes providing flotation atop the snow, we were able to reach a ridgetop thick with fresh elk tracks. I decided the tracks were made by bulls. But still the elk eluded us.

So we stopped for lunch and I built a small fire. After toasting sandwiches, we crouched, holding our palms to the blaze. Steam rose from our woolens.

"It's a pity my sons won't be able to experience this," Greg said.

"Wha-a-at? Why won't they?"

"Anti-hunting. Anti-gun. It gets worse every year. Another ten or fifteen years and we'll no longer be able to hunt."

Stunned, I settled back against my tree, staring into the fire. He added, "You live out here in Montana, Roland. Maybe you don't hear so much about the problem. But I'm right there in Minnesota where it's thick."

Silence fell. I peeled an orange. A coal popped onto a trouser leg and was brushed away. The fire collapsed on itself amid a shower of sparks. They hissed where they kissed the surrounding snow. I added a couple more branches, then said:

"We're twenty-five miles from the nearest other person, in the middle of one of the biggest wilderness areas in America. There are only a few of us left this time of year, but still a few. Earlier there were hundreds of them. Fact is, hunters are virtually the *only* visitors to this wilderness in September, October, and November. Summer travelers go home after Labor Day."

"I can believe that ..."

"So half the justification for setting aside great chunks of wildlands for people to see what America was once like is that half of those visitors are hunters in the fall. It's difficult enough to save wild places for your kids and my kids without turning away half its constituency by ending hunting."

It was Greg's turn to fall silent. At last he said, "Have you brought up that point?"

"All the time."

The elk continued to make fools of hunters and their guides. Finally it was Friday evening, nearing the end of

our trip. Just two more days to hunt. We were gathered
around the cooktent table.

Vern balanced a bowl of gravy and scooped potatoes
onto a thick slice of roast beef. "Didn't I hear something
about Roland's wedding anniversary coming up soon?" he
asked.

Jack set a steaming pan of corn on the table. "That's
right," the cook said. "How long have you been married,
Roland?" He looked funny wearing an apron—the only
one of my cooks to do so.

"A while."

"When did you marry?" Vern said. "What year?"

"'Nineteen fifty-four. We've been married twenty-four
years." I shook my head and flashed a wry smile. "Tomorrow."

"Tomorrow! And you'll be in here with this rotten
bunch when you've got a wife like yours probably crying
her eyes out because you're not there? What's the matter
with you?"

I shrugged.

"Hey, I'm serious."

"So am I. I have an obligation to you guys."

"No way," the mayor said. "We're going out tomorrow.
I'm going to personally escort you to your door and hand
you over to your wife. No way am I going to be a home-
breaker."

The guy wasn't funning. I shook my head. "Can't. The
only transportation we have at road's end is the old stock
truck. There are five of us. Jane is supposed to bring the
pickup to the trailhead on Monday. Even if we get out to
the road, there's no way for us all to get home."

Vern snorted. "Then we'll ride in the back of the stock
truck."

"It's too cold."

"Then we'll take turns. Two in the back with the horses,
two up front with you until the guys in the back pound on
the cab, then trade. Roland, we *are* going to get you home
to your wife tomorrow night. Then Greg and I will take
you all out for dinner—right, Greg?"

So that's how we drove into our yard at 7:30 p.m. on Saturday, Jane's and my twenty-fourth anniversary. "Put on your best dress, woman," I shouted. "We're going out to dinner."

It takes time to unload horses and gear, then properly rake out a week of accumulated grime from beneath one's fingernails. But at last we gathered the troops—Jack and his wife Margaret, Jane and me, Rich, Greg, and Vern— then found a restaurant that was still serving.

After the waitress had taken our drink orders, Vern instructed her to bring a second round with the first. "We have a very important date to commemorate here," he told her, "so it has to be done properly." When she returned to take our orders, Vern again took charge.

He pointed at the ladies. "They'll have lobster tails," he said. Then he pointed at me, Jack, Greg, and himself. "We will each have *two* lobster tails ..."

"Are you serious?" she said.

"Madam, I could not be more serious." Finally he pointed to Rich, who'd already told the man he did not like lobster, "And bring him *two* T-bones—the largest in the house—with an extra side dish of mashed potatoes."

The waitress hesitated, gazing wide-eyed at each of us in turn, then began scribbling. "And, oh," Vern said, "we'd like two bottles of your finest chardonnay."

The poor girl was dozing at a corner table when, long after midnight, we prepared to leave. But she brightened considerably when Vern began peeling bills from the roll pulled from his pocket. He added several to her tip. "And this for the cook," the mayor added, laying a fifty atop the pile.

<hr />

I left before daylight with the stock truck, short on sleep, but long on memories of a delightful anniversary evening with a most delightful woman. The plan was for me to pack in alone to break camp, then return to the trailhead the following afternoon. Jack was to meet me there in our pickup to haul the gear and pull the tack trailer home while I brought the last of our horses in for the winter.

It was a good plan. The error in it was that I failed to properly calculate the season. The blizzard struck while I was still driving to the trailhead, and I had to chain up the old Ford to bust through deepening, drifting snow to reach the eight horses in our end-of-the-road corral.

I made good time despite the snow. At camp, after unsaddling and caring for the ponies, then scattering the last of their hay, I started shoveling snow from the tents. The work went fast, and I took down and made packs of all but the cooktent before full dark fell. At last I debated whether to pull the plastic fly from the remaining tent. The snow had stopped and stars winked back. I lit a lantern and used the light to pull the fly, then opened a can of chili and one of peaches, ate a hurried dinner, and crawled into my sleeping bag.

That night it snowed sixteen inches and turned bitter cold. Up at four, I knew the snow-laden tent represented trouble. I built a roaring fire in the stove and began to shovel the roof, cursing all the while at the stupidity of my trying to save a few minutes by removing the plastic. Ice froze to the sides of the tent as fast as it melted from the roof. I worked as swiftly as I could, but it was noon before the horses were saddled and loads slung. The last to be loaded was the iced-up 14 X 16 tent.

That tent weighed seventy pounds dry. Now, as I stood panting, it felt like two hundred and I could in no way lift it. I managed to get one end up on a block of wood by the side of my most gentle packhorse. Then with the last of my ebbing strength, I lifted the other end, tilting it until it crashed against the side of the mare. Thank God she stood still for it. I wormed the huge load up her side onto her back, then lashed it there.

Exhausted, I knew if the pack slipped alongside the trail I would have to leave it. As I clambered into the saddle and headed my horse string for road's end, it began snowing again.

We made it to the road just at dark, the frozen tent still in place. Jack was waiting. "I had a hell of a time getting here," he said. "The road is almost blocked and there's been no traffic on it until we get down to the Spotted Bear Station, then not much from there."

"Let's hurry," I said, swinging from the saddle. As I leaned against my saddlehorse Buck, forehead on the saddle pommel, my hat fell to the snow.

Jack handed me the hat, then began pulling packs and loading them into the truck.

The first two miles of road was uphill. The snow was so deep that every time I took a run at it, I busted through a few yards, then bogged down. There was no alternative except to back up in the tracks I'd just made, then take another run at the packed snow. It took two and a half hours to bust our way to the crest of the hill and begin the seven-mile descent to the main forest road at Spotted Bear.

The snow, even with gravity in my favor, was too deep to simply drive down the hill. Again and again, I had to back up and take another run at it. I was exhausted. I grew sleepy in the overheated truck, stopping twice to rub snow on my face, trying to will myself alert. My reactions were slow and I killed the engine time after time. "What the hell is going on?" My brain cried out that danger lurked just beyond the windshield. After all, the left side of the road, for most of the way, fell several hundred feet down to the river. Still, I grew woozier and woozier. I felt the truck going over! "Oh, no!"

Then it stopped tilting and I opened the door and fell out into the snow on my face.

Jack rushed forward from the pickup to help me sit up. "What's the matter with me?" I cried.

My friend helped me to my feet, but I again collapsed. "Monoxide," he said. "You've been carbon-monoxided."

I stayed down this time, rubbing snow into my face. Then I rolled over to peer at the truck. Instead of going over the embankment, it had nosed into the barrow ditch on the other side. In my deluded state, I'd not been able to tell the difference. I began crying. Jack patted me like a baby.

"How long before I get over this?" I asked.

"You'll still have a headache tomorrow. The best thing we can do is get you home."

"The horses!"

"We'll have to unload them."

"But they've got to eat."

My friend said nothing. So I asked, "Why? Why did it happen?"

"The snow. You've got an old muffler on that truck. It's probably leaking exhaust. The snow is holding it under the truck and some of it creeps up into the cab."

I struggled to rise. Jack helped. Then I stumbled to the pickup, back to the truck, back to the pickup. I climbed into the truck cab and slipped the still-idling engine into gear. Through the rearview mirror I saw Jack standing in the pickup lights shaking his head.

Surprisingly, the truck backed from the ditch on its own. I rolled both windows down and again started for home, driving like a drunk determined to stay out of trouble.

I was finding out what <u>tough</u> really was.

God, it was cold in the windswept cab! But my senses were gradually creeping back. The deep snow took its toll on more than just me, however. Halfway home, I ran out of gas.

With no alternative, we left the horses standing in the truck and I jumped into the pickup. We lurched home through blowing and drifting snow, pulling into our yard shortly after midnight. That was when we discovered there was no tack trailer behind the pickup—the trailer ball had sheared off and both safety chains had broken.

With several cans of gasoline, Jack and I returned to the stranded truck at two a.m. and we were on our way to civilization shortly thereafter. We found the tack trailer nosed into a roadside bank not far from town. All we needed to bring it on home was a new trailer ball.

"That's tomorrow's project," I said.

I stumbled into the house at four a.m. Jane waited at the door. "Sell the outfitting business," she said.

I shook my head, then sprawled in a kitchen chair while she rattled pans on the way to breakfast. But when she turned to set the bacon and eggs on the table, she discovered my head was in her way. ■

Chapter 23

Kiss of Death

We're almost there," I told Jane in April, on our way home from the Los Angeles Sport Show. "Our summer bookings are strong and hunting season is almost full. If we can do this well for two years in a row, then we'll know we've arrived."

She nodded, snuggling against my side as road signs ticked off the distance to St. George, Cedar City, Provo, Salt Lake. Her confidence was innocence, mine stupidity.

I'd cooked up yet another unconventional promotional scheme, hosting a Skyline Outfit reunion during the long July 4th weekend. Past guests from all over America attended: from Pennsylvania to Oregon, Minnesota to Texas. We scheduled a lodge at Spotted Bear, and Jane labored for days sewing a giant nylon fly that we spread over a portion of the parking lot as shelter in case of inclement weather. Rows of hay bales provided seats. Guest speakers were brought in. A few of our past clients also provided entertainment: two accomplished violinists, a country-music singer.

We had our horses on hand for short trail rides and our inflatable rafts for whitewater floats that were piloted by our guides. Jane led wildflower hikes. An airplane was available for scenic flights over the Bob.

It was our intent that the reunion would provide an

opportunity for guests from one part of the country to get to know guests from other parts, other years, other trips. That way, we reasoned, the best possible publicists—satisfied customers—would spread word of our various types of adventure options.

In retrospect, though the reunion was well-attended, the success of our innovative promotional effort was uncertain because our struggling enterprise was soon to be overtaken by an unforeseen recession.

1979 was the year Jane came into her own as an accomplished outdoors woman. The year before, she had demonstrated mastery of campfire cookery for paying guests. But 1979 was when she actually began developing mere culinary skills into the gourmet art she unveiled in subsequent years.

Our first party of the summer adventured without her, however. They were a big group of guys who'd attended dental school together, then remained friends by pledging an annual joint fishing trip. This year they chose our horseback-in, float-out fishing trip through the Bob Marshall Wilderness.

We used four inflatable rafts—each carrying two fishermen and a boatman. I piloted one raft. The other three guides were experienced river-rat friends who closed their businesses in order to participate in the adventure.

It was late in the float, and at the moment I piloted the last of our four rafts. John and Norman, my anglers, were both expert with a flyrod. We rounded a bend onto a long straight reach of what looked like trout-laden riffles. "Ohh," Norman murmured. "Go slow."

"Go slow?" I said as the fast water gripped our raft—the bank sped by faster than I could walk. Both anglers whipped their rods, delicately dropping presentations behind this rock, by that submerged log, alongside that undercut bank. John yipped, and the guy his friends called "Normie Neptune" grunted shortly after. Both reeled in and released a fish, then began feeding line, waving their magic wands.

I bent to the oars, rowing methodically against the current in order to slow our rush downstream. "Uh-huh," John said as his rod bent. Normie's line arced again and again until he settled his fly behind a chair-sized boulder, where the water exploded in an instant as a fifteen-inch cutthroat trout went for a slam dunk!

The first raft in our little flotilla had already rounded a distant bend when we hove into view, and the second soon disappeared. Only the third drifted between us and the far-off bend, and I could see that the guide, Bernard, was making no attempt to hold his vessel back. This stretch of river was ours—just as long as I could hold our raft in it.

For their part, Norman and John were so engrossed in catching and releasing fat cutthroat after cutthroat that they were oblivious to the effort I made to keep them in that superb trout water. Then I spotted a guy standing on shore. He wore only a pair of cut-offs and sandals and he had his hands thrust deep into his pockets, standing with his back half-turned to us, watching the third raft as it disappeared around the distant bend.

"Uhh," grunted John. "Ohh!" said Normie. The shore loiterer heard them and turned as we drifted near.

"How you doin'?" I said for courtesy's sake.

The guy pushed hands deeper into his pockets. There was *something* about the wistful way he stood. Beyond, upon a gravel bar, perched a small tipi-type tent of white canvas. The canvas door was jerked aside and ...

"Sure looks like fun," the guy on shore said.

Normie paused in the middle of his backcast, his fly and leader and twenty feet of line falling alongside the raft with a plop ...

John had a fish on and he abandoned it, line stripping from the reel in a noisy whir ...

I shipped oars and the raft picked up speed, drifting in a lazy circle ...

... because from the tipi stepped a bronzed Scandinavian lovely, stretching to snap the back loops on what I can best describe as a three-piece bikini. Straight blond hair hung below the long-limbed beauty's waist. She walked like a runway model.

The guy had his back to the exquisite blond when he'd said it sure looks like fun.

Normie, eyes entranced by the man's tentmate, murmured, "Sure looks like fun."

And John echoed, "Sure looks like fun," as his trout spun the backing from his flyline, came to the end, and snapped free.

Our raft, still drifting without direction, swept into whitewater. Norman and John grabbed for safety ropes as my mind turned from fun to survival.

———

Bob Fox intimidated me with a gravelly voice and an unsmiling no-nonsense style. When I learned he was a Los Angeles attorney whose firm negotiated labor contracts, I turned as wary as a spotted fawn lying undetected while a

A raft, with Roland and two fishermen into the abyss.

pack of timber wolves trot past. Later I discovered the big, gruff, grumpy guy with the stiff shock of crewcut, iron-gray hair was an ex-marine who'd been sorely wounded on Tarawa. You'd have been intimidated, too.

Bob and his wife Jean had paused at our Los Angeles Sport Show booth. They were sufficiently intrigued by what they saw and heard to return and schedule a horseback-in, float-out fishing trip. Even while writing a check for their deposit, the man had a disconcerting way of chilling my clumsy attempts to be pleasant by pinning me with his glass eye while the other eye roved around the pavilion. "This is one trip you must go on," I told Jane as the couple strolled away. "It's possible we'll need your more refined diplomatic skills."

The couple made it easy to include Jane when they scheduled a third member for their adventure—a diminutive lady who, late in life, decided to do all the things for which she'd yearned. Learning to fish, and experiencing a wilderness adventure were two.

As it turned out, my fears were groundless. Bob Fox was indeed big and gruff. He was also profane. He limped from his wounds and groaned from shrapnel he'd learned to live with for thirty-five years. But he was also a kind-hearted pussycat who loved his wife and was loved deeply by her.

Still, the guy proved less than charming to newcomers and, as a fisherman, could be considered a tad inept. Most of his fishing problems stemmed from failing vision in his only eye. He fumbled his way to outrageous knots in his fishing line, airily brushing off all attempts at assistance. Then when at last ready to cast, he inevitably snagged shoreside brush, our raft's safety rope, or someone else's clothing, at which time he'd curse, break his line, curse some more, and begin anew. Meanwhile, his wife rigged up quickly and expertly, cast accurately, and reeled in fish after fish, innocently contributing to her husband's annoyance.

After a proper interlude, both Jean and I asked if we could help the guy rig up. My suggestion was dismissed with a rude one-finger wave; Jean's offer met a string of angry curses.

Bob did catch a few fish. Though he was clumsy with their release, he again was abrupt in dismissing offers to help. Finally I lapsed into angry silence. And so went the morning and the evening of the first day.

It was around noon on the third day when Bob hung his line in shoreside bush yet again. By then he was growing so short on lures that we were attempting retrieval when possible. I pulled for shore and beached the raft. Bob stomped back upstream, cursing all the way at wife and fate and the sky above. While he was away from the raft I could no longer contain myself, apologizing for the man's behavior toward his wife.

Her features stiffened, but she said so softly I had to lean forward to hear: "Bob was one hell of a man, Roland. You must realize that. It's unfortunate that he can no longer do all the things he once did."

We both watched as the topic of our conversation angrily jerked his spinner loose from the bush, snapping the line. He bent to pick up the lure from among the stones as his wife said in an ominously low voice: *"But he ought to have the chance to try."*

A flush crept from beneath the neck of my lifejacket as I realized what an ass I'd made of myself. What a woman! What great fortune that they had such love.

I also learned about the power of poetry from Jean Fox.

That's one thing about spending five days in proximity to someone while drifting down a remote wilderness river— one is able to get into the other's mind. I was forty-four years old at the time and I confided to the lady that I had never understood poetry and still didn't. "Actually, it leaves me cold."

She shook her head. "Yet stories told in verse can be so powerful, Roland. Much more so than prose; so descriptive. A few lines of verse would take several pages of prose to properly capture a scene. For instance, Barbara Fritchie:

Up from the meadows rich with corn,
Clear in the cool September morn,

The clustered spires of Frederick stand
Green-walled by the hills of Maryland.

Round about them orchards sweep,
Apples and peach tree fruited deep,

Fair as the garden of the Lord
To the eyes of the famished rebel horde,

On that pleasant morn of the early fall
When Lee marched over the mountain wall …

"Don't you see, Roland? How could a novelist write so powerfully in such short, declarative terms? Why, it would take reams of prose to develop such a scene."

And it was like a door opening!

―――※―――

Ted Modlens was a retired Pennsylvania machinist who saved and scrimped for years to make his first elk hunt with our Skyline Outfit. Ted fell in love with the land and returned home to sing its praises to his wife and daughter.

It was Ted's daughter Sandi who made the family's wilderness trip happen. Sonya, the mother, was a matronly woman anyone could love, with an appreciation for wild places and wild things that put my own rudimentary love for the outdoors to shame. For instance, Jane and I once visited in the Modlens' home and watched Sonya trap spiders and release them outdoors because she did not wish to kill them.

The trip had barely begun when Sonya was exclaiming at sights I considered humdrum. "If you think this is okay," I told the ladies, "just wait until we get into the heart of the Bob."

Sonya had some physical hurdles to overcome. She was a bit stout for one thing, and had painful arthritis that made it a chore merely to hold bridle reins. But cheerful? And full of enthusiasm? The lady knew that, at her age, this would be her one and only chance for adventure into the Bob Marshall Wilderness.

It was near the middle of their trip when I took the family to the top of the Wall Creek Cliffs. The ride up is tough. But one can work horses near the cliff top without newcomers being aware that the land falls away for a thousand feet just a dozen steps from their horses' hoofs.

We tied our ponies to stunted limber pines and walked the rest of the way toward the cliff, Sonya leading. She faltered twenty feet from the cliff edge while the rest of us continued to the brink, "oohing" and "ahing" at a stunning view that included seventy-five miles of mountain ranges stacked one after another clear into Glacier National Park.

Open meadows dotted the nearer hillsides, while avalanche chutes and late-summer snowfields capped the distant peaks.

I glanced back at Sonya, who'd obviously had an attack of acrophobia. I did a double-take. With clinched teeth, the woman was crawling toward the cliff on hands and knees. When I made to help, she shooed me away. Then she fell to her belly and crawled on with eyes closed.

She stopped three feet from the edge, swallowed, and opened her eyes. Then she began weeping, so moved by a vista she knew she'd never again be able to view.

Her husband went to sit by her side, comforting his wife of nearly fifty years. So did daughter Sandi. I stood off to one side, wondering whether I'd done the right thing by bringing such a sensitive woman to such a wondrous place.

In over two decades of leading others to adventure, I've never been as moved as I was that still day when the only sound was the quiet sobbing of a lady in love with a land.

❦

The Mason children, eight and eleven, were precocious and well-mannered, but we were hardly prepared for them or their parents. Sally Mason had scheduled their family adventure over the telephone, and there'd been no direct in-person contact. It was not until they drove into our yard that we discovered Harvey Mason was black, his wife Sally an attractive blond. Though it embarrasses me to write this today, I'd be less than honest about our learning curve during those outfitting years if I told you we were culturally prepared for the shock of that discovery.

Guiding Harvey, Sally, Hop, and Heather Mason proved to be one of our more personally rewarding adventures. They were fine people, courteous and considerate of us and each other. Harvey is a Hollywood studio musician and one of the top drummers in the world. Sally is an accomplished musician in her own right. The couple met in music school, fell in love, and married.

Such a talented family! I later played both golf and tennis with Harvey and was soundly trounced. Several years later, Hop (Harvey, Jr.) developed into a star guard for Arizona State's number one rated basketball team, and Heather developed into an equestrian of renown. Jane and I led the family on a roving gypsy trip, moving camp often, riding deeper and deeper into the wilderness. During the lengthy journey, we developed the kind of friendships that permitted me to ask Harvey searching questions about his background. I discovered that the man was the eldest of eight children raised in an Atlantic City ghetto.

I was amazed to learn that six of Harvey's seven siblings were also college graduates. "How can that be," I asked, "given your background?"

"My mother was a strong woman," he replied. But Harvey had no high regard for his father, who "only returned home long enough to make a new baby."

Harvey shared one tantalizing personal belief: the man favored school busing to achieve a degree of educational equality. He said busing was an experimental project in Atlantic City schools while he was in his elementary years. He made friends with children of privilege, visiting in their homes, and the experiences provided him with a yardstick to measure his own future achievements.

Harvey helped his next sibling through school, and then the two of them helped the next, and the next. "How about you?" he asked. "What about your college?"

"Uh … it's time for me to round up the ponies."

That evening, Harvey picked up a teapot and tapped it with a knife. Then he tapped a cup, a glass, the sugar bowl, an empty pop can. Hop joined him, and soon the two had an impromptu array of Jane's cookware and dishes and were tapping out a recognizable tune with a couple of tableknives each.

I shook my head. Joe Rogers had it right—I'm a klutz.

Jane began to jerk to the beat, humming along. So did Sally. I started to grin, tapping one foot, then two.

Fred Wuthrich was hands down the finest flyfisherman I've ever guided, yet he fished the least. The reason? Fred brought his two sons, thirteen and sixteen. Though the father usually held his flyrod at the ready, he spent most of his time coaching the boys in the fine art of fishing dry flies.

Occasionally, though, Fred would spot a missed "honey-hole" as our two rafts drifted downriver, and he unerringly cast to that spot. More often than not, he would pull out a lunker cutthroat. It was thrilling to watch.

The fourth member of the group was an oral surgeon from Fred's Denver office complex. My second guide was a retired school superintendent, Hazen Lawson, who'd also served for many years as a seasonal ranger in Glacier Park. Hazen was an outstanding horseman and a superb river guide. He was so energetic at bouncing in and out of the raft, pulling it over rapids, swimming for the zest in it, that our guests named the sixty-five-year-old "Amazin' Hazen."

Fred told me he took his kids somewhere on this type of vacation trip every year.

I leaned on the oars. "That's interesting. What do you mean by 'this type of vacation'?"

"Oh, to a ranch for riding, perhaps hiking, skiing."

"But always guided?"

"Yes."

"Would you share your thinking with me?"

Fred watched his fly trailing behind the drifting raft. "Actually it's more for the boys to be exposed to people like you and Hazen than for the adventure."

"Huh?"

"They need to meet people with your kinds of values, self-reliance, discipline—and dozens of others. Those are values that aren't always prevalent in the city. I want the kids to grow up having another type against which to measure new friends and acquaintances."

I stared across the water at Hazen's raft just drifting around the upstream bend. "That's a heck of a tall order to have to meet, Fred. I hope we're filling the bill."

He smiled and rollcast to the slack water gurgling against the far bank. The water erupted. ∎

Chapter 24

A Team at Last

Jane feels her greatest contribution to the actual operation of the Skyline Outfit was her insistence on making life easier for everyone—husband as well as guests. And that's true. The woman's forté was an ability to diagnose potential trouble spots and reduce tension, or help guests understand and thus ease any distress caused by ashes in the coffee, sand in a sleeping bag, or gnats in the atmosphere.

Of course, the lady gave more, much more. Until diminutive Margaret "Mike" Wagner sent her deposit for an adventure with our Skyline Outfit, we were told the aging grandmother had never been allowed by her stern, recently deceased husband even to write a check, let alone ride a horse. But riding for thirty miles through a wilderness, then shooting whitewater in a raft piloted by our son Marc and accompanied by Jane, the woman took on such a spirit of adventure that she returned two additional times for other adventures, toured the Holy Land, and joined an archeological dig. We took great pride, Jane and I, that it was with our little guide service that Mike first experienced life on the wild side.

We were very fortunate that Jane was into the outfit in a big way. It was Jane who insisted on more rest breaks for Sonya Modlens than her not-so-understanding leader would have provided. It was Jane who brought games to occupy the kids around camp of an evening. And it was Jane who rode the trails behind the kids, scooping up a dropped glove here, a flashlight there, glasses at a lunch stop, a hair barrette along a creek bank.

In addition, Jane turned campfire dining into one pleasant surprise after another. She was the one who turned Dutch-oven cooking from theory into art. Our meals had been robust: steak and mashed potatoes and brown gravy—you get the picture. But after Jane took charge, there were always fresh salads and out-of-this-world desserts. Her entrees included pork tenderloin, roast Cornish game hens, stuffed flank steak, leg of lamb. And did my eyes ever pop when the woman first served lobster tails three days and sixty miles deep into the Bob Marshall Wilderness!

It was Jane who gave my own wildflower education a kick in the rear, much to the delight of our guests. And it was she who proved more attentive to a lady's needs than her callous outfitter husband could ever be—toilet times along the trail, for instance, and better arrangements for modesty and tastefulness around camp.

As our busy summer of 1979 wound to a close, I realized she would no longer be there by my side during the coming hunting season. By then, the gal had wormed into the outfit's infrastructure. For the first time, I gave serious thought to making her a part of the hunting camps.

"No way," she said. "That's too much of a 'man' thing. I wouldn't be welcome there."

Then one of my key guides was hurt in a truck crash. We were strapped.

I was mantying packs for a party of Oregon veterans who'd been with us many times. Kenny Averill worked by my side. "Kenny, it looks like Rich won't be with us on this trip."

The old man nodded.

"Looks like it'll be just you and me. You think we can handle it?"

"Aw, I don't know why not."

That was vintage Kenny—never a complaint, always willing. But Jane, who never before wanted in on a *man's* hunting adventure, stepped to the plate. "I'm going with you."

I collapsed on a pack in surprise.

"At least I can do the cooking and save you from that work."

I rubbed my jaw thoughtfully. "The Sayres are veteran hunters personified—the very type you feared. Are you sure?"

"But they are also nice people. Too nice not to know you need help. They'll have to make accommodations to the fact that I'm a woman. If there's a problem, they'll get over it."

So we packed the long distance to our White River camp. Jane led the hunters, Kenny and I came along with the packstring. We arrived at camp around dark. Jane set up the kitchen while we unloaded the horses—and it took a while for me to get over how she arranged "my" cooktent to suit her left-handed ways. But as soon as I lit into her tasty supper, I decided the lady could do anything she wished with "her" kitchen, and all I'd do was rub up against her and purr.

Jane removing chaps at hunting camp.

During the hunt, she wrangled the next day's horses while Kenny and I were still afield. She was out of bed at five a.m. Hors d'oeuvres were always waiting for early returnees to camp. Meals were always ready, always tasty, and always plentiful.

It was Jane who provided fresh trout for dinner. And it was Jane and our world's greatest grouse dog, Hunter, who brought in enough of the tasty birds for a second meal.

Most of all, she babied me.

Hunting camp, Jane found, was different from summer trips. She had the days to herself. Up in the morning before daylight, true. To bed long after dark, true. But after the hunters disappeared into the surrounding mountains at first light, she could spend her day reading, hiking, riding, or sunbathing as the mood struck.

The patriarch of the Sayre clan watched in bemused silence as the woman worked. Bud saw her kindle fires, shoot heads from grouse, then skin and gut them with a flick of her wrist, bring in a stringer of fish. He heard her tell me of fresh elk tracks at the upper wallows or atop the Long Ridge. He saw her saddle horses and whip up biscuits, bake cakes and cut wood, pick leaves for "trapper's tea," and help bag elk quarters.

"Aren't you outdoing yourself?" I asked one evening as we settled into our sleeping bag.

"What do you mean?"

"I mean I know you're good—a rootin'-tootin' outdoors woman without peer. But it seems to me you're going out of your way to demonstrate it."

She laid her head into the crook of my arm. "I have to, you know. I'm compelled to prove I can be just as good as any man."

I laughed and pulled her close.

It was late in the trip when Bud and I stood outside the cooktent at dusk as sounds of the rustling vittles came from inside—pans rattling, a spoon dropped into a bowl, meat frying. Bud took out a cigarette paper and cupped it, then shook tobacco into it from a sack he closed by pulling the drawstrings with his teeth.

"You know, Roland," he said after striking a match and holding it to the smoke, "if I was you I wouldn't teach that little woman one more thing."

I stared in open-mouthed surprise. The veteran hunter grinned and added, "'Cause she seems to learn pretty good on her own."

It was, I'm sure, one of the choicest of all the many compliments Jane had received over the years. Bud Sayre is not one to pass out superlatives on a whim. And praise from such a veteran outdoorsman at the beginning of her outdoors career had to be a tremendous ego boost to the lady who was throwing another long loop around my heart. ■

Chapter 25

Pushing a Dream

With Jane's full-time entry into our outfitting business, my life seemed complete. The lady provided a dimension that had been missing while the outfit's macho leader set the standards. Now, we were a *team*—a first-rate team. Both of us had grown until we were competent and disciplined. We were *professionals*. The Skyline Outfit was staffed by experts, no doubt about it—our business seemed firmly on its way.

In addition, with Jane on the starting squad there were no more long separations. I was proud of, and in love with, the woman. And she seemed to share an equal pride and respect for her husband. In such an atmosphere of endearment and encouragement, is it any wonder that our romance kindled anew?

"Don't you find it ironic, dear, that we have an oversized waterbed at home, but more than not, we end up snuggled together in zipped-together sleeping bags in a wilderness?"

"Mmmm."

"And at high noon, with hunters in the field. What would they think if they knew their outfitter and their cook …"

"Mmmm."

If camp wasn't practicable, we found the softest meadow grass or the mossiest ledges for planned assignations. There were beds of pine needles and alpine tundra.

"You're becoming a nuisance, you know," Jane said, toying with my shirtpocket.

I lifted my hat to peer up at her. "You can always ride out."

"I might. You're not getting any rest this way."

"I couldn't be more at peace with my world than I am right now."

She sighed and sprawled in the grass at my side. Two golden eagles circled above and a marmot squeaked from the field of boulders at our right.

It was a gorgeous spring that began the century's eighth decade. Our bookings were again strong, despite all the ill-founded rumors of recession spreading from the land's financial centers.

"Okay," I told Jane, tapping a sheet of statistics I'd compiled. "It's certain now—our business has arrived. We're paying our bills and retiring some of our debt load, and we even have a little left over to buy you some new shoes."

She sat at our kitchen table, chin cupped in palms, trying to keep her eyes from glazing over.

"We're running somewhere close to eighty-percent repeats, Jane." I bent forward to lay my paper before her, punctuating the figures with a tracing forefinger. "What this means is that we can cut down on the dollars we're spending to attract new customers. See? No need to pour money down a rat hole. Why should we spend money on new customers if we have no room for them?"

"Really? I'd feel better if we had another year or two behind us."

I chuckled. "Trust me. After what we've been through to make a success out of this business, you think I'll risk anything now? Nope, I just want to increase our net, maybe buy me a new pair of shoes, too."

So I made plans to cut our sport-show schedule down to zilch during the '81 sale season and began preparing for our first party of the year—four spring bear hunters from

Los Angeles.

Then, while I was packing extra horsefeed into the mountains for the coming spring hunt, a strange dust cloud rolled in from the West. It turned out that a mountain six hundred miles away blew its top, and airborne volcanic ash fell upon Montana. The governor proclaimed an emergency, closing five western counties to any nonessential activity.

Fortunately, a soft rain fell before the arrival of our hunters. The ban was lifted. Unfortunately, the rain continued, falling harder and harder, weakening the hold of tree roots. They crashed across trails and down hillsides. Creeks rampaged over their banks. The rain turned to wet snow. Our small aluminum-framed summer tents collapsed, mostly with tired and half-frightened hunters asleep inside.

At last a day came when four hunters stood bedraggled amid deepening snow, snuggling up to a campfire where Jane struggled to cook. One hunter said to another, "You know I read in the paper just before we left that it's supposed to be ninety degrees in Palm Springs this weekend."

The man he was talking to shook snow from his cap and brushed it from the shoulders of his thin nylon jacket. "That so? Maybe we'd ought to ride out and take a look."

"Boys," I cut in, "I'd like to see you give it another day. See if it'll quit. This can't go on forever."

So I talked them into staying one more day. That was the day our horses ran away and the snow collapsed our last piece of reliable shelter, our big dining fly.

I tried to get the hunters to stay longer, but when I proposed giving the weather another day one of them laconically said, "There's nothing in the world can make me do that."

So we rode hard for neon lights and civilization. And at our home, toasty warm in front of a roaring fireplace blaze, with cocktails in hand, those four hunters scheduled a fall hunting trip with the Skyline Outfit.

Except for me, it was an all-female party—an adventure at the peak of wildflower season in late June. Actually there were only three women, one of whom was my wife. She knew better than to entrust those two ladies' welfare to me without her in attendance. As usual, Jane proved remarkably astute—I needed her protection right from the outset.

Doris was a school librarian from our hometown, a thoughtful, intelligent teacher with a rugged outdoors zest and a Montana ranch background. Elene was a lovely, willowy Pennsylvania lass with wavy auburn hair and eyebrows that arched provocatively at the slightest sign of a blush from the outfitter. In fact, I suspect that "Leanie" must have stayed awake nights thinking of ways to make her eyebrows arch.

Doris and I debated the relative merits of poems and prose. The Pennsylvania lass thought mostly of wild country sightseeing. Both of the ladies loved to ride horses and could sit in the saddle all day and well into the night. Between them, the three women wore their outfitter to a frazzle.

One day the four of us rode from White River Park to Haystack Butte along the crest of the famed Chinese Wall. The ride is a long one—nineteen miles round-trip. Though the day was cool and windy where mountaintop snowbanks still lurked, we found it blistering hot upon our return to the valley floor. And for the last five miles back to camp, the ladies talked of little else than bathing in the swift little river.

As soon as we reached camp, they left me to grain and unsaddle the ponies while they hurried riverward, towels tucked beneath their arms, rushing to catch the last of the sun before shadows crept in from the West. I watched them pass—especially that slick young one. Wow—what a beaut! Then I thought of ticks.

Ticks are pests seldom encountered in this region, except in the spring. But undetected, they can bore into your flesh and become nasty irritants. At worst, they can even carry such diseases as the sometimes fatal Rocky Mountain Fever. So, too, is the tick-borne Lyme disease rumored to be spreading westward.

By late June, spring had, of course, already come and gone at the lower elevations. But up in the high country it was just now in full swing. So it was possible for each of us to have come in contact with the little varmints.

"Hold on, ladies," I called, stepping away from the horses and thumbing back my hat.

They all turned at the authoritative tone. Leanie said, "Yes?"

Jane asked, "What is it, Roland?"

"We may have gotten into ticks today. I'm suggesting you check yourselves over real good as you bathe."

"Good idea," Jane replied, and she and Doris again headed for the river. But Leanie just stood, head tilted, staring impishly.

"You do know what ticks are, don't you ma'am?" I said. "They get on you and crawl to some juicy place, then start boring. You should check yourself over for them. That's all."

I saw Jane turn.

Leanie's eyebrows arched. "I thought that was the out-fitter's job."

It hurt that Jane laughed hardest.

<hr>

Our first float trip of the year had six guests. We used three rafts and three boatmen.

She nodded her understanding that there was simply no place for an extra passenger, but that didn't keep her face from hanging to the ankles. So when our next party of two fisherfolk went out, she struck:

"You only have two fishermen this time. And I know you don't want to take just one raft downriver in case something happens. So why don't you let Marc take the smaller raft down and I'll go along to help you cook?"

I took her into my arms and whispered, "And you'll learn to be a boatman, won't you?"

She leaned back to stare innocently up into my eyes. "And would that be so bad?"

Gary Akers, it turned out, was a wildlife biologist with a master's degree in ornithology. He was the best person I've ever seen at bird identification, sometimes recognizing the species by calls I could not even *hear*. That alone would have made it a memorable trip. And it was the morning and the evening of the first week when Jane took her initial fumbling steps toward becoming a full-fledged whitewater guide.

We'd first packed the Phelps party into the wilderness in 1978. They returned to float and fish the South Fork in 1980. It was while we were riding through the big yellow-pine and bunchgrass meadows at Murphy Flats that John Phelps turned his full attention on our roving Brittany spaniel, Hunter.

Back and forth across the trail, to first one side, then the other, the dog roamed. Ahead and back and forth. Occasionally the dog would trot back to the horse string to make sure all riders were there. Then he was off again. If we traveled twenty miles per day, Hunter traveled fifty.

A huge grin spread across John's face as the dog worked. "You know," he said at last, "that has to be the luckiest dog who ever lived."

I, too, watched the dog and decided John was right. Then I thought of the life I led and decided what the Illinois orthodontist had to say about the dog was also a fitting metaphor for my own life.

Besides the spring "explorer" trip at the peak of wilderness wildflower season, we also developed a second value-added adventure during the summer of 1980: a horseback trip through the high country with a focus on geology.

We were lucky—there never was, and never will be, a better interpretive geologist than ours. I became acquainted with Dr. John Montagne through a friend, one

Hunter, the world's greatest grouse dog.

of the professor's geology students at Montana State University. Bernard Windauer had occasionally served as a float trip guide. The young man heard me talk about putting together a high-country trip with an interpretive geologist, and he suggested contacting his college professor. Dr. Montagne agreed to accompany a party on an experimental basis. A yearly tradition was born.

John Montagne (he does not care a great deal for titles) retired from teaching and is now professor emeritus from MSU. He is still active in geological research and dissertation, an expert in snow avalanche prediction, and he's the greatest teacher I've ever known. What may be more to the point, the guy is a friend, my hero, and one of a mere handful of people who have had an inordinate influence on my life.

Besides all that, John opened up an entire *world* of geology to the staff and guests of the Skyline Outfit, beginning by offering evidence of glaciation and mountain thrusting, moving on through sedimentary layering, continental drift, and origin of recognizable life on our world.

Providing John Montagne with a horse, food, and shelter for a yearly wilderness week may have been the best single academic investment Jane and I ever made.

Diminutive Margaret (Mike) Wagner, the Rolling Hills, California, grandmother looking for a second adventure, was first to sign up for this new experience. "Mike" was accompanied by friend, Beverly Menze, also from Rolling Hills. Vicky, a computer programmer out of Minneapolis, completed our party.

Vicky was originally from Montana and was what you might call "Western" inclined. She wrote prior to the trip asking if I would be kind enough to provide her with a spirited horse. I obliged. It was a mistake—Vicky was an accident waiting to happen. Like the time she was out of her saddle, leading her horse along a steep sidehill trail. I heard a shout and wheeled. Vicky, stargazing, had walked off into space and was dangling from her steed's leadrope while the animal stood with all four feet planted to keep from being dragged into the abyss. No, Vicky wasn't hurt by her spirited pony. Nor did she hurt the horse. But it wasn't because of Vicky.

Our first night's camp was near the Pentagon Guard Station, close to the headwaters of the Spotted Bear River. I jerked packs from horses, then unsaddled and grained the animals. Finally, I went to set up the dining fly. Off to one side, Vicky talked earnestly to Rich as he unmantied duffel packs.

"Oh, no you don't!" he said, obviously replying to something she'd said. He pointed at me. "You'll have to talk to *him* about that one."

So Vicky came over as I wrestled with aluminum poles. "Yes?" I said.

"We have a problem," she said, twisting a hanky in her hands.

"We do?"

"Uh-huh."

"Okay, Vicky. What's the problem?"

"Well, there's a ranger station over there …"

I snorted. Hell, we could both see the station from where we stood.

"… and there's an outhouse for the station over there."

I looked where her finger pointed. "Yes, I know that."

"I used it."

"Vicky, I'm sure the federal government won't care …"

"What I want to know," she said, "is what do you do when a guest of yours drops their prescription eyeglasses down the outhouse hole?"

———

We managed to retrieve the spectacles, but relations with the United States Forest Service could not always be handled so smoothly. The problem surfaced when the agency denied my application to guide the same number of summer guests I'd led the previous year. Instead, my written request was returned with the slot we'd not already filled scratched out, denying the opportunity to schedule should the opportunity arise. The application also carried the notation that I must sign the amended version and send in my fees in order to validate my permit. I tried to learn the reason for the denial, but the District Ranger in charge would only say that I was guiding too many people into the wilderness.

I pointed out the previous year was the best ever for our struggling enterprise; that even then we'd led only twenty-three summer guests and twenty-six hunters over a seven-month period—not exactly earth-shattering.

"I believe I can demonstrate that fifty clients is the break-even point for us," I told the Ranger. "If you reduce our permitted numbers below last year, you're taking away any chance for my wife and me to maintain a viable business."

His answer was to send out the same amended permit cutting our use days, this time with the threat that should I fail to sign and return it, I would be in violation of my permit and subject to revocation.

I went up the ladder. The Forest Supervisor heard my plea and said he would look into the matter. "I'm sure something can be worked out," he said. "But you'd better pay your fees prior to entry."

With the Forest Supervisor's assurance that things could be worked out, it was easy to agree to guide Rod Allers and his wife when the Connecticut attorney called to request the very dates still in question. I should have guessed I was sailing into reefs, though, when I filed my proposed itinerary for the disputed trip, wrote a check for the season's use fees in advance, and was met only by stony bureaucratic silence.

The Allers were fine folks who were unusually fit. The previous year, Rod had won the National Downhill and Slalom Ski Championship for his age group. Anne raced sled dogs, hauling her dogs alone to Alaska and the Yukon in order to compete.

Meanwhile the wheels of justice ground exceedingly slow and the U.S. Attorney's office in Butte, Montana, eventually filed suit in Federal District Court on behalf of the United States Forest Service, charging me with the crime of conducting business on National Forest land without a valid permit. At the time, I knew nothing of a pending imbroglio with all the might and majesty of the federal criminal-justice system. ∎

Chapter 26

Competing with *Men*

It had been a superb summer for Jane. For me, too, but for her 1980 was a year of unfolding wonders. She was learning to row a boat through whitewater. She'd learned from a birding expert how to identify songbirds by their calls. And now geology!

It's probable Jane had difficulty grasping the dimensions of an earth-building process occurring over millions and millions of years. So did I. But with those Irish eyes at work, she became an overnight sensation at finding evidence of fossils in surrounding limestone.

At the beginning of the year we'd hunted shed antlers and the woman brought in more antlers from winter range hillsides than her macho husband. She also bested me seven ways to Sunday in wildflower identification. Bring on the whitewater! Listen to the pine siskins chirp. "Can't you tell evening grosbeaks by their call? Want to see rocks with shells in them? Follow me."

Then it was hunting season and the lady fairly *panted* to prove she could be—well—one of the boys on a tough, man's adventure.

"Roland," she said even before our summer season began, "I could go on every *other* hunting trip. Just my handling the cooking chores on alternate trips would make it easier for you, wouldn't it?"

There was no way, of course, that she could accompany every party because she had an essential role to fill on the logistics end, at home. She must do the purchasing. Airport shuttles were her domain. Because ours were demanding, deep-penetration adventures far into wilderness, weight was critical and prior food preparation essential. Beef roasts, turkey, and ham were all cooked at home, sliced into meal-sized portions, and frozen in order to save weight. Glass containers were discarded before the trips, the contents repackaged in plastic or cardboard. Flour, cornmeal, bread—everything—was pre-measured and repackaged. This she did prior to every trip. She discovered, however, that she could prepare for *two* hunts in advance.

So the lady became a regular fixture on alternate hunting trips, entering into a macho world in which she was becoming increasingly confident. She found her perfect foil on our first hunt.

Mike Post hailed from the tiny Pennsylvania community of Wrightsville, a few miles down the Susquehanna River from Harrisburg. Confederate cavalry had raided through the region during Lee's march to Gettysburg. Remnants of the burned railway bridge are still visible today.

Post began his working life as a town policeman in Columbia, across the river from Wrightsville. Later he became a construction laborer, moving steadily up the ladder until he founded his own earth-moving company. He's tough, gregarious, the spitting image of a man's man. He had firm ideas about hunting camps being off limits to women.

Our camp was not the one of choice for Mike and his friend Tom. Their first choice had been Wyoming, but they failed to draw Cowboy State elk licenses. Then Tom called Mike to say a couple of fellows from his factory had scheduled a Montana hunt into the Bob Marshall Wilderness and there were two openings left.

We received their deposit and I forwarded newsletters about our Skyline Outfit, the country, and our method of hunting. Mike and Tom were pleased. Then, a month before they were to begin their hunt, I wrote to them about our crew:

> *I will, of course, be part of your team, a regular guide, wrangler and packer. The other guides are our 18-year-old son Marc who has logged many thousands of miles in Bob Marshall adventure and is an experienced elk hunter and guide; Kenny Averill who has over thirty years' experience as a guide in the Bob, including ten with me.*
>
> *The final member of our party will be my wife Jane as cook. She's among the most competent outdoor-swomen I know and can and will produce some of the most bellytickling meals you'll ever eat.*

"Tom!" Mike shouted into the phone. "Did you get that letter from the outfitter we hired."

"Yes. Why?"

"Why! Didn't you pick up on the fact there's going to be a *woman* in our camp."

"Well, yes, I noticed that."

"My God! Aren't you upset?"

"Upset? Why should I be?"

So Mike called Bill. He got no more satisfaction from Bill than from Tom. He called Chuck. Chuck yawned.

"What in hell is the matter with you guys?" he cried, back on the phone with Tom. "Don't you understand? This creep is taking a *woman* into hunting camp. A hunting camp is no place for a *woman!*"

Tom leaned back in his swivel chair and gazed out over the factory he managed. "Aren't you being a little melodramatic, Mike? The man is a veteran outfitter—remember? We checked on that. Don't you suppose this woman is also competent or she wouldn't be going on the trip?"

So Mike's cherished tradition of hunting camps as masculine bastions was about to be sundered. On their long drive from Pennsylvania to Montana, as Tom later told me, Mike spent an inordinate amount of time grumbling about this *woman* who was invading their bailiwick. "I'll bet—if she can cut the mustard—that she's a real battle-axe. Probably with shoulders as wide as window headers."

Tom laughed.

As the four Pennsylvanians drove into our yard, we had no hint that Mike was still surly about "*that woman.*" They seemed jovial, though I thought a couple might be a little out of shape. They all seemed pleasant enough, especially the one with the mustache—the one name Mike.

I introduced them to Marc and Kenny, who were stacking hay into our pickup truck. Then the last crew member was called outside to meet our year's first hunters. She stepped out wiping her hands on a towel.

"She's still packing food for tomorrow, guys. Jane meet Tom, Chuck, Bill, and ..."

"This must be Mike," Jane said, holding out a firm hand.

Mike took it, mumbling something unintelligible. At the time, I didn't know the man's views concerning women on hunts. But we later laughed at how foolish he'd been, and he even atoned by admitting the sort of remarks he'd made to Tom. But that was still to come.

"She may be a knockout," Mike told the guys as they drove away from our yard. "But tomorrow will tell the tale. Hell, she's no bigger than a church mouse."

"Mike," Tom said, "I'll make a prediction that you are digging a hole for yourself."

The following morning, even the reluctant Mike congratulated Jane on her sourdough biscuits. Then they all hopped in the wagon. Jane negotiated the winding road in our station wagon like it was a Jaguar at Le Mans, while I tagged behind with a truckload of saddlehorses. Marc and Kenny were well along in saddling the ponies when the rest of the party arrived at the corral shortly after daylight.

"You guys will go ahead with Jane," I told them while adjusting stirrup lengths. "I'll stay here and help sling packs, then come along with the packstring."

"You mean you're not going in with us?" Mike said, his mustache trembling.

I grinned up at him, still not understanding that a problem existed. "Don't worry, Jane knows the way. Besides, we'll probably catch you before we get to camp—unless you guys can keep up with the little woman."

"Keep up?" He jerked his saddlehorse around. "Don't worry, we'll get her there one way or another, even if we have to pack her face down over the saddle."

I thumbed my hat back and stared. Tom was chuckling. Then Jane swung into her saddle. "Everybody ready?" she called. "Then let's go."

Our grouse dog, Hunter, a veteran of hundreds of these excursions, bounded away. Jane twisted in the saddle to wave, calling to me: "This time we'll beat you to camp if it kills all of us."

I grinned and waved back.

Jane explained to her hunters as their string moved through the forest that she tries to walk a few minutes every hour, leading her horse just to stay limbered up. "Otherwise you can get saddlesore before twenty-seven miles go by."

Two miles farther along, she swung from her horse to walk. When the others dismounted, she told them that it was also imperative to keep moving: "Remember, the horses can only walk as fast as we do. So walk like you're late for dinner."

Three miles later she was still swinging along as her saddlehorse trotted to keep up with the woman's ground-eating pace. Bill and Tom and Chuck, realizing they were outclassed, had already remounted. Mike still stumbled on, beginning to have inklings that his ideas about female inadequacy might not be entirely accurate.

Then Hunter put a grouse into a tree and Jane paused, whipped out the little Ruger Bearcat she packed on her hip, and shot the head from the grouse. She snatched it from Hunter's retrieve and, while walking back to where Mike was gasping for breath, gutted and skinned the grouse with one quick flick of her wrist.

"Mike," she said, "we'll make better time if you'd just go ahead and get on your horse. That's what he's there for, to take you to hunting camp."

Mike told me later that he wiped sweat from his face and eyed that slip of a woman standing before him; the lady held a smoking revolver in one hand and a slick-skinned grouse in the other. It was then that he decided whatever *that* woman told him to do, he would do. Not only would he do it, he would *expedite* the doing.

Jane, for her part, wheeled back to the front of the string, grabbed her pony's halter rope, and continued walking up the trail at a pace that kept the saddlehorses trotting—except when she paused to shoot the heads from additional grouse.

Mike said his only concern during the rest of a long first day wasn't how tiring the trip was, or even if there were any elk in the country; only that when *that* woman turned to glare back at her tarrying hunters he would no longer attract her attention—or what was worse, her scorn.

"Whatever you guys do," he pleaded with the rest of the hunters at lunch break, "don't let on to that woman about me having any doubts about her."

"I like Snickers," Tom said, eyeing the candy bar Mike had begun unwrapping.

His friend handed it to him.

"And I like cookies," Bill said.

Our packstring did catch the hunters, but it was a close race. Jane shrugged and held out her hands, palms up as we went by. The hunters sprawled in the bear grass at the top of the pass, where they had a good view into the valley beyond. Jane was the only one standing, holding her pony's leadrope, eager to go. Mike's hat lay at his side; gray-flecked black hair was soaked with sweat.

"Do you know the way?" I said to my wife, grinning down at her.

"You just have the cocktails ready and see if I can find it," she replied.

It was several days before Mike shamefacedly admitted his doubts about having Jane in hunting camp. By then, he'd let two notches out on his belt, partly due to the tasty trout she caught and cooked and the finger-licking fool hens she relieved of their heads and fried. "I can't get over what an ass I made of myself," the man said.

For all his misguided macho notions, Mike was not what

you'd call an accomplished woodsman. It was the fourth day of the hunt when I left him to hunt the forest back to camp. He was worried about being alone in the big woods, so I explained how the little creek running nearby was the same one that gurgled by camp. As long as he stayed within sight and sound of it, he simply could not get lost. "Then when you hit the old fire-scarred area—there's camp."

He nodded hesitantly.

I tried another tack. "Mike, your best chance to get an elk, since they're not bugling and it's so hot and dry, is to still-hunt alone. Move slow. Sit often. Listen. Take three or four steps and listen again."

"Where will you be?"

I pointed to the mountain towering above. "I'm going to climb above those cliffs and check out a smaller basin for elk sign, then return to camp by a trail along a goat ledge."

"What happens if I do get something?"

I handed him a roll of bright orange flagging ribbon. "Tear off foot-long bits of ribbon and tie them to a tree branch just close enough so you can still see the last one. Keep flagging in that manner either to the creek or the horse trail we followed on the ridge. Then when we come back with the horses to pack in your elk, we'll simply follow the creek or trail until we strike your flagging ribbon and follow the ribbons back to your elk."

He nodded. "I'll give it a try.

My watch read 2:15 when the first report from Mike's rifle rolled up from the forest below my ledge. Four minutes later another gunshot rolled from the same location—the kill shot.

"I got him!" cried a distant voice a moment later.

"MIKE!" I shouted.

"I got him!" came the distant voice again.

"FLAG TO THE TRAIL!"

"What?"

"FLAG TO THE TRAIL!"

Several moments went by. Then: "I'm not leaving him!"

On the night before our return to civilization, Mike asked how we were promoting our business. "We're not," I said, nodding complacently to myself. "I've decided to drop the sport shows we've been attending and rely on repeat business. We're running around eighty percent, you know."

"That's insane," he said. "Don't you realize the country's going into a recession."

"I haven't seen it," I said.

"Maybe it's not here yet, but it's going on and it'll hit here. Dammit, man, my business is struggling, and it's been a going concern for ten years."

When I said nothing, he said, "Do you know the annual show in Harrisburg is the biggest sport show on earth?"

I thought he was joking, so he added, "Pennsylvania has a lot of hunters."

"That's true, I guess. We've guided a lot of folks from Pennsylvania."

"You should do the Harrisburg Sport Show."

I heard no more about it until I came out of the mountains at the end of the season. The first thing Jane said, after I pulled my boots off, was, "Did you tell Mike you'd do the Harrisburg Show?"

I laughed. "Is he still on that kick? No, I didn't. I didn't say flat out NO, but I didn't tell him I would, either.

"Well, the people who put on the show called to thank us for scheduling with them."

"W-h-a-a-t!"

"They sent us an information packet with our booth space marked on it."

"They'll change their mind when we don't send them the deposit."

"Roland, the deposit has already been paid. I asked them how that could be, and they told me it was paid by a man named Michael Post. The show is in early February." ■

Chapter 27

The Enemy Strikes

This is a matter of the United States of America versus Roland Cheek, intoned the U.S. Magistrate. *Is the government ready?*

We are, your honor.

Unless you've been there....

Few honest, well-intentioned Americans have ever been faced with criminal charges in any court, let alone a Federal District Court. All should pray God it never happens; a crushing, lonely, heart-rending feeling. As I gazed at the sea of faces in a crowded courtroom, I saw that most were bureaucratic and legal officials. Were they here because of a perverse sense of curiosity? Or were they here with the objective of destroying everything for which our family had worked so hard, sacrificed so much?

I'd received the summons in January. The charge was that I had knowingly and willfully engaged in a criminal act during 1980, to wit: outfitting and guiding on National Forest land without a valid license and without paying appropriate fees.

The trial had been postponed several times. At last—May 26, 1981—came our day in court. Before the sun set, Jane and I would know whether the Skyline Outfit still existed. Or whether our investment of blood, sweat, and toil for a decade had been destroyed by invidious officials determined to squelch non-sycophantic critics.

The forest ranger who had initiated the charge was first to the stand. As the federal prosecutor questioned the man he outlined his denial of my requested summer days on the permit application and my obdurate refusal to passively sign off on the amended permit he offered. He also provided testimony that I had been observed by a number of U.S. Forest Service personnel throughout the summer, conducting guided trips into the Bob Marshall Wilderness without proper authorization to do so.

But under cross-examination from my defense attorney, a different picture began to emerge. Some of the prosecution's own exhibits that had been introduced into evidence demonstrated clearly that I had repeatedly tried to resolve the impasse: letters, telephone calls, chance meetings on trails. It was conceded that I had repeatedly brought the subject of agency evaluation of my permit brouhaha to a higher level.

One of the government's claims was that I had not followed proper Forest Service appeals process by formally requesting the procedure in writing. But among the evidence introduced by government attorneys was a letter written by the ranger, stating that I could appeal either *orally* or in writing. The man also admitted to attending a June 17th meeting with the Flathead Forest Supervisor and me, during which my permit imbroglio was discussed.

But the most damaging testimony to the government's case was when the ranger admitted under oath that the reasons given for my permit denial (overgrazing at one camping spot where we always fed supplemental feed, and at another that our journey would not approach within fourteen miles) was invalid.

There were five hours of testimony, and yet the case eventually came down to criminal intent. Did Roland Cheek knowingly and willfully intend to commit a criminal act? My repeated letters and phone calls to the forest supervisor and district ranger, and repeated queries of forest personnel on the trail while attempting to find out the status of my appeal, weighed heavily in the verdict that my intent was *not* criminal.

The U.S. Magistrate's summary was swift:

"I can't see any intent. I feel that Mr. Cheek did make every step to comply with the law. I think that there's a lack of communication all around here. But, based on intent, I'd have to find Mr. Cheek not guilty of the crime as charged."

I found it ironic that the first person to congratulate me on victory was the federal prosecuting attorney.

"Justice was served today," he said, vigorously pumping my hand and then my defense attorney's.

But a different picture began to emerge over the next couple of weeks when both the district ranger and forest supervisor asked for meetings. I saw the supervisor first. Though we disagreed at times over management prescriptions or philosophies, we'd always been cordial. But during this meeting, I found it more difficult to remain composed.

"Well, Roland," he said as he backed into his office chair, "we thought we had you this time."

My eyes must have flashed, but instead of blurting what came to mind, I lifted my water glass and sipped, staring at him over the rim. *Sonofabitch*, I thought. *This is a game with him!*

Much the same happened at Spotted Bear Ranger Station when I visited that remote bastion of wilderness administration to discuss my 1981 itinerary. The meeting was uncomfortable for both the ranger and me. To his credit, the administrator tried to break the ice by saying:

"I'll certainly give you credit, Roland. You didn't strut out of the courtroom, gloating about winning."

I moved to the window, sliding my hands into the pockets of my Levis. *So he thinks it's a game, too. He thinks it's about who's number one. Don't these turkeys realize that I'm fighting for life and family, not glory or prestige?*

But what I said was: "I'm out thirteen hundred dollars in attorney fees, another twenty-five hundred from a spring bear hunt we couldn't schedule because my license and permit were in question, and I've endured the censure of my peers. And I'm supposed to feel like a *winner?*"

⟨ ━━━━ ⟩

When Jane and I had walked out of the courtroom arm in arm that day, we at least were full-fledged outfitters once more. But we were far from out of trouble. "Well," I said, "all the judge really gave us was the *chance* to try to save our business. How we'll do it though, honey, I'll confess I haven't a clue."

She nodded. She knew exactly what I meant—that forest officials' effort to keep us in penury could have been avoided by simply waiting for the 1980s recession to do the job for them. The recession took a year to reach us, and had we been better business heads, we would've used that lag time to formulate ways to ease its shock. Instead, I squandered that cushion by complacently cutting our advertising budget when we should have increased it. Our 1981 bookings were down by half—half of our income was wiped out while I was distracted by writs and bureaucrats and government lawyers.

There was one bright spot—the Eastern Sport, Vacation and Travel Show, held annually in Harrisburg, Pennsylvania. The Harrisburg extravaganza really does rank as one of the largest outdoors shows in the world. For the simple reason that one of our hunters, Mike Post, insisted on our participation in the show, we had a foot in a door that held lots of future promise.

In retrospect, I believe Mike may have saved our way of life. It's ironic that anyone cared. After all, the idea was to save a Skyline Outfit that had almost ruptured our love … and for which, more than once, I had nearly died.

⟨ ━━━━ ⟩

"I'm going to go for the book, Jane."

The sudden decision caught her by surprise. We were in the midst of attempting some post-trial financial planning.

Bills, receipts, canceled checks, and pages of scribbled notes cluttered the kitchen table. It was apparent we would, in short order, need an infusion of capital to survive. But here I was, letting my attention wander from the alligators at hand.

She knew exactly which book I meant. For a couple of years, our sport-show booth had been across the aisle from one promoting houseboat vacations on northern Arizona's Lake Powell. Stan Jones was one of the Del Webb Marinas' representatives in that booth. And Jane, my extroverted wife, had made friends with the man.

Stan was, in my opinion, a tasteful and expert promoter of both his employer's marinas and *his* own self. He'd written a book about Lake Powell, illustrated it with his own photographs, and produced an excellent topographical map of the mammoth reservoir and its surrounding area. Both map and book, I could readily see, sold like hotcakes.

One evening, as people stood in line to buy his publication, I blurted, "Could we do that?"

"What?" she said. "Take a houseboat vacation?"

"No, no—do a book about the Bob Marshall."

"I don't know why not," she replied. "You have the photos."

"Most of them. I'd still need to take some, but there are no books out there about the Bob Marshall Wilderness. And it's one of America's best-known really wild places," I muttered.

But our busy 1979 and '80 seasons allowed no time for such an endeavor and I more or less forgot about it until the bottom dropped out of our 1981 outfitting season. Jane was, I knew, sympathetic to this venture—unlike starting up an outfitting business from scratch. Books she understood. *Picture* books she understood even better. On the other hand, she also had a woman's intuitive practical streak.

"How could you possibly come up with that kind of money?" she asked, waving a hand at the table full of bills. "Haven't you already investigated its cost? Didn't you tell me a book like that would cost fifty thousand dollars? How can you even think of going further into debt with our business crashing around us?" Then she took my hand and looked slyly from narrowed eyes. "Of course, you could always sell the Skyline Outfit."

I ignored the suggestion. "Janie, I don't know if this is going to make any sense, but here goes: You're right, it may be that no one will loan us the money. After all, we have no track record in publishing a book. But I think it's worth a shot. What I *can't* do is do nothing. We have a half-empty guiding schedule, and we have to do something—something with a promise of contributing to future revenue. As long as we try something—have some plan under way—then there's hope. If we do nothing, there'll be failure at the end, that's certain."

"Can't we drop our prices and perhaps still attract a few clients?"

"Honey, we tried that when we started out. All we wound up doing was trading dollars."

A gloomy silence fell; then I added, "If all we're going to do is trade dollars, we might as well keep the few dollars we have and use them to visit the places we haven't been, and shoot the remaining photos for the book."

When she still said nothing, I added, "I'll write it, too."

Marc and I left home late in June for an eight-day odyssey through the Sun River country on the east side of the Bob Marshall Wilderness. A month later, Jane, Marc, and I made a four-day forced march through the southern portion of the Bob Marshall. We went in via the North Fork of the Blackfoot, over a low divide into beautiful Danaher Meadows, then out via Youngs Creek and Pyramid Pass.

Since the entry and exit were many miles apart, I left our station wagon at the Pyramid trailhead while the three of us journeyed to the jumping-off place in the loaded stock truck. The plan had a flaw, however. When we reached the station wagon, we discovered someone had borrowed its tires and wheels.

We had barely enough time to get our packstring down from the mountain before dark, then find a suitable place for a tent and enough grass for our worn-out ponies. The next morning I trotted my old saddlehorse Buck ten miles into the hamlet of Seeley Lake to make a telephone call for help. Crouched in a phone booth along a highway was not the way most cowboys spend in-town time. But there I was, holding onto Buck's leadrope, trying to stall an operator while I fumbled for my telephone credit card.

State Highway 83 through the Swan Valley is a busy one, with constant logging-truck traffic. In all his years, my old pony had never been to town. His head was up, eyes wide, ears working like radar antennas at cars and trucks whirring by on the highway, and people and dogs coming and going with no apparent rhyme or reason. I'd finally reached my party and was explaining our plight when a logging truck went by, hitting his air brakes. "*SSSShhh-hhh*," went the brakes and away went Buck—with me holding onto him through a closed telephone-booth door.

I did hold onto the horse, but the booth, skidding across the parking lot, was something else. When Buck settled and quit stretching the phone wires, I was able to tell my rescuer what was going on. He laughed and said, "I wondered why your voice was going high soprano."

Another idea we explored for righting the wobbly Cheek family economy was expanding our guide service through cross country ski tours, using the "hut" system for overnight adventure. Marc and I hiked miles of mountain terrain during that summer of 1981, identifying two or three trail and road loops on which it might be feasible to lead skiers with intermediate skills.

However, each of the loops required some utilization of National Forest lands. And my currency with Flathead Forest officials was so low after our bitter disagreement over my outfitter permit that there was no chance I would be considered.

Still, I submitted a request to establish a crosscountry ski-guiding operation. It was taken under advisement. That evaluation process is apparently still under way after

twenty-five years. Federal officials are thorough, if nothing
else.

Jane and I worked at selecting photos and writing the
text for the book about the Bob Marshall Wilderness. In
order to utilize our time efficiently, I lugged an old manual
typewriter to the trailhead where I could use breaks
between trips to create and organize my first fumbling
attempts to write something of consequence.

Passers-by stared at the incongruity of a sweat-stained,
grimy cowboy, seventy-five miles from the nearest neon
lights, pounding at an obsolete typewriter while he waited
for his string of horses to clean up their oats.

Jane helped in every possible way, just as she had always
helped in everything else about which I became obsessed.
She kept me supplied with typewriter ribbons and typing
paper, got copies made and film processed—not to mention supplying groceries and clothing changes. Gradually, a
coffee-table book about the Bob Marshall Wilderness
began to take shape from a most unlikely quarter.

Despite all the divergence of energy in other directions,
we still led many wonderful people to summer adventure:
the Jensen family on a high-country gypsy tour and the
three-generation Keller family on a float-fishing trip. Ann
Jensen, at six years of age, was our youngest guest ever.
Ellis Keller, eighty-four years young, was our eldest.

Ellis proved to be a fascinating octogenarian. He'd been
an officer in Pershing's cavalry in World War I and had
served on Patton's command staff in World War II; after
that, he had been a military attache in Iran—vulnerable
while leftist Mossadegh rose to power in the early 1950s—
and a professor at Penn State. My best recollection of the
elderly gentleman was how he first showed up at our corral
wearing his World War I campaign hat, and how he sat his
saddle with all the rigid appearance of a cavalryman riding

from the Fort Belvoir parade ground.

When hunting season rolled around, we hosted Tom Blakey for the first of his many hunting trips—a guy who joined the army on December 18, 1941, and saw duty as a top sergeant in the 82nd Airborne throughout the big one, with jumps on Sicily and Italy and Normandy and "The Bridge Too Far."

There was also a professor of wildlife science from the University of Georgia—Billy Hillstead, who went on to become Director of Fish & Game in the Virgin Islands. And there was a Trans World Airlines pilot from Florida who wistfully told me at the end of his cold, wet, ten-day hunt that he was ready to go out into the civilized world and find himself something "soft and warm."

There were other Floridians: the guy who owned Stetson Hats, and another whose daughter had just been selected Miss Florida and was on her way to the Miss America beauty pageant.

We guided our first international guests: Canadians Ron Hinchey and Gordon Burrell. It was for Gordon that Jane cleaned her first big-game animal—when he shot a deer near camp while no other guides were in the vicinity.

The West family from North Carolina was back again, too. And I was still trying to give Robert back some of the money I'd won from him in poker four years before. The World Series was on when we went in, with the Yankees leading the Dodgers two games to zip. I told Robert the Dodgers were going to win.

"You wouldn't care to put fifty on that, would you?"

"Consider it done," I replied. "And I'll bet another fifty that you just made a bad bet."

Ten days later we came out of the mountains to discover Los Angeles had swept the next four games. And I had another hundred of Robert's disposable income.

We also had the misfortune to host a couple of Florida hunters who, in turn, had the misfortune to assume that I was both guide and man servant. And we hosted a New York hair stylist and a Brooklyn police sergeant. The latter expanded my understanding of Big Apple law enforcement:

"Joe, what do you think of the criminal justice system?"

"Mug a judge," was the police officer's quick and descriptive reply.

I thought of the policeman's answer throughout much of the following winter.... ∎

Chapter 28

Overtaken by Events

"You're Jane?" the statuesque blonde asked, holding both of my wife's hands as introductions were made. "After what Mike said about how capable you are, I expected someone … um … different."

"Like an eight-hundred-pound gorilla?" I asked, laughing.

"No, no. Not at all," Julie Post said. "But, Jane, you are *little*."

Her husband had not only paid our deposit for booth space at the Harrisburg, Pennsylvania, sport show, but he had designed our display and had arranged to have huge backdrop signs painted. As if that weren't enough, he and his charming wife, opened their home to us for the duration of the show.

We moved into a choice corner display space during our second Harrisburg year. That was the year when 116,000 visitors passed through the turnstiles on opening day and nearly a million clicked the counters before the ten-day show ended.

What a madhouse! Aisles were so full of sightseers that anyone who wanted information from our booth had to shove their way through a mob to reach our counter.

Jane meets people easily and well. By the time we began attending the Harrisburg extravaganza, she was

experienced enough to field most questions about our
business and the wilderness land where we offered our
guide service. Conversational ease has never been my long
suit and for me, meeting strangers is a chore. But, as a
necessity, I've developed a set-piece opening. Jane and I
repeated the same thing over and over again to different

Julie Post and Jane atop the Chinese Wall. Hunter the Brittany crouches at their feet.

people—hundreds of times each day, thousands during a show:

> "First off, we don't take any _easy_ trips. All are by horseback, deep into one of America's largest wilderness areas. We don't try to make our trips tough; but it's tough country to get into. But once you get there ..."

It was plain that a lot of people were interested in the kinds of trips we offered, but by 1982 the latest economic recession had a tight grip on the nation, the industrial East in particular. Even those who could afford our services elected to postpone such vacations until the economy improved.

"Well, it's clear I was a dunderhead to cut our advertising budget at the beginning of this recession," I told Jane as we drove home from Harrisburg.

"What will we do?" she asked. "What can we do? What other form of advertising can you try when people simply aren't spending their money?"

"That brings up another strategic blunder I made," I muttered. "I wanted the Skyline Outfit to serve middle America—even held our prices down to be within their reach. But the recession wiped out their ability to take the vacations we offer. We should be promoting our adventures to people who do have the money."

"Like who? And how?"

"I don't know."

The coffee-table book, _Montana's Bob Marshall Wilderness_, began reaching bookstore shelves on May 1, 1982. As the first book of its kind about one of America's best-loved wildernesses, it was a modest success—but only because Jane was relentless in promoting and distributing the book. So was I in seeking out radio, television, and newspaper interviews. She traveled the Treasure State end to end: Billings, Bozeman, Butte, and Dillon; Havre, Helena, Townsend, and Thompson Falls; Shelby, Darby,

Polson, and Browning; Lewistown, Libby, Kalispell, and Wolf Point; Glendive, Cut Bank, Choteau, and Great Falls.

"Roland, I see your book *everywhere*," was a common refrain from folks we knew. In grocery stores, supermarkets, convenience stores, motels, gasoline stations, resorts, convention centers, chambers of commerce offices, and novelty shops. It was *the* regional release of that summer and fall. And we sold 13,000 copies that first year.

Still, like everything else to which I applied my superior business acumen, it made us no money. Again, a business-school drop-out could've predicted failure. In order to raise the necessary capital to print the full-color book, Jane and I borrowed $55,000 dollars at 18 percent interest during the depths of the worst recession to hit the country since the Great Depression. What genius! In order to obtain that money, we mortgaged everything we owned: our home, pastureland, Skyline Outfit assets, *and* our inventory of unsold books.

By New Year's Day, 1983, there remained 4,000 hardcover copies and 6,000 in softcover—somewhere around $60,000 worth of books in inventory. But because of the economic drain from our wobbling outfitting business and the always annoying need to eat, we *still* had a debt load of $31,000 at that bloody 18 percent interest.

❦

Mike and Julie Post were our first guests during the 1982 season, out from Pennsylvania for our spring explorer trip during the peak of wildflower season. We traveled twenty miles the first day to Salmon Forks, then moved camp five miles upriver to White River Park. Because we planned to cover such a short distance that second day, we treated the move casually, leaving Salmon Forks shortly after lunch.

Puffy white clouds pushed over western mountains, turned gray, then ominously black, and filled the sky as we arrived at our planned campsite.

"We'd better hurry!" I called as I began dropping packs from horses. Like a well-oiled machine, our little crew flew

into action: Jane pulled ropes and canvas from the packs
while Marc and I jerked saddles from the ponies.

"What can we do?" Mike called.

"Firewood," I said. "Dead pine limbs. Bring in an armload or two and pile them beneath that tree."

Marc strung a highline rope between trees, tied horses
to it, and began graining them. Jane scurried to the edge of
the high bank overlooking the river and started erecting
our sleeping tents while I wrestled with the big dining fly
and its aluminum poles.

Lightning crackled in the west. I glanced toward it and
saw the bottoms of huge, black thunderheads sagging
lower and lower below mountain peaks.

"Mike! Julie!" Jane called as a gust of ground wind
struck. "Bring your duffel bags and throw them in this tent
to help hold it." A moment later another gust hit, and only
an unladylike diving tackle saved our tent from jerking
loose from its moorings and sailing off the bluff. I ran with
our duffel bags.

Marc pulled nosebags from the ponies, then belled and
hobbled and loosed them to graze. I kindled a campfire
and assembled our cooking grill. Marc erected his smaller

Jane and Roland leading their horses across the South Fork suspension bridge at Black Bear.

tent amid rising, crossgusting ground winds and ominous grumblings from overhead. I threw anchor ropes over the dining fly and secured them to give extra support against the alarming power of the williwaws.

Meanwhile, Jane and Mike carried buckets of water from the spring; Marc pitched his duffel inside his tent and zipped it shut; Julie gathered another armload of firewood, and I began gathering up odds and ends left scattered on the ground—tarps, ropes, saddlebags—and throwing them beneath the dining fly. A big splat of water struck my arm, and another atop my hat.

"Here it comes!" I shouted. Everyone converged on the dining fly as the heavens opened their floodgates. I glanced at my watch. From the time we pulled into this campsite until now had been thirty-two minutes. I grinned at my companions and said, "Just enough."

As if to dramatize our thin margin of escape, a mighty bolt of lightning blew the top from an ancient larch tree, only two hundred yards from where we huddled. There was no detectable lag between the flash and the mind-numbing roar of thunder.

"My God!" Mike breathed. Horses streamed back to camp.

"I hope it don't get any closer," Marc muttered.

It didn't. Soon the storm front had moved far enough away so that we were counting as many as five "one-thou-sand-and-ones" between flash and thunder. But there the storm stayed. And stayed. Lightning seemed as steady as if someone were standing at a bank of electric switches, and the rumble of thunder actually impeded the flow of chatter between friends.

Fortunately the rain soon quit, but the thunder and lightning continued for hours, changing eventually from cloud-to-ground bolts to cloud-to-cloud. Darkness fell and the storm still raged, its lightning remaining so frequent that one could've hiked trails by the regularity of its flashes.

The celestial display was still going on when Mike and I finally quit watching it at one o'clock in the morning.

The next day we set out in search of the *flower*.

"The flower" is a Franklin ladyslipper (*Cypripedium passerinum*), and it's apparently rare in our part of the country. Thus far, our family had spent four years in the search. We'd been informally drafted into the quest when U.S. Forest Service silviculturist Danny On told me the orchid had, years before, been sighted in a particular area of the Bob Marshall by a Vanderbilt University botanist. Danny showed me a letter from the botanist, even giving coordinates. Danny knew we frequented the supposed area of the rare flower, and so we began a long odyssey.

My silviculturist friend provided a photo of a flower similar to, but distinctly different from, our more common mountain ladyslipper (*Cypripedium montanum*). In order to recognize the plant, I thought I must see it in bloom— during a narrow window of time that exactly meshes with the time period for our spring explorer trips.

The big problem, as we quickly discovered, was that the coordinates given in the Vanderbilt letter were impossibly wrong. That made searching for a needle in a haystack more like searching for it in a hayfield. And the search during our trip with Mike and Julie proved as fruitless as those during previous years.

⁂

Hortense Friedman had served forty years as assistant treasurer for the University of Chicago, responsible for that prestigious university's endowment fund. When she came on her adventure with us, the 82-year-old lady said this would be her *sixteenth* packtrip into the Rocky Mountains.

When I asked Hortense why she'd taken so many horseback journeys, her answer was simple: "Because I like horses and I like mountains."

At the scheduling stage, when the lady forwarded deposits for herself and her niece, she called attention to the fact that future correspondence should be addressed to Miss Hortense Friedman. We were happy to oblige, of course. But might there be a problem? "She sounds pretty

Puritan to me. Do we dare take the mixings for evening cocktails?"

"Ask her," was my wife's common-sense reply.

So I did, with considerable hemming and hawing. "I should mention, ma'am, that Jane and I enjoy a cocktail of an evening. We don't want to offend, and we could do without, but if it makes no difference and wouldn't offend ..."

Hortense cut in: "Isn't that remarkable? I was wondering how to ask you the same thing. I drink bourbon, myself. Only one each evening. With only as much water as would melt from two ice cubes, hear?"

We'd come off a long ride, and Hortense was relaxing on her sleeping bag, spread under the dining fly. Her niece Patty was out cantering her horse through the meadow while I grained and pulled saddles from our other ponies. The coffee pot burbled over a blazing campfire and Jane busied herself with supper preparations.

After I'd loosed our saddlehorses and washed my hands, I poured cocktails—a dash of bourbon for Hortense with two ice cubes' worth of water.

"Thank you," the lady said, leaning back on her bag.

Just then our old Brittany spaniel wandered over and sprawled beside her, laying his head in her lap. I opened my mouth to call the usually impeccably correct dog away, but closed it when I saw Hortense absently begin scratching his ear.

She continued to scratch as she sipped her bourbon and branch and gazed dreamily into the campfire. I sipped my own drink and studied the picture of repose.

"I don't know why dogs and humans never learned to purr," the lady suddenly said. "It would be a perfect response to the way I feel right now."

***

I worked with Jane on advanced whitewater training during our next venture—a fishing journey down the South Fork with only one guest, Stan Jones of Page, Arizona.

Stan had kindly provided advice and editorial help with our Bob Marshall book; now it was payback time, and he

was interested in learning more about whitewater rafting techniques.

Most of all, Jane and I picked up marketing tips from Stan, an expert publicist who successfully provided informative books and maps of regional (Lake Powell) interest to a clientele three million strong. And at last, it began to sink in that our Bob Marshall market was a mere fraction of the one Stan served.

It was on this trip that Jane learned respect for the power of a river. While wading a riffle above a log jam, she slipped, was swept downstream, lost her flyrod, and only saved herself at the last moment from being swept beneath the logs by scrambling and clawing her way hand over hand up a submerged log.

Our daughter Cherie and Jane (looking for fish) drift through Black Bear Canyon

By the fall of 1982, I considered Jane my equal as an outdoors person. She lacked my acumen for direction-finding, but understood well how to select campfire wood and how to build and maintain cooking fires. She was developing an eye for spotting wildlife, could read tracks in a trail, and had an unerring sense in adding touches for guest comfort:

"Here, Bill, I've heated some rocks. Wrap one in a sock so it won't burn your skin, then put it against the small of your back. By morning it will be better."

Or, "Here, Beverly, you take my flashlight. Then if you hear any sounds during the night you won't be frightened."

It was she who suggested we collaborate in keeping two members of a hunting party separated as much as possible. The men had a falling-out over, of all things, golf scores. When they were in camp together, Jane kept one occupied in the cooktent while I talked to the other around a campfire. And vice versa. Worked beautifully for the entire ten-day hunt.

* * *

Perhaps my favorite recollection of the 1982 hunting season was one day when I was guiding John Detwiler and Joe Somers on a hunt along the sloping side of the Chinese Wall.

These fellows had hunted together for years out of Jackson Hole and had only booked with us because they failed to draw a Wyoming license. Six inches of light snow had fallen during the night, and there was not a fresh track in all the country to set a hunter's heart pumping as we labored up the mountain. We were soon wet with both melting snow and sweat. When we stopped for lunch, I kindled a big fire from the rotting remains of a fallen tree.

Joe ate his lunch, licked his fingers, then stood to get a better view of the surrounding peaks. Silvertip Mountain towered to the northwest, Lone Butte to the west, Turtlehead and the Flathead Alps to the south, Ibex to the north. All were shrouded in snow.

Joe turned a full three-sixty, staring all the while. Then he said:

"You know, in Jackson Hole the Grand Teton stands out like an exquisite painting." Pause. "But this ... this is like a whole damned gallery!" ■

Chapter 29

Ooo-La-La

We found the flower!

Or should I say Jane found the flower?

Or maybe her horse should get the credit.

Our guests were Jack Campbell and Asta Bowen, along for our spring explorer trip. Jack and Asta were both nature lovers, intrigued by the mystery of the disappearing Franklin ladyslippers, and they eagerly joined in the search. Finally, however, with the orchids still elusive, we elected to spend a day riding to the top of the Chinese Wall for a spectacular four-compass-points view from the Great Plains to the Idaho mountains and from the Canadian Rockies to the mineral mountains that make Montana the Treasure State.

The weather was hot and muggy for late June. It was late in the afternoon when our little cavalcade clattered onto the flood plain, just prior to the trail ford. The river crossing here can be tricky, particularly during spring's snow melt. And this morning's crossing in the swift current had been no different. My thoughts were on getting back across the swollen little river. Besides that, I was growing cross and irritable from the muggy heat, the already long day, and a wife who was chattering endlessly with two totally absorbed guests about all the colorful wildflower ensembles with which God had cloaked this land. I was getting impatient to reach camp.

Jane, leading, reined her pony to a halt alongside a bleached mule-deer antler that had obviously been shed some years before. "Aww, Jane," I called over the heads of our guests, "let it go. Let's get on back to camp."

"Okay," she replied. "I don't know what I'd do with it anyway." The lady clucked at her horse, but before he'd taken a dozen steps, Jane dropped a bridle rein. Her well-trained saddlehorse stopped. Then he bent to sniff a tiny white orchid at his feet. Jane leaned forward to retrieve the rein, saw the pony sniffing, and in a hoarse voice called, "R-R-Roland!"

Damn! That woman will be the death of me yet. "Now what is it?"

"My ... my horse is about to eat your flower."

"Oh for God's sake, Jane, let's get this outfit ... *My flower! What flower?*"

The long-sought flower, Cypripedium passerinum—the Franklin ladyslipper

All thoughts of dangerous water crossings and timely camp arrivals vanished. I leaped from my horse and rushed past Jack and Asta and their ponies to where Jane's horse still sniffed the flower at his feet.

There could be no doubt. The tiny white orchid was indeed a Franklin ladyslipper. And there was another growing beneath the limbs of a spruce tree. And two more beyond!

We lashed our saddlehorses to nearby trees, then did a quick inventory of the immediate surroundings. Scattered throughout the sparse young forest, dozens of the little flowers bloomed—always near seeps and wet spots. The mystery *really* was how we could have missed them for the past five years!

❦

Our little guide service still struggled in the wake of the '80s recession. Hunter numbers seemed stalled at eighteen in both 1982 and '83, and summer business was nearly zilch. Still, those few who did have the inspiration, intelligence, fortitude, and spirit to take advantage of our dynamic, superior, inspirational services, proved without exception to be remarkable folks, many of whom wound up our lifetime friends.

Mike and Julie Post returned for a float trip, and Alex Tully, the Wests from North Carolina, Tom Blakey, and Mickey Morris were all into their long run of seasonal hunting trips. A few new friends also entrained with the Skyline Outfit: Keith Sensabaugh and Gary Bryan were two who returned again and again; so were Bob Shelton and Russ Barnett. Of those '83 guests, however, none were as remarkable and intriguing as Dieter and Ulla.

Dear Mr. Cheek,

From Mike Markels in Alaska I got your address and would like to kindly ask you to inform me about the best possible time and the costs for a 14 days hunt on elk and puma with you in 1983, as well as to send me your book "Bob Marshall Wilderness," which seems to give good information on this kind of hunt.

> *With best regards,*
> *Dieter Assmann*
> *Humboldstrasse 13*
> *5880 Ludenscheid*

"Where is this letter from?" I asked Jane, handing it back to her.

"Ludenscheid is all I can see." Then she asked, "Will you answer it? Or should I?"

"You do it. Nothing will come of it anyway."

Two weeks later her reply to this Dieter guy was returned as undeliverable. Our local postal people said it wasn't deliverable because the address had no destination country on it. "Well, that's that," I said.

Not exactly:

> *Dear Mr. Cheek,*
>
> *We refer to our letter of October 7th, 1982 and would like to remind you to inform us about the best possible time and the costs for a 14 day's hunt on elk and puma with you in 1983. We also asked you to send your book "Bob Marshall Wilderness."*
>
> *Thanks in advance.*
> *Dieter Assmann*
> *Humboldtstrasse 13*
> *5880 Ludenscheid*

"Ashcan it," I told my wife. "There's still no proper address."

Instead she visited a neighbor who lived on a farm a mile from ours. Heinz Irriger took one look at the letterhead and said, "Why, that's West Germany. Ludenscheid is but thirty miles from where I was born."

I caught Jane working on a second reply. "What's the use, honey? The deadline for obtaining a Montana hunting license is only a couple of weeks away. There's no time to fill out an application and get his money for a license—not to mention our deposit."

"I don't care. I'm doing it anyway."

She sent her letter, properly addressed, via airmail.

Within days Dieter called. I happened to answer the phone. When I explained the time crunch, the German cut through the red tape like Wotan besieging a Roman column—wire-transferred sufficient funds to our account and gave me all the information necessary for completing his license application over the phone. He told me he had hunted over much of the world and his wife always accompanied him. "Ulla does not hunt, but she goes with me out in the field."

Dieter and Ulla Assmann make a striking couple; she's a tall and beautiful blonde, he a handsome businessman dealing in electronic components, with offices in both West Germany and the United States. His English is passing fair; hers less fluent, but enough to allow us to converse.

I don't know what I expected from European hunters, but I imagined problems foreign to anything I'd learned through my Western heritage. Dieter fulfilled much of those fears in his choice of a hunting rifle—a side-by-side double of custom Czech manufacture. It had more silver on it than Lone Ranger's horse, and each barrel was big enough to swallow a "shooter" from my grade-school marble days. Naturally, it was engraved, filigreed to a fare-thee-well. The stock was hand-carved walnut, and its sling strap was of the finest hand-tooled leather.

When the German handed it to me to examine, I could only stare in horror. "Dieter, I don't have a saddle scabbard to fit this weapon. There's no way we can carry this on your horse."

"I will carry it on my back, no?"

"For twenty-seven miles? My God, man!"

But he did. Without a murmur. Without a complaint. What's more, he also stowed the rifle behind my truck seat on the way to the roadhead.

"Oh, no!" I gasped. "There are tool boxes rattling around back there."

He laughed. "Is all right. It is also a tool."

"Yeah, right," I muttered. "A ten-thousand-dollar tool."

Ulla was frightened of horses, fearful of the pending ride. As she told Jane, she was afraid her horse would "galoop" with her.

As always, my wife rose to the occasion, leading Ulla's horse all twenty-seven miles so the docile old mare, Fertiliza, could not "galoop."

"Fertiliza. Is strange name. Why so?"

I grinned, but only told the lady that we called the horse "Liza" for short.

The experience in horseback travel was not at all what Ulla feared. In fact, she considered it great sport and even talked of actually guiding Liza a bit on the way out of the wilderness, at trip's end. Ulla credited the success of her ride to Jane's leading her trustworthy steed. But most of all, she credited her saddle.

Western saddles, the German lady discovered, differed from the English-style saddles she'd ridden in her Hessian countryside. The high cantle of her cowboy's saddle was much easier to relax against. And the horn! So easy to grip when her horse must plunge through mud or clamber over rocks. English saddles aren't so equipped. How clever are these Americans!

I told her the saddlehorn was a speed- control lever. "Push it and Fertiliza will go faster. Pull it and she'll slow down."

Hunting guest, top-flite artist Tom Saubert, at his easel near camp.

The blonde lady looked puzzled for a moment, then laughed. "You are, how you say? Kid me. No?"

Kid her? Yes. Besides having a fine sense of humor, Ulla had almost a kittenish curiosity about everything strange to her—which meant *everything* about this northern Rockies wilderness adventure.

Other guests on this particular hunt were rising young Montana artist Tom Saubert and Kalispell orthodontist Bob Windauer and his twelve-year-old son David. Bob had guided float-fishing trips for us and had hunted from our camp. A couple of years before, he'd brought his elder son Michael on a hunt. This year was Davey's turn.

The name Windauer is, of course, German, and Bob's grandparents were immigrants from the old country. As a child, he had spent considerable time with those grandparents. In addition, he had served much of his army hitch stationed in Frankfurt. As a result, he could speak a modicum of Deutsch—a talent Bob had not revealed to Dieter and Ulla.

At one point on the long ride in, Bob rode directly behind Dieter, who trailed Ulla. The couple carried on a running conversation in their native tongue, laughing and bantering. As it happened, Ulla's horse had a gas attack— one reason we named her Fertiliza—and there was a loud report from beneath her tail. Ulla and her husband laughed. A couple of hundred yards farther and there was another burst of flatulence from the horse as she climbed over a log. Dieter called in German, "Ulla, is that you?"

Bob replied in German, "No, I think it's her horse."

It was my practice during hunting trips to clamber from bed two hours before daylight, light the lanterns, kindle a fire in the cooktent stove, then wake the guides so they could catch and saddle the day's horses. Meanwhile, Jane would arise and begin making breakfast. Upon her signal that she would be ready for our guests in fifteen to twenty minutes, I'd pass the wake-up call throughout camp.

It was then that Ulla would pad along the path to the creek, clad in a bathrobe and slippers, on her way to her morning bath. Rain or snow—and a couple of mornings there *were* skiffs of snow—the woman bathed before daylight in the ice-cold creek. No wonder, if they routinely whelp such women, that the Krauts nearly whupped the world in two wars!

Naturally, the thought of the blonde beauty bathing nude in our creek conjured up all sorts of images. And I joked that this trip was the first when I had no trouble whatever getting my guides up in the morning. "Instead, my problem is getting them down from the trees."

Her laugh was again throaty. "You are again kid me, no?"

One day Jane said that Dieter would ask me to sell Ulla's saddle to him.

"What? What in the hell would he do with one of our saddles? For that matter, what would *she* do with it?"

"I don't know. But he says tomorrow is her birthday and she's in love with that saddle."

"Well, it's not for sale," I snorted. "We'd just have to find a replacement."

That night at the supper table Dieter asked how much a saddle like the one Ulla rode to hunting camp would cost.

"Search me," I said. "It's been a while since we bought any saddles."

When he said nothing, I took a sip of coffee. "That's a used saddle, of course—it was old when I picked it up. I know what I paid for it, but it would cost twice as much to replace it today."

"Ulla would like to have that saddle. Tomorrow is her birthday and I would like to buy it for her."

"Aw, Dieter, I don't really want to sell it. I'd have to find another."

"What would it cost if you did replace it?"

I shook my head.

"How much to replace it?" he persisted.

"Oh, say *three* hundred."

"Say four hundred."

I laughed and spread my hands. "Say four hundred. Done."

Jane boxed and air-freighted Ulla's saddle to Frankfurt. Some years later, we had occasion to speak with Ulla on the telephone and I asked if she'd ever ridden her saddle in Germany?

"No, no," she chuckled. "But is on pedestal in foyer. How you say? Is piece for conversation."

Dieter dressed in the German style for his daily hunts: leather knee-length breeches (lederhosen) held up by leather straps that crossed in the back. The straps were held together in front by a breast-high cross-strap. Also included were knee-high green stockings and an olive-drab wool coat that reached to his thighs. Atop his head was a pointed, narrow-brimmed wool hat with a traditional tight, long-chamois hair bundle clipped into a narrow leather hatband. The hat, too, was of green wool. His feet were clad in ankle-high leather hiking boots that showed the wear of many miles of rough mountain travel. His ensemble looked as though it came right from the Austrian Alps.

And indeed, as it turned out, the man owned a hunting lodge in the Austrian Alps.

German Dieter Assman reading prepared initiation rites for Tom Saubert's and twelve-year-old David Windauer's first "high game."

Tom Saubert took his first elk—a five-point bull—on that hunt, and David Windauer took his first mule-deer buck. These achievements required, according to Dieter, that each man be initiated into the fraternity of "high-game" hunters. A ritual message marked the ceremony and required a stroke with the flat of a sword each time one of the three elements of the message was invoked: *The beauty of the country; the splendid company of his fellow hunters; and the magnificence of the animal.*

Actually the ceremony was colorful, albeit a tad sobering. However, there was one minor hitch. Since swords were scarce in our hunting camp, Dieter used a stout limb to inflict the strokes of salute. Mature Tom Saubert accepted the ceremony with equanimity and interest. And twelve-year-old David took his strokes like a man, though he seemed a little bewildered by it all.

Shucks, I was bewildered by it all. ■

Chapter 30

International Flavor

I was dragged kicking and screaming into globalization. First there was the Englishman who arrived via Calgary. Then there was Dieter, the German hunter, and his wife, the beautiful lady our guides thought of as "ooh-la-la."

Despite my reservations about hosting foreigners—people who might not have the proper sensitivity to the wild places and wild things turning my crank—I realized that those people would not be visiting our wilderness if they had access to comparable public wildland treasures in their own back yards. And in weak moments I had to admit that visitors from distant countries were fascinating. But language and cultural barriers meant added difficulties for the guy with whom the buck stopped. I told Jane, "It'd be okay with me if we stuck to guiding Pennsylvanians."

❦

I picked up the phone on its second ring. After listening a few seconds I said, "Huh?" But after another minute I cut in with, "Hold on a minute," and handed the phone to Jane. She covered the mouthpiece, raising her eyebrows.

I shrugged, "I don't know—couldn't understand 'em. Sounded something like 'meat-sooey issue-talky from

*Mitsue
Ishitake*

Tokyo.' See if you can make sense of it."

My wife conversed with the caller for a few minutes, then hung up. "Who was it?" I asked.

"Mitsue Ishitake, from Tokyo, Japan. She just scheduled our August 22nd trip for three."

"Japan? Tokyo, *Japan?* They're coming here to ride horses in a wilderness? Didn't you tell them what they'd be getting into?"

"Stop it, Roland. It will be an exciting, educational adventure, and you know it. Methinks he doth protest too much."

Mitsue Ishitake presided over an educational foundation in her native land—sort of like our American National School Assemblies. The foundation was established by her late industrialist husband.

Each year Mitsue toured America, primarily to review books and movies suitable for translation for Japanese schoolchildren, but also to indulge in her passion: riding horses. Like Chicago's Hortense Friedman, Tokyo's Mitsue Ishitake loved horses and loved to ride trails in western America. Each year, too, Mitsue would bring a couple of her foundation employees as a reward for outstanding service and a chance for them to grow educationally.

Michi Sakai, a young woman and Toshiaki Tatsuda, a young man, were puppeteers with a show they took from school to school on behalf of the foundation. Each of the visitors spoke a little English, Mitsue best of all. None was bilingual enough to allow easy conversation.

As Jane predicted, I found my learning curve turning upwards with these people. Each was as polite as I'd been led to believe the Japanese people to be. Though I saw no overt display of cultural differences, there were enough glimpses to make them fascinating—like their eagerness to learn, their wide-eyed absorption of our culture of "big" and "broad" and "roomy." Any cultural problems appeared to be mine or Jane's, brought on in large part by our inability to converse readily with our guests. Nevertheless, it was apparent the Japanese were willing to make every effort to fit in.

For instance, I knew of the Japanese fetish for cleanliness, sometimes bathing several times per day. One evening at supper, I mentioned that it was hard to stay clean on horseback packtrips. Mitsue didn't understand, but she appeared interested. So I groped for the right words and spoke slowly enough to convey the message. When at last the lady grasped what I'd meant about staying clean, white teeth flashed and she said, "But ver-ry comfortable."

Jane, who at 5'3" towered over both the Japanese ladies, bumped squarely against the culture thing when she paused to help Mitsue bridle her horse.

"No, no, no!" Mitsue brusquely said, dismissing her with a wave and quickly moving between Jane and horse. "I will do it."

A couple of minutes later I hurried past, saw Mitsue struggling on tiptoes to reach the pony's ears with the headstall, reached out and took the bridle, slipped the bit in Baldy's mouth, and hooked the throat latch in place.

"Ahh," Mitsue said, bowing politely. "Thank you, thank you."

"You're welcome, ma'am. Anytime." And I hurried on.

Jane, who watched the exchange, tittered—but her smile never reached her eyes. "She

Toshiaki Tatsuda

wouldn't let me do it. Ordered me away. Told me she wanted to handle her own horse. Then *you* come along and she has a melt-down."

I squeezed my wife's shoulder. "Maybe it's because theirs is a male-dominated society, honey. They definitely are patriarchical. To Mitsue, you may be inferior, whereas I'm superior merely because I'm a man."

"Sounds flaky to me," Jane sniffed.

Michi Sakai

Each day we rode long and far. The favorite ride both for our Japanese guests and us was into alpine country along the Continental Divide. It was a land of vast meadows and open ridges rising to tundra-like country at the crest. We spotted mountain goats along the cliffs, mule deer at forest edges, even a black bear feeding on mountain-ash berries. Mitsue was ecstatic at day's end. "Your trails, they are so … so wide!"

I smiled and nodded and slipped the bridle from her horse, then offered the lady the pony's nosebag and watched until she managed to secure it over his head. The truth was we spent the day riding where there were few trails. But I could see little reason for correction.

A few minutes later a soft rain began. I dashed about gathering things left outside the shelter of our tents or the big dining fly: saddlebags here, a jacket there, a shirt, sunglasses, empty nosebags for the ponies. Mitsue's camera was lying lens up on a stump. I snatched it, too.

"No, no, no," the Japanese leader cried running toward me. "Is underwater camera."

I skidded to a halt and examined the camera. Indeed it was: a Nikonis; a very expensive camera. "Aw gee, how foolish of me," I said, handing the camera to Mitsue, grinning down at her.

"Is all right," she said, turning the camera over in her hand. "I give it to you."

"What! What did you say?"

"I give it to you."

I took a step back, holding out hands to stop her. She followed anyway. "Ma'am, I just can't accept that. It wouldn't be right."

"But I want to give it to you."

"No ma'am I can't ..."

"Shut up, Roland," Jane interrupted from the side.

Michi was the quiet one, inscrutable as a brick, yet as absorbant as cotton. I have a tiny toy Japanese automobile that, at the end of our trip, she dropped into my hand, then turned and dashed away.

Toshi was tall for a Japanese, over six feet, slender as a cornstalk. The young man, who lives in a city of ten million people, obviously was overwhelmed by much of what he

A mountain meadow where Mitsue thought our trails are so wide.

saw in wilderness America—the horses, a lonely land, the lack of people most of all.

Our little outfit would turn our attention to hunting season as soon as this trip ended, and guides had already set up the 14 x 16 hunting-camp cooktent. One day Toshi and I sat in that tent drinking coffee. The lad's eyes kept roving the tent. "Is *big*," he said.

"This tent?"

He nodded.

"Well, how big is your Tokyo apartment?"

Toshi frowned, so I pointed a finger at him and said, "Tokyo apartment ..." He nodded and I held my hands out far apart. "How big?"

"Oh," he said and looked around. He cut the tent space in half with a figurative chop from the side of his hand. "This big."

"Half?"

Both resignation and disgust were mirrored on the young man's face. Then the fire went out. "Half," he repeated. "Stove here. Table here."

Silence fell between us until I asked, "Do you have a car?"

"Not understand."

"A car. An automobile." I pantomimed driving, then pointed to him. "Do ... you ... have ... automobile?"

Again his expressive face turned blank. "No. Motorcycle."

"Oh, a motorcycle. What kind is it?"

Resignation again. "A Honda."

"A *Honda*. That's a good motorcycle, isn't it?"

"Yes ..." The lad's eyes drifted to the far corners of the tent. "... but I would rather have a Harley Davidson."

On the way back to civilization, Toshi rode with me while I hauled horses home in the stock truck. On the way he taught me to say, "*Sayonara mataaimashou*," Japanese for "Goodbye, til we meet again," so that I might surprise Mitsue and Michi.

It worked. The ladies both gasped, then each smiled and bowed politely with palms together in front of their breasts.

1984 saw other fascinating people, heartwarming events, hilarious episodes, or curious medical occurrences.

Like the time Leslie Billet's straw hat—the one I'd spent six days trying to trade her out of—got knocked off by a tree limb and before she could get off her pony and retrieve it, her trusty steed lifted his tail and proceeded to fill the hat with fresh, hot-from-the-oven horse biscuits.

The lady, of course, screamed. The next thing she said was, "I'll trade! Roland, I'll trade!"

Like the float trip where Jean Miller picked up giardia for the second time. The first time was on another float trip with the Skyline Outfit in a previous year. Oddly, there were several other people in Jean's party on each float, and none of them contracted giardia. To further compound the conundrum, Jean's husband is a physician—actually he's *my* doctor, operating a clinic in Whitefish. Husband/doctor Ron could not prevent his wife from ingesting the microscopic giardia-carrying snails, but fortunately he did know how to allay its effect.

Oddly enough, we never had another guest contract giardia during twenty-one years of outfitting. Dan Cherry picked it up, however. Dan was one of my guides. Like Jean Miller, Dan contracted giardia twice. And as with Jean, no one else on Dan's many wilderness sojourns ever picked up the annoying disease.

Like Jack Oliver, vice-president of Westinghouse, out of Pittsburgh, choosing a horseback travel vacation with our little outfit.

"How did it happen, Jack, that you even knew about us?" I asked.

"I wanted to know about the Bob Marshall Wilderness," he said. "Our company was doing a lot of work with some of the folks at Butte and when I asked for information, they sent me your book."

"And then you wrote us?"

"Hell, yes. I wanted to go with the fellow who wrote the book."

In 1984, as in other years, some of our guests wrote to us after they got home:

> *Dear Roland and Jane:*
>
> *Words fail me in trying to express the magnificence of our experience last week. It exceeded all of my expectations—which were pretty high.*
>
> *The skill and thoroughness with which you two worked together in planning and carrying out the intricate logistics of our trip continues to awe me. And it was all done so unobtrusively as to make it seem simple. I know better, however.*
>
> *Thanks again, more than I can say, for a wonderful experience. You helped us to see that inspiring country through your eyes, and learn why you feel about it the way you do.*
>
> *If my money and body hold out, I'd like to think we can do it again and see parts of the Bob Marshall that we missed.*
>
> Good luck!
Jack Oliver

> *Dear Roland, Jane and Marc*
>
> *Roland, us folks who have returned to hunt with you are grateful for the friendships and enjoyable times that you and your profession have made possible for us. People that I have met and experiences I've had with the Skyline Outfit will be in my mind forever. The kind of people that we spend time with in the "Bob" get harder to come by all the time!*
>
> Thank you, your friend
Robert West

For four long years, the number of guests finding their

Some of the country where Skyline Outfit took their guests.

way to our struggling little northern Rockies guide service was hardly enough to permit us to live: twenty-four in 1981, twenty-three in '82, twenty-seven in '83 and again in '84. Then our numbers began a slow climb. It was clear, however, that by 1984 we neared the end of our tether.

Jane, bless her, had given her all to make this thing work, but it just wasn't to be. Though she, too, was now devoting her life to what had become a mutual love for the outdoors, I could no longer deny the mounting evidence. Loan payments were overdue; we'd sold another tract of land and it still wasn't enough. Horses and trucks were aging and some must be replaced in order for our business simply to function. Sales of our Bob Marshall book were tapering off. We were backed into a corner with but one alternative.

"Jane," I said at the supper table one evening, "I guess you'll like what I'm about to say."

It was our anniversary and she'd lit candles and opened a bottle of wine. There was a tossed salad and a thick, juicy tenderloin steak done to perfection. A fire blazed merrily in the fireplace and she'd moved the dining table so it was just in front. And most importantly, the woman wore the traditional anniversary orchid that I never forgot through a lifetime together.

My wife raised her eyebrows and said, "Go on."

I shook my head as if to clear it. "There's no way we can continue. I've made up my mind—we must sell the outfitting business and I'll have to …"

"NO!" she cried, eyes widening in shocked surprise. "No!" Tears began to flow.

"No? Jane, am I hearing right? Are you saying no? After fifteen years of trying to get me to sell this confounded business, now you're saying no? What in the world has got into you, woman?"

Tear streaks were all over her carefully prepared face by now. "How … how will we meet … our wonderful … friends?" she sobbed.

And I knew there was nothing this woman could do to keep me from loving her the rest of my life. ■

Chapter 31

Some Woman!

If our life had been a fairy tale, virtue would have triumphed over all adversity when Jane realized she, too, was overcome by a love for our way of life—and we would've lived happily ever after.

But ours was not a fairy tale. Instead of a straight line to success, riches, and glory, our tracks were as erratic as the footsteps of W.C. Fields staggering along a center stripe under a traffic cop's baleful glare. But willpower, desire, love, and teamwork count for something. Thus, just when my drive to succeed flagged, Jane's burned hotter and brighter. We sold two more tracts of land and refinanced our debt load in order to benefit from lowered inflation and loan rates. That was how we squeaked through our latest financial crisis.

By 1985, however, we'd sold so much pastureland that what we retained was insufficient to support our horses. So Jane searched for and found pasture for lease.

And at long last, just when I'd despaired, our bookings began to climb. Though we were still too far removed from the pulse of economic America, the back of the 1980s recession had been broken and we scheduled thirty guests for our Skyline Outfit's fifteenth year. True, those thirty guests represented less than two-thirds of the number we needed to eat and show a business profit. But now there could be no doubt we'd succeed. After all, we were positively committed—*together!*

Lacy and Colleen Sayre visited the Bob in the spring. Sandi Morris returned with Bill Pogson and Jack Phalaric. This time Sandi chose a geological gypsy adventure. Keith Sensabaugh and Gary Bryan and Ted Modlens, Tom Blakey and Dale Stockstill and Tom Saubert, Mickey Morris and Bob Shelton and Russ Barnett all returned as hunters, bringing many fine friends with them.

Newcomers Gary Ernst and Lloyd Gummo and the Wellborn family all began long hunting-season strings; and Bill Kittredge and Annick Smith joined the geology trip.

But of all our 1985 guests, none were as intriguing to our family as Leonard and Irma Shapiro. The couple hailed from Philadelphia. Lennie was a graying, curly-haired gynecologist in need of R & R, she a striking blonde. Their children were grown, immersed in successful careers. Had we not been so innocent, Jane and I might have guessed from the name Shapiro they were "of the true faith."

Lennie Shapiro works hard at replacing pork Jane tried to feed him. Jane is at work, too.

On the first night, Jane served pork tenderloins roasted over an open fire—savory, dripping delicacies of the finest campfire cuisine. The Shapiros tackled their dinner with gusto, licking all twenty fingers at the end. Then they asked about the cuts of meat.

Naturally, Jane glowed from their praise and their obvious relish of her culinary art. "Pork tenderloins," she said. "We buy them in bulk and I … is something wrong?"

Irma and Lennie exchanged horrified glances. At least Irma's was horrified. I thought Lennie's mouth corners twitched as he waited to see what his wife would do. "We … we're Jewish. Didn't you know that?"

I thought fast. "What does that mean?"

"What does that mean?" she said. "Don't you *know* we can't eat pork?"

"Why?"

The question was lost in Jane's anguished moan. "But all our breakfast meats are pork—ham, bacon, sausage. And I've planned porkchops for one dinner!"

"Irma, it's not that important," Lennie said.

"Didn't you know we're Jewish?" she asked again.

"Did you tell us?"

"No, but our name …"

"Well," I said, "I'm sure I sent out a letter stating that if you had any dietary needs …"

"You did."

"Well, why didn't you tell us at that time that you couldn't eat pork?"

"Irma, let it go," her husband said.

Instead, she said, "We were on a trip down the Colorado last year and we did tell the outfitter. So he changed his entire menu to accommodate us and we felt like everyone else suffered because of our faith. We decided this time we wouldn't inconvenience others on our account."

Our daughter Cheri, along for the adventure, said, "Well, the river is full of fish. I can't see what the big deal is if they can eat fish."

"That's right," the doctor said, fitting a reel to his fishing rod.

I nodded. "Besides, that means lots more bacon and sausages for me."

As it turned out, there weren't too many extra slices—not after Lennie helped his surreptitious self to as many pieces as he could get past Irma's watchful gaze. And they did eat fish. Lots of fish. Usually two or three fat ten-inch trout with every meal.

Meanwhile, I was intrigued by the first people I'd every met who were honest-to-God practicing Jews. So began the questions that apparently edged toward embarrassing, perhaps forbidden ground.

Lennie gave only evasive answers. Irma seemed more direct, even confrontational. One evening as Jane busied herself with supper and the rest sprawled on the sandbar, cocktails in hand, Irma said, "All right, I will tell you what it's like to be Jewish."

Lennie tossed off his drink, stood and reached for his flyrod.

Irma watched him walking along the river. "Lennie can't talk about it," she said. "But I can. The reason I'm telling you is because you seem genuinely interested and you haven't said to me how easily I could avoid being pegged as a Jewess because of my blonde hair."

For the next two hours, Irma held forth on their perception of being Jews—the necessity for them to cloak

As the "Charlotte" wildfire rages along a distant ridge, Irma Shapiro sets up a camera tripod. Jane trots back to camp to check on supper.

themselves in the faith, against the prejudices that surround them. European pogroms were discussed. So was discrimination in America. Eventually Lennie wandered back to the sandbar. He reached us just as Irma admitted that their children are not as adamant as she about the need to adhere strictly to their Biblical code.

"Lennie doesn't believe as strongly as he should, either. But it's the children I'm worried about. They spend altogether too much time with friends outside the faith. I tell them the day will come when they'll be disappointed in those friends, but they won't listen."

We listened—Jane and Cheri and me. We listened, but I'm not sure we understood. We did understand how people gain strength from tradition and a feeling of unity; how single reeds can be broken, but how a reed lashed with others into a bundle can withstand powerful forces trying to destroy it.

We learned that Lennie and Irma had visited the Soviet Union—this was in the pre-Gorbachev days.

"Why?" I asked.

"We went with a purpose," Irma replied.

"What purpose?"

Lennie waved to Irma, then said: "To provide hope. To prove solidarity with people from other lands who care about their plight." Pause. "No, we could not offer escape. Neither could we offer money, or relaxation from oppressive regime set against them. But we could offer hope; the certain knowledge that others, somewhere, care."

The lightning strike had occurred a month earlier. Camped at White River Park, we had watched bolts strike Charlotte Mountain again and again. The next day, as we headed out of the wilderness at the end of our trip with Lacy and Colleen Sayre, Lacy looked back over his shoulder at smoke boiling up and predicted, "That one might amount to something."

A few weeks later, heading upriver with the Shapiro party, we could see that the Charlotte fire had indeed

The South Fork near Salmon Forks. Note camp on gravel bar at left.

amounted to something, crawling up and over first one ridgeline, then another, creeping toward Holbrook Creek.

There was considerable interest in this first "let-burn" wildfire in the Bob Marshall Wilderness. The Charlotte fire signaled a major change in U.S. Forest Service policy of suppressing all wildfires by 10 a.m. the morning after detection.

We packed on upriver. The weather continued hot and dry. Two days later, as we drifted comfortably downriver in our inflatable rafts, the Charlotte fire "blew up," running before strong, gusty winds blowing from the west. The fire advanced on a broad front, climbing a shoulder of Scarface Mountain, moving inexorably toward our river-pipeline to the outside world.

We camped on a huge gravel bar only three miles downwind from the fire. I thought about continuing downriver before camping, trying to run past danger's path. But this particular open gravel bar, with little or no flammable fuel scattered about, in my judgment, offered the safest place to camp.

Still, the advancing fire gave us pause. After dark, we sat on rocks watching the fire burn two hundred-year-old larch trees.

"There it goes again!"

"Wow, look at that!"

All were spellbound as another burst of flames shot one, two, or three hundred feet skyward; first to the left, high on a ridge where it butts against the open rock face of Scarface Mountain; then to the right, lower down the same ridge, where the advancing fire marched in our direction.

"I don't know if I'll sleep tonight," Cheri said before crawling into her tent and spending the night snoring softly.

I clambered from my bag twice during the night to check on the fire's approach. As expected, the inferno's energy dissipated with cooler nighttime air, and at two in the morning Charlotte appeared no more sinister than a hundred campfires in the distant night.

⚜

That was the year my spirits ebbed. Jane, with her entry into the essence as well as the mechanics of our business, saved it—saved us.

My last image of the lady's outstanding competence came during that watershed 1985 season's last hunt. It was mid-November. Bitter cold had seized the land, and we had to chop ice from the creeks in order to water our horses. Finally the hunt ended and we broke camp to return to civilization. Jane started early, leading our hunters, while I stayed to help load packhorses.

Five miles from camp, Jane and her hunters encountered a major hazard—a stream that had not only frozen from bank to bank, but had repeatedly overflowed and refrozen. With subsequent rises in water level, the creek had undoubtedly deepened. How much, she couldn't guess.

She tested the crossing with her small horse, urging him onto the ice, breaking though, until he was swimming. Then, with amazing presence of mind, she returned to shore and picked her biggest horse and his rider to break through the remainder of the crossing. Bill and the big horse Flame, with Jane's pilot track already broken part way, busted through and the other horses followed.

At times the horses were swimming. Riders' feet were soaked—a serious danger in the bitter cold. But again, with a mind sharpened through years of experience, Jane halted her party on the far shore and kindled a roaring bonfire where they dried their boots and stockings.

I approached the dangerous ford with a loaded pack-string only a few minutes after Jane and her hunters had ridden away from their fire. I studied the stream crossing, then shook my head. *Some woman.* ■

Chapter 32

Heroes Gone, But Not Forgotten

The Skyline Outfit's guest numbers continued to inch up—from thirty in 1985 to thirty-nine in '86. Though still below survival level, our income was supplemented by the modest but steady sales of our *Bob Marshall* book, as well as occasional sales of northern Rockies' adventure stories to regional and national magazines. At least the extra revenue allowed us to eat.

Unfortunately, it was not until late in July that we were able to schedule our first guests of the season—Pete and Betty Lou Merkle of Hanover, Illinois. Then geologist John Montagne put together a mid-August trip with family and friends. But it was my old Pennsylvania nemesis Elene Hitz, returning this time with her daughter and husband for a float-fishing adventure, who most sticks in my memory and Jane's.

"Leanie" was the beautiful young lady who, six years before, so embarrassed me in front of an all-female party (including Jane) by suggesting it was the outfitter's job to pick ticks from blushing maidens. Naturally, I expected all-out psychological warfare between the outfitter and the articulate lady, and was thus properly prepped. What I didn't expect, however, was for Leanie to enlist her dashing, mild-mannered husband (Lee) and attractive twelve-year-old daughter (Leigh) on her sharp-tongued side.

"Leanie" Hitz—this lady is one of the more polished females at shredding outfitters the world has ever known.

River flows were down in 1986, a result of light snows during the previous winter and little rain during the summer. Without sufficient regard for the low flow, I launched too far upstream to float our loaded rafts over most riffles. As a result, we spent a great deal of time outside our rafts, dragging them through shallows.

In order to get some respite from Leanie's digs at a guy she *surely must* have admired (why else would she be so implacable toward me?) I assigned her to Jane's raft while I escorted Lee and young Miss Hitz downriver in my boat.

I was able to drag our raft over the first few riffles without asking my passengers to help. But later on, the river turned more and more braided, splitting into two or more channels, and the riffles turned ever shallower. First Lee was out in ankle-deep water tugging on our raft, then Leigh. Back upstream, Jane and Leanie heaved their raft downstream together like Volga boatmen.

For mile after mile.

Late in the day—two hours after we should've reached our campsite—the river braided and the braids braided. The watercourse I selected to follow grew shallower and shallower. Large stones dotted the surface, then smaller ones reared their ugly heads. Our raft, loaded with four hundred pounds of gear, drew only two inches of water, but that was twice too much for the shallows we tried to breach.

Tug. Pull. Rest. Tug. Lift. Pull. Just a little more—perhaps fifty feet—and we'd be able to float down into a pool where several river braids came together. Our faces turned red. Breath came in gasps. "Goddamn it, Cheek!" Lee suddenly shouted. "We're beaching the sonofabitch."

The irony of the man's exasperation struck me as hilarious and I fell into the water laughing. He began laughing, too, then Leigh joined him. It was the cackling that broke the tension.

"How long … how long you been a-doing this, Cheek?" the man gasped at last. "You been an outfitter long?"

I clambered to my feet and started wading upstream. "Come on, Lee," I said. "Let's go up and help the women get that other raft down here—they have the food."

That evening, as we sat around a campfire devouring the roasted trout that Jane dropped on our plates, Leanie leaned tiredly across her daughter to say, "I give up, Mr. Outfitter. We're even now, okay? Let us float tomorrow instead of pulling barges down the Yangtze."

Later in the week, after drifting miles down a stream joined by countless feeder creeks, the South Fork of the Flathead turned into a real river. Now there was no longer any need to drag rafts over shallows. From here on, our only concern was to avoid upsetting our rafts in the whitewater rapids yet to come. Usually, when we came to particularly nasty stretches I would take my raft through, then hike back upstream and row Jane's craft through the worst of the rapids. Gradually, however, Jane was growing more and more confident and insistent on tackling bigger white-water challenges.

Our boats drifted beneath the suspension bridge near the Black Bear ranger cabin. Below was an exciting, but not dangerous, section of whitewater. I knew it well. At the foot of the rapid, the stream butted against a boulder-studded bank and bounced off, turning ninety degrees to the left. I led off in my raft, and Jane held hers against the current's slow drift while she studied my route.

I hit the standing waves head on, the raft cutting through them or riding up and over. In mid-passage I spotted a flurry of activity on the river-bend boulders—naked men diving into the water. Probably a Forest Service trail crew skinny-dipping on their day off.

They must have spotted our craft and noticed Leigh's blonde hair flying like a pennant, revealing that a female sat up front. Heads bobbed along the rocks as we shot through the rapids, then drifted through the pool they occupied.

But damn! That water ran off remnant snowfields and glaciers and was damned cold! So as soon as we had drifted a few yards downstream, the men began clambering back onto their sunbathing rocks. All eyes were upon us—none focused back upstream where Jane's raft crashed through the waves, heading directly for them.

Leanie snatched up her camera and screamed, "If you got it, boys, flaunt it."

Her words carried easily down to us and we turned to watch. It looked as though someone had emptied a bucket of frogs on that rock as white-skinned men flung themselves from their perch back into the frigid water.

⚜

"We'd like to talk to you about an elk hunt."
I looked up from the letter I was writing at the Harris-

burg sport show, into the blue eyes of the speaker—a fortyish, sandy-haired, freckled man of medium height and slender build. "Sure," I said. "What is it you'd like to know?"

"Everything." There was a slight frown on the speaker's face, but each of his three buddies flashed encouraging smiles.

"Well," I began, "we only do horseback packtrips deep into the Bob Marshall Wilderness. We try to tell people we don't make any easy trips." I saw the man tense and wondered why. "We don't deliberately try to make 'em tough, but it's tough country to get into and tough country to hunt after you do."

I talked to the men for the next hour. The reserved sandy-haired one did most of their talking. His questions were well-thought out, concise, and pertinent to a hunt with us. But something nagged me about the guy. Unlike the others, he seldom smiled. His reserve seemed impenetrable—as if he had a chip on his shoulder.

"How about a man with one leg?" Sandy-hair asked abruptly.

That stopped me. I glanced into his buddies' eyes. Each smiled encouragingly. There was no guile. "What about him?" I murmured to gain time.

"Would there be any problem?" Sandy-hair shot back.

I hesitated, thinking of the long ride in, and the steep mountains surrounding our hunting country. My wife, who was standing at my elbow, said I was silent for at least a full minute as Sandy-hair shifted nervously, his reserve turning to what I thought was belligerence.

"Yes," I said at last, "there would be a problem. But not from our standpoint. The problem would be his. There's no way he could avoid the long ride in. But after we arrived at camp, there are certain ways to help him hunt."

The man stared back, his features softening ever so slightly. Then it hit me! "Are ... are you the one with an artificial leg?"

"Yes."

Our eyes locked. "I don't know what you can or can't do," I said.

"Pegleg" Mitchell straddles Baldy...

"I've never found anything I can't do," he replied.

"Let's go hunting," I murmured. He smiled.

Ron "Pegleg" Mitchell has to rate as a most unusual guest for our small outfitting service. And a pack of his, swaying atop one of our pack-horses, rates as the most unusual load we've ever carried. Pegleg hails from Manchester, Pennsylvania. He grew up there, is married, and has three fine children. From the age of six, Pegleg and two of his childhood chums had dreamed of a horseback elk hunt in the Rocky Mountains. In a tragic accident over twenty years before, the man had lost his left leg from the thigh down. He had learned to cope with his handicap, however, continuing and solidifying his friendship with his childhood buddies during many Pennsylvania hunting and fishing trips.

But their dream of a Rocky Mountain elk hunt remained only a dream as each man pursued a career and raised a family. Finally the friends determined to make their lifelong dream come true. They so impressed Jane and me that we determined to get Pegleg to our distant hunting camp, despite his disability.

The trip was indeed difficult for Pegleg. But he's a gritty guy. The artificial limb had, by the halfway point, so chaffed his stub that he decided he had no choice but to remove it and ride into camp without it. When he handed it to me and asked if I could somehow lash it atop a pack-horse, I stood mute for a moment, then said, "Hell, we can do *anything*."

So on we went, through bogs, over rocks and logs, over a high pass, and down to the valley below. For thirteen more miles and five long hours, Pegleg grimly sat—not quite astride—his saddlehorse. He and the horse arrived at camp with the rest of us. He was tired, his face wreathed in pain, but grimly determined—and triumphant!

...while his artificial limb goes atop another horse.

There *really* wasn't much that Pegleg could not do. Obviously he couldn't walk as far as most folks, but he was more mobile than some we've guided. We discovered the man walked better around a mountainside in a direction that allowed him to swing his artificial leg on the downslope side. Boredom wasn't a word in the man's vocabulary, and he was tireless on a stand. What was more to the point, he was determined not to allow favoritism because of his disability. And he had an unflagging sense of humor to go with an ingrained cheerfulness that was all the more refreshing when one saw him struggling into his artificial leg an hour before daylight.

Pegleg's companions were cut from the same solid Pennsylvania oaks—a finer crew we never had. Poems could be written about them.

In fact, poems were written *by* them. A band of elk escaped from Pegleg's companions via a cliff ledge. When I returned to Harrisburg the following winter, they presented me a 1987 calendar illustrated with a picture of the famed Chinese Wall. Beneath the photo were these words:

> *The Chinese Wall has seen it all.*
> *But none stranger did it peek*
> *Than when the elk ran out the goat ledge*
> *And escaped from Roland Cheek.*

The Pennsylvanians had given us all nicknames. Guides

Dan and Kevin were named Dangerous Dan and Recall. I was Iron Cheeks because of the hours I spent in the saddle. One of Pegleg's companions, Roy Thoman, added this poetic image of camp life:

> *Oh, it's morning say the sounds*
> > *that filter through my head,*
> *As Dangerous Dan and Recall*
> > *dress for what's ahead.*
> *Yet from my peaceful slumber,*
> > *it's not waking that I dread.*
> *It's Iron Cheeks and his lantern—*
> > *for then I must get out of bed.*

From our point of view, the most telling statistic from our 1986 season was that of our twenty-six hunters, half were repeat guests and five new ones came with repeat guests. Clearly the nation was emerging from its latest recession and our former guests' spendable income was rising. Optimism was a watchword for the folks who most cared about the Skyline Outfit: Jane and Roland Cheek. ■

Chapter 33

On Top At Last

1987 was the year when I almost killed my wife. It was during an early spring adventure, before trails were free of snow, cleared of fallen trees, or replaced after being obliterated by floods, landslides, or snow avalanches. Lacy and Colleen Sayre, long-time friends, accompanied us on the journey.

"Tell you what let's do," I told my companions, eyeing a game trail that snaked up a nearby hillside, "let's cut cross-country."

"Oh, I don't know," Colleen said, shaking her head. "I've followed you cross-country before. And I don't relish getting lost in some jungle."

I laughed. Lacy said, "What's the alternative?"

"The alternative is to go back the way we've come, then catch the horse path up to the main trail. But I think we can cut up here, follow that elk trail until we get on the bench above, then pick our way over to the Forest Service trail. Save us maybe a couple of miles."

"Well, I'm game," Lacy replied.

I looked at Colleen.

"I'm with you guys, I guess."

Jane said, "Promise me one thing—if it gets too bad we'll turn back."

"I promise."

Jane and Colleen walk along beach at outlet of Big Salmon Lake

Fifteen minutes later we were nearly atop the forested glacial bench—just another hundred feet to go. But the trail ahead did not look good. "Hang on," I shouted back to the others and pointed my aging horse Buck right for the steep spot. He's always been catfooted, that horse, and he hit it at a dash, clawing his way up the bank as I gripped his mane behind the ears with one hand, leaning ahead, urging him on.

Atop the flat, I twisted in the saddle to watch Lacy. He, too, bent over the saddlehorn, willing his steed up the last pitch. In a moment he was beside me and Colleen was racing up the last stretch. Then it was Jane's turn. "Roland, I don't like this."

"Just hold onto the horn, honey."

Her horse was a good one, but slight-built. It may have been because she was fearful of the challenge ahead that she didn't allow her horse to gather sufficient momentum for the dash. Whatever the reason, he ran out of steam just short of the top; then, with Jane hanging helpless from a vertical saddle, he toppled over backwards.

It began in slow motion. I screamed, "Get out of the saddle!" But she had no chance before the horse was down on top of her, somersaulting end over end with her stuck in place.

"No! No! No!" I cried.

She lay in a crumpled heap when I reached her, blood trickling from one ear and a cut on her forehead. I straightened her out as gently as possible, afraid to move her more than necessary, certain that she must have broken bones. *At least, dear God, she's breathing.*

Then the woman's eyes popped open. "How did you get here so fast?" she asked.

I squeezed tears, then brushed my lips against hers. "Try lifting a foot." She did. "Now the other." She did. Then with Lacy's and my help, she struggled to sit up.

"Where do you hurt?" I asked.

"Nowhere."

"Not even your head."

"No. Oh, my neck feels a little stiff. Maybe it'll hurt later, I don't know. But now I remember—you promised to turn back if the trail got bad."

Jane did, of course, have a headache, as well as a plethora of other aches and pains. For a while, she also lost confidence in her guide, her horse, and herself. But she was not seriously injured, despite the horse repeatedly rolling over her. Only Providence saved the woman— because I damned sure didn't!

<hr />

It was not a good summer for Jane in more ways than her horse wreck. We were float-fishing down the South Fork with Jack and Jo Heeringa of Grand Rapids, Michigan. I had the Heeringas in my boat, while Jane worked with a smaller back-up raft, carrying some of our camp gear and her faithful dog Tess.

It was mid-July, the river flows still strong, and Jane piloted her raft on a powerful river that was charged with remnant spring flows. It was when she reached the "Rock Garden" that her adventure went awry. …

I cast a quick glance at the two lifejacketed passengers who leaned forward in anticipation. "Okay, he-e-e-re we go!"

The raft careened down the chute, and I let it run, dipping my right oar twice to keep the correct angle. We nudged one onrushing boulder only hard enough to spin the raft so we missed the next.

Jo turned her spray-splattered face to ask, "Did you do that on purpose?"

"Look sharp!"

I put my back into a half-dozen deep oar strokes that swept our stern past a jagged rock by mere inches. Then a couple of quick "portagee" forward strokes and we nudged a second boulder so that we spun past yet a third.

"Masterful!" Jack exclaimed. I hardly heard the man as I concentrated on the outsized downstream boulder—the most hazardous in the Rock Garden. Whitewater gushed halfway up its upstream side. Jo gasped and Jack's hands tightened even more on the safety ropes.

"Which way?" I muttered. "Right or left?" I pulled right. Only one deep stroke was needed and I could then lean on the oars as the last boulder in the Rock Garden rushed past.

Reaching calm water at last, I pulled into an eddy. "Better wait for Jane," I said. "Make sure she comes through okay."

It wasn't really dangerous, this section of river upstream from Salmon Forks on the Flathead's South Fork. Low water sometimes requires rafters to drag their boats through the rocks; high water and you'll float over them. But on occasion, the prominent "dragon's teeth" and a certain water velocity can combine to be challenging. This was one of those combinations.

Jane, rowing the smaller, more maneuverable raft, positioned herself carefully at the head of the rapids, then shot into the maelstrom. Rowing strongly, she avoided the first rock, but slammed into the next, caroming away. She reminded me of a moth doing battle with a lampshade, with oars like wings a-flutter. Then she got her act together and, with her Brittany spaniel still perched atop the prow, pulled past the next onrushing rock.

She got her breath, paused to take stock—and smashed directly into the next boulder. The lady's raft was so lightly laden that it bounced back upstream and, with the dog scrambling to stay aboard, she managed to keep one oar in the water long enough to spin away. Now she bore down on the real obstacle—the monster boulder with water gushing halfway up its side. Flustered from her minor mishaps, Jane rammed both oar blades deep and pushed with one while pulling the other, spinning wildly.

A raft claws out of South Fork whitewater.

"No!" I muttered.

Her raft broadsided the perilous boulder, shooting halfway up its side and sticking there. Water poured into the canted raft from upstream. The dog leaped for safety atop the huge boulder only seconds ahead of her mistress. Once there, Jane stood with fists on hips, staring down at me and shouting, "Roland!" as if I'd had anything to do with it.

I was too busy laughing to take the woman's dilemma seriously until Jo pointed to a slowly sinking creel washed from Jane's waterlogged raft. The creel carried at least a C-note's worth of lures and flies. From that moment I was busy swimming after equipment that should've been tied securely in my wife's craft. After the equipment rescue, I went after Jane, dog and the raft.

It was only after I'd safely escorted her to shore that my honey pointed out—somewhat stiffly—that I had my priorities skewed.

June Gehringer was almost the death of me. A pistol and a half, the feisty lady would have finished the demolishment begun by Leanie Hitz the year before, had it not been for her kindly (and longsuffering) husband. I can still hear Ken Gehringer chuckling, saying, "Now June ..." while I covered my ears and shuffled out of range of the lady's barbed wit.

June was not particularly different from most other women who seem to relish seeing me blush—but June was better at it than most. And for some perverse reason, my own wife seldom came to my defense when I suffered psychological abuse from ladyhood.

The Gehringers and their friends made up a great party, yet another group of Pennsylvanians. Ed Gilbert could call great horned owls—we actually watched him call them into camp. June, meanwhile, spent her adventure keeping the outfitter off balance. She seemed almost on a *mission*.

We hiked and rode horseback into the high country, swam in the streams, enjoyed a wonderful campfire camaraderie. One day we sat eating lunch atop Switchback Pass on the divide between the Spotted Bear River and the North Fork of the Sun. I'd pulled off my boots and socks and was happily wriggling my toes in the rarified atmosphere when a large group of riders appeared. They dismounted a short distance below us and the outfitter leading the group ambled our way to exchange pleasantries.

He was fully decked out in all the garb of the trade: chaps and spurs, gloves and ... and sunglasses. "Look at him," June said, loudly enough for God to hear. "He's dressed right. Ken, why didn't you find us an outfitter who followed the dress code."

"Now, June ..."

"Shucks, ma'am," I said, "I got all that stuff back in camp."

It was December when we received the following poem from June:

> *T'was the month of August—year '87*
> *when we rode the trail to that corner of heaven.*

We Bob Marshalled West, so to speak
*   with an engaging couple, namely Cheek.*
We rode, we hiked, we stared in awe;
*   most incredible views we ever saw!*
We fished, we climbed, sometimes we'd walk,
*   we ate good food and talked good talk.*
Sometimes we went up, where the angels appear.
*   Sometimes we went down, our guts filled with*
*   fear.*
Our feet got sore, our hinds how they ached,
*   and sitting in ice water, by the sun we got*
*   baked.*
And what to our wondering eyes did appear?
*   I beg of you, Jane—this you must hear!*
Mr. Elwood Cheek resembling a lark,
*   in chaps and spurs and glasses dark*
Come Ed! Come Ken! Come Dolores! Come June!
*   D'you suppose this creature came from the*
moon?
But we put our fingers beside our nose,
*   And up the campfire the apparition arose!*
So we heard him exclaim as he drifted from sight,
*   Happy trails to all and to all a good night.*
But you wait a minute; don't go away.
*   The Gehringers have a bit more to say.*
Our heartfelt thanks to both of you,
*   for sharing a world we never knew.*
Not only that God-made beauty of land,
*   but your thoughts, philosophies, your guiding*
*   hand.*
We enjoyed it all and when we did depart,
*   we embraced knowledge and wisdom we lacked*
at the start.

Jane and I led two more summer groups; one consisted of another family party.

Ted Johanson owns a major boot-manufacturing company in Lewistown, Maine. The man was so intrigued by the rigors we put boots through that he returned home and sent each of us two pairs of boots with Dunham and L.L. Bean imprints for us to test.

During the course of their adventure, I learned more about the complexities of boot manufacture than I'd gleaned throughout my earlier years. I also learned a bunch about the art of rock climbing—these were prodigious Eastern hiking and climbing enthusiasts.

Our summer season ended with another visit from the "Carbondale Seven," who were now becoming a featured fixture for a late-season float trip. "Those guys are fishing fools," I told Jane before the trip. "God, they don't just fish *every* day. They fish *all* day *every* day."

The arrangement with these guys was I'd give them a significant price break for their trip if they'd pilot their own rafts downriver. I would guide one raft downstream and ride along for the journey. Jane and I would figure the groceries and provide all the necessary horses and equipment, but they would supply the manpower.

The truth is, they were magnificent. And the further

The "Carbondale Seven." You don't see seven. They exaggerated about other things too.

truth is, I've never been out with a better bunch.

There are several recollections. For one, I remember how that old hand, John Phelps, grumbled about having to wear a lifejacket when we pushed off our starting spot near the headwater stream where the South Fork begins. "Roland, I don't remember having to wear a lifejacket before," he said when I told him to put one on.

"Memory is the *second* thing to go, John," I said.

So he reluctantly donned his safety jacket. On the second river bend, Carbondale barber Ronnie Benton, lost control of his raft in a rapid and smashed into a log jam, toppling John into the same hole where Jane almost drowned a few years before when she lost her footing while fording upstream shallows.

John said he knew he was gone. Then his life jacket brought him back, gasping, to the surface. The way he later told it, Ron Moutadier was looking anxiously over the side of the raft when John popped back up, still carrying his flyrod and wearing his straw hat.

"Hand me your pole," Ron said. And John did—it was an expensive graphite rod. In the process, the raft passed over the near-drowned angler. He grabbed the safety rope and, still wearing a now dilapidated hat, hung on until Benton rowed furiously around the log jam and brought him to shore.

I was following, piloting the next raft. I saw John's mishap and cried out in alarm. Then I nosed the second raft into shore where John crouched, shivering like a drowned rat. He was clearly heading into shock, so I leaped out and kindled a roaring bonfire where he warmed up and dried his clothes.

From that point on, I never had any problems with the Carbondale boys when insisting on safety procedures. That made the circumstances somewhat strained when, on the last evening of their voyage, I wanted to "fanny bump" through the most dangerous rapid on the river.

Fanny bumping is a procedure where one dons a life-jacket and leaps into the water at the head of a rapid, drifting feet first downriver, bouncing over rocks and through whitewater. Jane and I, as well as all our regular river guides, did it for the fun of it.

"I'm not getting into that water deliberately," John said. "You have to be out of your mind!"

"Come on, John," I said. "Do you want to live forever?"

"I'm going fishing." And they did; all seven of them lined up along the river near our last night's camp, flycasting for cutthroat after cutthroat.

I walked upstream, clad in a swimsuit and a lifejacket. At the rapid's head, I lit a cigar, then jumped in.

With the lifejacket, it was a cakewalk. I drifted through the big reversal—my cigar still smoking—then floated through their fishing grounds, puffing clouds of smoke as I went.

Within minutes, the guys were in lifejackets and swim trunks, fanny bumping through whitewater with their outfitter.

Nine of our twenty-three hunting guests were repeats, and they brought along others. All were fabulous people. Tom Trosko most sticks in my mind from that year. The guy's a doctor from the Pennsylvania coal region, a general practitioner. His patients love him. Perhaps Dr. Tom's nine humorous health hints explains why:

1) Check your birth certificate and look for the part that states life is fair and don't be disappointed if you cannot find it. Then check the obituaries and if your name isn't there, don't complain. You're having a good day.

2) As Socrates said, all things in moderation. Even too much sex can cause a sore back. An occasional egg or cheeseburger will do no harm. But remember, in moderation.

3) Choose your medical advice wisely and with a grain of salt. This year's medical fact may be next year's medical myth. Whether it is in the New England Journal of Medicine, Prevention Magazine or

Reader's Digest, it does not have the status or immutability of being printed on two tablets of stone and handed down from Mount Sinai.

4) Forget this nonsense of "no pain, no gain." Leave that to John Wayne, Vince Lombardi and adolescent males (or females) developing their identity.

5) Be childlike, not childish. Some men (and women) never grow old, and some never grow up. Those who grow up are those who never grow old.

6) Wear your age proudly. Don't insult yourself by joking about celebrating another 39th. Whether 39, 59 or 69, wear it proudly. You worked hard for it, and you earned it.

7) Don't let youth talk you into being old. America is the only culture where age and maturity are not respected.

8) For all of the men out there (ladies, read this for your mates), don't get concerned about your sexuality. If you're like most men, you are not as good as you think and not as bad as you fear, and your mind wants to do it one more time than your body is capable of. A normal phenomenon—don't get concerned or panic.

9) Relax. None of us is getting out of this alive. We all have a bullet with our name on it. Don't race to find the one that says "to whom it may concern."

⚜

We served 54 guests in 1987. Six long years after the U.S. Forest Service tried to crush our little guide service, we'd struggled back to the numbers of clients needed to survive. At long last we could sit back and draw a deep breath. And why not? We were in the black! We'd also weathered a recession and my own idiotic business bumbling.

Not only that, Jane and I were deeply in love, committed to an admirable life style in a wholesome environment.

We enjoyed good health, owned a successful business, employed great people, and had a sound string of reliable horses and serviceable equipment.

In addition, we were becoming respected in our field: I was elected President of the Montana Outfitters & Guides Association, and Jane was appointed by the Governor to a three-year term on Montana's Tourism Advisory Council. All this despite the fact that our guide service could only be classed as a small—real small—"Mom & Pop" operation.

We were perched squarely atop our world. ■

Chapter 34

Awake to Reality

Despite our optimism during the previous year, it was
apparent by spring that we were staring at another
financially disastrous year. Our summer season was shap-
ing up poorly, and by the mid-April sellout date for
nonresident licenses, we'd managed to schedule only
eleven hunters. Why? Why?

This time we had none of my unconventional (or idiotic) business maneuvers to blame. I was playing the game
straight up, utilizing management and promotional strate-
gies taught in business curriculums anywhere. That's why,
when the bottom dropped from beneath our feet in 1988,
the will to continue in such a volatile roller-coaster occupation ebbed.

Jane suggested that my duties as president of the Montana Outfitters & Guides Association might be interfering
with efficient management of our Skyline Outfit. I pointed
out that her own position on the state's Tourism Advisory
Council could also be distracting.

The unusually hot and dry summer throughout the
mountain West may have killed our hopes. Lightning
crackled across the high country. Wildfires broke out by
the hundreds, then thousands. The "Fires of '88" were
born. Yellowstone burned. Folks who might've been leaning toward a western mountain vacation turned to New

Brunswick or the Washington Monument instead.

Two lightning-caused wildfires raged in the country we roamed: the 220,000-acre Canyon Creek fire to the south raced across the Continental Divide to sweep out onto the

Smoke from the Gates Park Fire billows above a distant skyline as riders pause in a mountain meadow. Left to right: Hugh Cullman, Tommy Medlins, Nan Cullman, and Frank Holding.

prairie, threatening homes and ranches and even small communities; and the 55,000-acre Gates Park fire burned uncontained, near the heart of the Bob Marshall Wilderness.

1988 wasn't all bad, however. It was Hugh Cullman who alerted us to the fact that we'd been recommended by *Hideaway Report*.

"Who?"

"*Hideaway Report*. It's a high-quality newsletter published by Andrew Harper about exclusive vacation retreats all over the world. Your Skyline Outfit was mentioned as *the* guide service into the Bob Marshall Wilderness."

"I never heard of Andrew Harper. Or *Hideaway Report*, for that matter."

Cullman chuckled. "I'm not surprised. Harper visits resorts incognito, then reports on them. In your case, he was responding to a subscriber question about reliable horseback guide services, and he gives you high marks based on his research."

Hugh, Vice-President in charge of overseas operations for the Philip Morris Company, scheduled a mid-August horseback packtrip along the Chinese Wall for himself and his wife and two other couples.

Hugh and Nan were into adventure vacations. Or, properly said, Nan was into adventure vacations, and good-natured Hugh went along for the ride. They'd skied in Austria and Switzerland, hiked in Tibet, and toured the Soviet Union before *glasnost*. This was their year for a horseback trip into the northern Rockies.

Nan's sister Lu and the lady's husband, Tommy Medlin, and Frank and Ella Ann Holding, North Carolinians all, completed their party. These were especially striking and talented people. Ella Ann was an accomplished pianist, as was Nan Cullman. Both were trained in voice and provided tony lungs to enhance our lusty voices during campfire sing-alongs on their Rockies' wilderness adventure.

Sisters Nan Cullman and Lu Medlins. Lu is riding Buck.

Lu Medlin was a statuesque beauty—in fact, the lady had been Miss America runner-up about the time I graduated from high school. I let Lu ride my favorite saddlehorse Buck during the trip. Watching her on Buck, I told Jane, "In my next life, I want to return as a saddlehorse in the Bob Marshall Wilderness."

She smiled.

One day Jane caught Hugh rifling through her food boxes. "Why, Hugh!" she exclaimed. "Whatever are you looking for—perhaps I can help?"

He straightened, flashing a smile. "Oh nothing, really. I'm just doing a little market research, checking to see how many Philip Morris products you brought along for the trip."

"Whew!" Jane said later. "Was I glad that we stood the test. Did you know his company owns Kraft, General Foods, and Miller beer?"

Jane was a particular hit with this party, as the following incident I wrote in my newspaper column illustrates:

> *Sweat trickled along the inseam of my undershorts and coursed freely down a dust-caked face. I smiled encouragingly at our guests. "A tad warm, isn't it?"*
>
> *They were tired. It had been a long, dusty ride to view the "Chinese Wall" cliff formation and it showed on these folks' faces. It was during a prolonged drought, the third hot and dry day of their week-long packtrip through the Bob Marshall Wilderness.*
>
> *One of the ladies plopped down on a block of wood. That was when my wife handed her a strawberry daiquiri. Her mouth fell open and she squealed in delight. Jane handed the other ladies a daiquiri, also. The second lady shook her head in wonder. "This has ice in it," she mused. "How do you do it?"*
>
> *"That is our ice," Jane said. "I made them up at home, poured them into Seal-a-Meal bags and sealed them by machine. Then I froze them solid and we use the frozen drinks, as well as the other frozen foods, to keep our perishables cold." She turned to a pan. "See, here's tonight's meat. It's still frozen."*

One of the men walked over and stared at our pack-aged steaks, poking the wrappers with a forefinger. "It sure is," he said finally. "Are you saying you don't use ice?"

"Yes. We quit packing ice years ago. Who needs it? We found with ice we fought water spoilage as much as weather spoilage. Besides, when we car-ried ice we found we needed another ice chest. This way, we cut down on weight carried by our horses.

"It takes a little more time to do it this way," she continued, "and a little more trouble. But it's worth it."

"Explain," the man said.

"Well, for a party this size, we get by with one 48 quart ice chest. The bottom layer is this...." She handed the man a beer she'd taken out earlier to thaw. He smiled and popped the top. The other men walked over in interest.

Jane went on: "The second layer is the frozen meat we plan to use the last days of our trip. I try to fill it layer by layer, planning the meals by the layer." She handed the other two guys their daily beer ration. "Of course, this is only after I pre-cook the roast, ham, and turkey, then slice and package just what we need."

"My, my," one lady said. "That's a lot of work."

Jane smiled. "There's no place for leftovers on a packtrip; yet we have what we need, when we need it. And pre-cooking saves us lots of weight. The Seal-a-Meal is tough and it assures no spoilage from moisture or air. Look, I even have tonight's three-bean salad, complete with oil and vinegar dressing, in one."

Our guests toasted her. "Who needs ice?" they said.

"Plush primitive" is what Hugh Cullman called their Rocky Mountain adventure with the Skyline Outfit.

Throughout the summer, smoke plumes from the Bob Marshall wildfires of '88 poked skyward beyond distant mountain ranges. And ashes fell on our tents clear into hunting season.

That summer of '88 also brought Pennsylvanians Ken and June Gehringer back to give June a second crack at verbally dissecting her favorite outfitter/target. They were accompanied by former hunting guest Foster Hilliard and his wife Blanche, from the Quaker State, too.

I also packed in a group of unusually competent young men from the Red Wing, Minnesota, Environmental Learning Center. Bruce Ause, ELC Director and the group's leader, said our outfitting business had been highly recommended by several Montana sources. So despite our inexplicable fall-off in clientele, word of the high quality of Skyline Outfit's services was getting out.

⚜

But Jane and I faced another crisis.

Confronted with yet another financial disaster, the two Skyline Outfit principals convened at season's end to discuss their business future. The truth was, my will to continue had ebbed, or at least begun to ebb. The last time I'd approached the subject, however, Jane's passion for our wilderness life burned hot and high. We'd struggled through that previous crisis by sacrifice and determination, finally reaching what appeared to be a successful plateau—only to have our dreams dashed once again. How did the woman stand now? I wasn't even sure how I stood until we had our "board" meeting.

Jane handed me a hot-buttered rum, plopped into an easy chair, and stretched her feet to a crackling fireplace blaze. "Roland," she said, "it has taken all last year's profits to get through this year. We're not getting any younger. How can we survive?"

I sipped from the mug, then licked my lips. The tamarack logs popped and hissed.

"Your arms are bothering you," she added. "All the hard work. You know you won't be able to continue much longer."

"We have some fine young men working for us," I murmured. "They're damn good help."

"But you won't turn loose. It's not in you to stand aside

and let others do the work. Be honest now."

I said nothing. But I did turn from the fire to stare into her big liquid-green eyes.

She sighed. "Another year like this and you'll not be able to pay wages anyway."

"What about all the wonderful people we meet?"

"I'm tired, Roland. It's been a wonderful life. But I'm tired. I'm tired of twenty-hour days and our never being alone for seven months each year. I'm tired of stacking hay in the summer and feeding it during winter blizzards. I'm tired of proving myself to macho men—I'd like to be a woman again, get dressed for social occasions, have a candlelight dinner with friends. Most of all, I'm tired of killing ourselves for no financial reward at the end."

The logs collapsed on themselves in a shower of sparks. I took up a poker and toyed with the embers. "What would I do, Jane? After working for myself for so long, I could never work for anybody else."

"Go back into the safety field. You could do that. You were very good at it."

"No."

"Do anything. The truth is, if you want to badly enough, you can do anything."

I threw another log on the fire. "The fact is, honey, you're right. I didn't really want to admit it, but I guess I'm ready to get out of the outfitting business. I believe my writing has progressed to the point where I can make a living for us from that."

"Then do it. I'll get a job to help out. But for goodness' sake, let's get out of the outfitting business while we're still healthy enough to enjoy life."

"Outfitting has contributed to our good health."

"You know what I mean." Her words were bitten off, short—I'd not heard that tone for years.

"I'm ready," I said.

"Ready for what?"

"To sell."

She raised her mug. "Let's drink to that."

"… but with one proviso."

Her eyes narrowed. "What?"

I placed the poker in its stand. "We can't sell when we're coming off such a disastrous year. Nobody would buy an unprofitable business. We have to hit one good year—like we had last year—then sell."

"Promise?"

"Promise."

From that point on, Jane must have collaborated with a Higher Order to take control of the Skyline Outfit's destiny. Our telephone began ringing off the wall. In the end, thirty-eight summer guests scheduled—joined later by twenty-three hunters. In all, the sixty-one people we guided in 1989 constituted our best year ever!

And at the end of that financially and psychologically rewarding season, the Skyline Outfit went on the market. ■

Chapter 35

Magnifico!

What a year! 1989 was chock full with sixty-one guests—every one of them superb. Roy Foulke scheduled our spring explorer trip for himself and his wife, Reni. The Crovetto family, who lived across the street from the Foulkes in Larchmont, New York, decided to tag along. Florencia Crovetto was of French extraction, Rudolpho (who represented a steel company) hailed from Italy, and their son Enrico was born in Mexico City—talk about an international bunch!

One day we rode eight miles from White River Park to visit the Big Prairie Ranger Station. It was while riding through the huge meadows at Big Prairie that I spotted a plethora of white balls dotting the newly greening grass. We paused to pick three volleyball-size puffball mushrooms. Rudolpho perked up when he realized what the huge fungi were, and what I planned to do with them.

"Look what we brought you, honey," I said upon our return to camp. Jane took the puffballs, sliced one, cleaned the slices, and threw them on a griddle.

Rudolpho picked one up and sniffed it like a guard dog approaching a suspicious package, then broke into a broad grin and exclaimed, "Magnifico!"

From that moment, he hovered around Jane and the fire until she asked him if he'd like to cook the mushrooms.

He accepted with alacrity, insisting on regulating the cooking and oil and doing the seasoning for each slice.

Everyone in our group stood around the fire watching the master at work. "Do you realize how much these mushrooms would sell for in Italy?" he asked.

Everyone shook their heads.

"Eighty dollars a pound!"

I immediately began calculations. There were easily a hundred mushrooms in that single Big Prairie field. At a weight of five pounds each …

15 year-old Enrico Crovetto holds a couple of puffball mushrooms picked alongside a Bob Marshall trail.

Our next party was the Carbondale boys, followed by another Big Apple group, then a local party anchored by Flathead Valley folks—physician Bruce McIntyre and his wife Imogene, and retired businessfolk Jim and Pat Meyers—friends, all.

Margaret (Mike) Wagner returned for another geological gypsy trip, bringing her daughter and family. The thing I most remember about this particular adventure was that our geologist, John Montagne, led us into some spectacular fossil-bearing formations; but the retired university professor became frustrated because the two boys, Ryan and Trent Kauffman, appeared to take those wonders of ancient nature altogether too casually.

That night, after I thought everyone else had retired to their sleeping bags, I took one last circle around our picketed horses. Upon returning to the campfire I found John scribbling in a notepad. "Whatcha doin', John, writing a letter?"

He lifted his head to stare thoughtfully into the night. "No," he said. "No, I'm just trying to outline a way I can reach those two boys. I've *got* to find a way to get across to them that they're looking at deposits made three, four hundred million years ago! I *must* get them to understand that."

"John, John. They're only twelve and fifteen. You *are* making an impression. It's just that kids that age don't always demonstrate what sticks in their mind."

Our trip geologist, John Montagne, goes over a few geological fine points as Ryan and Trent Kauffman look on from either side. "Mike" Wagner stands behind John, while the Kauffman boys' parents observe from the left and Joyce Fish listens from the far right..

Pat Whitworth was an accident waiting to happen. For one thing, the Chicago-suburb florist led a sheltered life (if one can call big city life sheltered). But her husband Bob dreamed incessantly about western adventure, finally talking his lady into trying a demanding wilderness horseback trip. A local couple, Jerry and Marile Garrott, joined the party.

I personally spent seven days helping Pat on and off her horse. Gradually her fear of horses and the wilderness subsided and the lady began talking of actually trying to dismount without help. Finally came her moment: it was in a flat meadow, lush with green grass. She swung down, stepped into a gopher hole and fell heavily, breaking a bone in her shoulder.

"Oh, no!" she wailed. "You'll never trust me to try riding again."

After walking all the way to the trailhead, leading Pat on her horse, I considered it. But when they called from the doctor's office to re-schedule for 1990, how could I say no?

Vern Mendel rates high on my list of all-time favorites. The guy was a professor of animal husbandry at the University of California, Davis. He was born and raised in a small, remote community in eastern Montana and never lost the charm and sincerity that seems inherent in rural folks.

Vern always dreamed of touring the Bob Marshall Wilderness. He called with a problem, however: his wife, Tink, was petrified at the thought of riding horses.

Forewarned is forearmed, and both Jane and I worked hard at caring for the fearful, but sprite, lady. Our training must have "took," because, after Jane and I retired from guiding, Vern and Tink have returned twice to tour the Bob Marshall with other outfitters.

<hr />

Over half of our hunters were repeats—thus friends—so most trips were like old home week: some of these guys had been hunting with us from five to ten times; for up to a hundred days (ten hunting trips) of autumn adventures. Hijinks and hilarity are the order of the day, every day, when you're with friends of similar inclination.

One of the better examples of how quickly the tables can turn was produced by Arizona cardiologist Bill Hull. Bill had hunted with us twice before. But the guy had never sufficiently succumbed to the taunts of guides and companions to join them for an afternoon bath in our camp bathing hole.

The bathing hole was a bathroom-sized pool, backed up at the junction of two streams by a log jam. Both streams were fed by springs and remnant snowbanks. It was common practice for our men to gather on the log and take turns diving into the pool. Quick in, quick out.

Finally Bill gave in to the taunts. "I'll be right down," he called as the rest of us trooped to the stream.

Ten minutes went by and we'd given the good doctor up when he hove into sight carrying his towel and several implements. He waded right into the pool, sat down with water up to his neck, and began brushing his teeth. After he finished that chore, he took out a razor and cold-shaved. Then he patted under his armpits, took a sip from a cocktail he'd brought with him, and clambered out to towel himself dry—to our amazed stares.

"How long was he in there?" Gary asked.

"Had to be ten minutes."

"How could he do it?"

Talk about quieting your critics!

<hr/>

It was during our last hunt of the year that we guided the Gypsies. Their surnames were Adams and Williams. They called from Los Angeles to schedule. It was when they introduced themselves in person, prior to our hunt, that they told me they were Gypsies.

Gypsies, Saudis, Latvians, or Norwegians—it made no difference to me. But they did *seem* different. Mr. Adams and Mr. Williams actually proved to have a modicum of customs with which I was unfamiliar. But as always, I viewed their visit as a chance for me to learn. And for the next ten days, I seized every opportunity to query them relative to their origins, experiences, customs, and beliefs.

They apparently viewed their women in a somewhat more confining light than I view mine. And it's probable they weren't as forthcoming about other things as I would have liked, but they proved to be personable folks who contributed enormously to my ongoing education.

Our big problem wasn't cultural differences, but several days of torrential rain. We began the hunt with a foot of snow in the valley bottoms and ended ten days later with virtually no snow left in the mountains. In between, our part of the northern Rockies was inundated by floods. The river near camp swelled to a brown tide and we depended upon rainwater for drinking; we could hear boulders grinding in the swollen waters, and entire trees were swept downstream.

Jane had taken my absence, while I was guiding the last hunt of the season, as an opportunity to visit her parents in Oregon. It was there that our daughter, who lived in Libby at the time, reached her by phone. "Mom, aren't you worried about Dad?"

"Why would I be?"

"The entire country is flooding. Don't you read the papers, watch the news on television?"

Jane laughed. It was a measure of how far she'd come during our decades of outdoors adventure. "Cheri, what could I do about it if he *is* in trouble? If it's flooding, chances are I couldn't drive to the trailhead. And what would I do if I could? He's miles back in the mountains."

"I can't help it, Mom, I'm scared for him. A house just floated down a street here in Libby."

"He's a big boy, Cheri. I have faith in your dad. In fact, I can't imagine anyone I would trust more out there."

The truth was, we *were* in trouble—we just didn't know it. Packer Dan Cherry had barely made it back from road's end with a horsestring loaded with hay. "Dean Creek is rampaging," the young man said. "The banks are caving away. I don't think I could have made it if it was any higher."

Others did indeed have trouble during that storm. One of my friends, a former backcountry ranger in Glacier Park who had tons of experience in using horses in mountain country, drowned when his saddlehorse and two pack-horses were swept from their feet while attempting to cross the Flathead's Middle Fork.

We crossed Dean Creek four days later, while the water level was dropping. It wasn't easy, but doable. The worst part was descending or climbing the vertical cutbanks that the torrent had ripped out on either side.

"Did you get wet?" Jane, who had returned from Oregon, asked when I crowded through the kitchen door.

"Well, honey," I grinned, "let's just say we had plenty of opportunity to wash under our armpits." ∎

Chapter 36

They Made It Happen

Starting an outfitting business as we did, on a shoe-string, requires a lot of guts. Taking ours through lift-off and into the formative years required a lot of help. That help began with volunteers who went along for a trip or two each year to wrangle or cook or guide. Their pay came in the experiences they had with fine companions amid fabulously beautiful country.

Gradually, as the outfit evolved, we required a more permanent staff and we hired full-time guides and packers. Making the transition from volunteers to a paid staff took quite a leap of faith for owners who had yet to take profit from the business themselves. Eventually the time came when we could no longer avoid the necessity. And, almost as if destiny intervened, each time we needed an eager, hard-working, clean-cut young man (or a man of any age who could cut the mustard), one would show up at our door looking for a job.

Kenny Averill was one who made the leap from volunteer to paid professional guide. The man had grown up around horses and ranches and had guided off and on for other outfitters. His first trip with me was in 1973, when he was sixty-one years old. His last was in 1982. Until the big "C" nailed him, Kenny was a craggy-faced old mountain veteran who could outride, outwalk, outdrink, outdance, and outtalk anyone half his age.

His favorite expression was "I'll be go to hell!" when something or someone surprised him—like the time he rode his cat-footed wrangle horse, Joe, out to bring in our loose grazing horses and brought them at a gallop.

Kenny
Averill

Our hunters gathered outside the corral to watch the show, and Kenny didn't disappoint them, riding pell-mell behind the galloping ponies, waving his arm and yelling. He sat Joe on his haunches right at the corral gate, and the athletic horse slid to an abrupt stop. Unfortunately for Kenny, he'd forgotten to tighten Joe's cinch when he headed out of camp, so when Joe stopped the saddle didn't, rolling around the pony's barrel, catapulting Kenny to slide on his nose at the hunters' feet.

"Well, I'll be go to hell!" the old man said as he dusted himself off.

Material assets never accumulated around Kenny, and he cared not a whit. He was a today person, not enamored by yesterday or tomorrow. Overshadowing even his talent with horses and the high country, the man's best trait was his pleasant good humor. During ten years of close association with him for up to six wilderness trips each year, I never once heard him mutter an ill-tempered word. He was an absolute jewel to be around.

Kenny and his wife Jackie might show up at our home

on their way from town. Maybe it was spring and I might've been laying plans for a couple of early wilderness trips. I might mention them in passing and maybe Kenny would pretend a bored indifference.

Then Jackie would pop up with something like: "What are you acting like you don't care for? If you don't care, why'd you say let's stop and see Roland and Jane?" Then she might turn to me and say, "If he don't get back up in the mountains pretty quick, he's gonna explode. Or I'll kill him."

And Kenny would grin and say, "I guess I can get away, if you want me."

The old man was a perceptive observer of our financial foibles in an occupation where most cards were stacked against us. "Just hang on a while longer," he would say. "Times are bound to get better if you can just make it a little longer." Then he'd tell me about one of his past failures when he'd have been better off if he'd tried a little harder to hang on. He always said he gave up too quick.

During one especially difficult period, I confided to Kenny that I wasn't sure we were going to be able to pull it out this time. I told him I thought our credit was extended about as far as anyone would carry us.

A few nights later, Jane was making little tinkering noises in the kitchen while I worked on a new financial statement for a loan proposal into tens of thousands that I was trying to carry through. Tiny snow particles spit against the window panes, while flames crackled in the fireplace. Kenny and Jackie knocked on our door. They carried a six-pack of beer and stood brushing snowflakes from their coats.

Usually Jackie would stay in the kitchen if Jane was there, but this time she followed Kenny into the living room. Neither was free with conversation and I saw embarrassed glances pass between them. "Is something wrong?"

Jackie said, "Well, ain'tcha gonna tell him?"

Kenny's eyes were on his beer. "Jackie and me, we just come from the Whitefish Credit Union, and they said we could borrow two thousand dollars against our place."

"Kenny, Jackie ..."

"It's yours, if it'll help you and you want it."

Jane came from the kitchen, drying her hands just as Kenny finished with, "... and you can pay us back when you're able."

"Roland!" Jane said. "What's wrong?"

I pawed at something in my eye. "Nothing's wrong, honey. On the contrary, everything is right." And I explained to her what Kenny and Jackie had just offered.

Everyone was embarrassed. When I could at last speak without a jerk, I told them what fine friends they were and how much we appreciated their generous offer. I explained to them that we could not accept the loan of what amounted to a big share of their material assets, but that we would never forget the spirit in which it was extended.

Larry Gleason

Larry Gleason is the most talented individual I've ever known —at least when it comes to the things I most care about. Everything the guy does is done well, whether it's hewing interior log beams for a new home or analyzing the qualities of a new bull he's thinking of buying for his ranch.

Larry and I once worked together for the same lumber company. Gradually our acquaintance turned into friendship and I learned more about the guy. He's a fine saddlemaker, welder, saw filer, mechanic, electrician. And he knows more about horses and what makes them tick than anyone I know. He worked on trail crews for the U.S. Forest Service out of Spotted Bear, learning to pack from the best of the old-time government packers.

He's an observant man, this guy Gleason, and he knows wildlife and plantlife so well it took me a decade or more of outfitting to catch up to his level of knowledge in my own occupation. Larry went in with me for the first time in 1974, with a swell bunch of guests from Wausau, Wisconsin. After that he was hooked.

At the time, the guy had been working on his ranch and his job much too hard, and the wilderness trip was exactly what he needed to unwind and restore. The deeper we traveled into the wilderness, the more he smiled and relaxed and gave off deeply satisfied sighs—until we topped out on a high pass where a huge open expanse spread before us. Then he let out with a resounding whoop of sheer joy in being alive! He guided for us one trip each year, during his vacation.

Larry always listens closely to what anyone else has to say and seldom disputes even the wildest statement. But his silences are eloquent, and I've learned that the man's mere suggestions are often tantamount to heady pearls of wisdom from other sources. And they're always delivered in a manner that invites the listener to do otherwise if he chooses.

Larry was sharp enough to know we struggled to survive in our outfitting business. But being a kindred soul in his love for the outdoors, he knew why we were doing it. One day he stopped by with his big Appaloosa gelding. "The way I figure it," he said, "you should buy Baldy."

"I'd like to," I murmured. "But right now we haven't the money."

"I'll drop him off anyway. You can pay me what you think he's worth anytime you're able."

Larry became our unofficial horse-purchasing agent, with a keen eye always out for good ponies. My present saddlehorse is another Appaloosa raised on the Gleason ranch. In fact, half the horse herd presently dwelling on our place and considering me their manservant are animals Larry spotted for us.

God! Do I remember! I remember when Rich Mattson first came to work with us and how he and Larry walked out into the meadow across the creek from camp. They carried halters to catch a couple of ponies, then use them bareback to haze in the loose-grazing stock. Larry caught Blondie, slipped the halter on, and swung up on her broad back.

Rich, meanwhile, ambled up to the next horse, a big wild-eyed buckskin named Jughead, and fastened the halter. It was when he swung up on Jughead that things come unglued.

Jughead was the only horse in our outfit that couldn't be

Ted deWerd

rode. He was a fine, nimble-footed pack-horse. But he considered it an insult for a human to dare straddle him.

Larry watched Rich halter the buckskin, smiling all the while. Then, of a sudden, Rich was on top. Larry said the buckskin rolled his eyes back in surprise and reached for the sky. They were still laughing when they reached camp— with Rich riding a big sorrel named Flame.

Larry said Rich counted three goats on Lone Butte on the way up, then two more on the way back down.

Ted deWerd guided during his vacations, beginning in 1974. A paradox of a guy, he held a degree in accounting but made his living driving Burlington Northern railway trains. He's a bachelor with a soft spot in his heart for kids—with whom he's at his tenderest, his most patient. He was a hunting-camp mentor for our son Marc during his formative years.

Ted usually guided two trips, always late in the season because of a near-maniacal belief that hunting and snow go together. As a guide, the man was one of our most effective, probably because of his analytical approach to everything.

The trained accountant shook his head at our struggling attempts to make a viable enterprise out of the Skyline Outfit. He demonstrated clearly with paper and pencil

The Skyline Outfit's 1987 crew, left to right: Dan Cherry, Kevin Menz, Scott Taylor. Roland is crouching in front. The boys pulled moss from surrounding trees for their beards.

how thin was our margin between income and costs. It was Ted who, though unable to change our minds about our life work, caused us to look beyond the romance of outfitting. And it was Ted who was always around to give sound advice, quietly rooting for us to succeed while advising against our trying.

There was Ed Ernst, always smiling, always laughing. As soon as he hired on and learned how, he was the one who began competing with me at everything—and winning, too, mantying his share of hay faster, slinging his packs faster and better—when I was still in my prime.

Ed took the same competition into his guiding. Because he wanted to succeed against the master, he and his hunters would disappear into God-awful canyons or brush-filled hillsides. But because he smiled a lot and kidded them beyond what they thought was their capacity, his hunters enjoyed more than usual success. And they loved him for what he did to them and for them.

John Cline was a guide who could talk to bull elk in their language like no other. And his enthusiasm for the hunt was infectious ... sometimes inspiring his hunters beyond their physical capabilities.

Scott Taylor hailed from the far-eastern Montana town of Wolf Point. He wandered up to my door, said he'd read my book, *Montana's Bob Marshall Wilderness*, and wanted a job from the guy who wrote it.

He looked clean, quiet, and eager, like he'd make a good hand. But I shook my head and told him there just wasn't a place for him.

"Yes," he said. "Well, I understand. I know I don't have much experience, but I love the mountains and I'd, well,

I'd work for you for a while for nothing, just to get the experience. Roland, I want to learn from you."

Scott did learn from me (and I did pay him while he was going through the learning curve). He worked for us for several years, then went on to guide for other outfitters in Idaho and the Yukon.

There were float guides, Hazen Lawson and Bob Windauer. and there were two on board at the beginning, Lyle Ausk and

Gary Ernst

Denny Swift. There was Bret Brash, from one of the most remarkable families ever to tread the Bob Marshall Wilderness. There was our son Marc, who may have been the best "pure" outdoorsmen of all our guides simply because he was exposed to it virtually from infancy.

There was another Ernst—Gary Ernst—from Pennsylvania (no relation to Ed)—who began as a guest and ended as one of our most valued guides. It was Gary, a veteran long-distance truck driver, who kept our rolling stock going by insisting on *maintenance* instead of *repairs*.

My most vivid recollection of Gary is how he would check each vehicle before and after each trip, no matter how tired he might be. It was Gary who found broken wiring, or tires that needed repair. It was Gary who serviced the rigs, changing oil and greasing their fittings. It was Gary who listened to engine "tics" and brought them to my attention. It was Gary who, while horseplay was going on in camp, could be found outside the tents repairing tack.

❦

There was Dan Cherry, the hard-driving, God-fearing young man who worked for us for five years while pursuing a journalism degree from the University of Missouri in his off-season. It was Dan whose belief in God was unshakable, but who never tried to impose his beliefs on others; who engendered respect and admiration from all who came into contact with the young man.

Sober young Dan was another go-getter who brought competition to his guiding, competing with his outfitter-boss in meat his hunters brought in from the field. And it was Dan who took it so personally when he failed in the hunt that I had to set him down and counsel him about the real world of guiding so that his psyche wouldn't be crushed by circumstances over which he had no control.

Sprinkling the ashes of Kevin Menz, my former guide, along the crest of the Chinese Wall. Kevin's family asked me to accomplish the tribute in keeping with the young man's final request.

There was Kevin Menz, the guide-school graduate who signed on when we needed help and proved invaluable, not just because he was extremely talented, but because he never considered his job done until he could find nothing else to do.

It was Kevin who was up before the other guides and who retired after they'd long since turned in. It was Kevin who coiled ropes and folded manty tarps. It was Kevin who policed up our compounds, picking up gum wrappers and cigarette butts, who nailed loose shoes on our horses, and cut firewood even when it wasn't yet needed.

And it was Kevin's ashes that I sprinkled atop the Chinese Wall when the young man was killed in a tragic highway accident in Iowa.

And finally there was Rob. He was the only regular staff guide we had left when we sold the business. Rob had had a bad experience working for another outfitter in another state, but he decided to give it a second whirl when we needed help. Rob was another of those who were always smiling, always full of laughter and good will. Rob was a guide-school graduate, like Dan and Kevin—and like them, he packed horses in driving rainstorms and thigh-deep snow and loved every minute of every hour of every year.

Most of all, I remember how much we owe those guides who were so vital to the Skyline Outfit. They were its backbone, the essential connecting rods that pumped the machine and kept it functioning. In some ways, perhaps Jane and I were the glue that held it all into a single cohesive unit. I hope so. Perhaps I was a bit of a teacher, too. But with those fine guides around, offering their selfless

Rob Johnson

assistance, I was a student, too.

If you're beginning to get the idea from this book that it's impossible for an individual to succeed in life without help, then you're beginning to get the picture as I see it. ∎

Chapter 37

Welcome to Mexico

We signed the sale agreement for the Skyline Outfit to long-time outfitter and guide Cameron Lee and his investor, Randy Funk, on May 9, 1990, with the proviso that Jane and I would not turn the business over until after the 1990 season was complete. We'd already scheduled several guests who were counting on us to provide the service, and I felt we couldn't let them down.

Jane wasn't sure, right up until we signed the papers, that I would actually go through with the sale. She knew how much the Skyline Outfit had been a part of my life and hers—and she was uncharacteristically quiet on our way to the realtor's office for the transfer.

She shouldn't have worried; it was time to move on. I suffered a great deal from tendonitis in both arms and shoulders—too many heavy packs lifted atop too many tall horses over too many years. And I truly had become disenchanted with the rollercoaster financial nature of our outfitting business.

A way of life was ending. I'd been a wilderness outfitter for over twenty years. It had been a struggle, but an exciting, health-giving, rewarding one. What I'd learned could be found in no books, no treatises, no reports, no theses. We'd met some of the most wonderful people in all the world, and neither Jane nor I was under the slightest delusion that that was the single most important thing we'd be giving up.

I wouldn't miss the incessant, idiotic, debilitating struggle with a faceless bureaucracy that cared nothing about a little guy's necessity for profit in providing a needed public service.

I tried to tell myself I wouldn't miss the uncertain financial ride, either. But the truth was, I didn't know how we were going to live, other than that I wanted to pursue a writing career. Writing, though, had all the earmarks of a rollercoaster route to survival, too, just like outfitting and guiding, despite the fact that I had already sold stories to major magazines, wrote a successful newspaper column, and had a modestly successful book behind us.

⌧

Though we conducted wilderness trips throughout the summer and fall of 1990, I made no diary entries, and therefore have only sketchy recollections of that season. Our last *Just Over The Skyline* newsletter was dated June, 1990. The following was our farewell to the wonderful people we had served for so many years:

RIDING INTO THE SUNSET

It is said a dying star flares intensely just before its gasses cool forever. Fading athletes usually enjoy a last great season, sometimes even after their decline has begun. Most animate objects tend to think young at the same time their teeth grow long. In truth, though, their bodies can no longer run apace with their heads.

So it is with my old saddlehorse Buck, who at 26 still begs to be allowed to do all the things he did two decades before. So it was with Hunter, our late, great Brittany spaniel, who many of you remember as the best hunting dog who ever lived.

So it was with Janie and me.

Was it just yesterday we wrote in Just Over The Skyline *that we were prepared to go it another 20? Did we say we would continue outfitting into our dotage?*

Today, reality set in. Like Buck, we want to do what we've done so well for so many decades, but the motor and the drive mechanism says, "Hey! Wait a minute! There've already been too many blizzards, too many tons lifted and shifted and saddled and paddled. There've been more rivers forded, mountains scaled, horses wrangled and ropes tangled than any dozen folks face in a lifetime. Why ask more?"

That's a tough question from the body. Head couldn't answer. Are my teeth growing longer? Hell, I don't know—I took 'em out and looked, but I still can't tell. However, there's no denying the truth; no denying Jane grows weary of uncertain income and a before-daylight to after-dark regimen, seven days per week, for seven months of the year; while I tire of wrestling with federal and state bureaucracies who seem single-minded in driving the entire outfitting industry into Chapter 11.

All the above is taking a long way around to tell you Jane and I will be hanging 'em up come Christmas.

We began the Skyline Outfit on a shoestring in 1970 and we'll end our role in the business this year. In between have been scads of beautiful vistas, mile upon mile of Bob Marshall trails, a panoply of wildlife one can see nowhere else, books published, scores of magazine articles, hundreds of newspaper columns—all about "the Bob." There've been endless sunsets, frigid coldwater baths, trout rising to flies, bull elk trotting to bugles, and a camaraderie with the greatest bunch of guests and guides any outfitter could ever call his friends.

Will we miss it? You bet. More so than you'll miss us because we're leaving the outfit in good hands.

> *Samezever,*
> *Roland & Jane*

Why I failed to keep a diary during that last outfitting

season is tough to understand, especially since the events
logged in during the first two decades of our guiding career
proved indispensable when the time came to write a book
about the odyssey. But I didn't. Perhaps I felt I'd failed in
what I'd planned as my life's work, and wanted to blank out
all thoughts of it. Perhaps I was merely marking time until
the end of the season. Who knows?

One thing was for certain, the weather gods made
damned sure my will to get out of the occupation never
flagged. Snow came early to the high country, followed by
rain, then bitter cold, and more snow. Crusted snow
became so deep that our loose-grazing horses could not
paw down to grass, and we had to cut and run for our lower
camp, only breaking through three-foot drifts at the pass
by the thinnest of margins.

We reached the lower camp just as evening shadows
stole across the land, only to find the cooktent collapsed
and shredded by the deep and crusted snow. Fortunately,
we had the tents from the upper camp with us and were
able to make substitutions. But first we had to shovel away
the snow and clean up the kitchen-tent mess. It was well
after midnight by the time I was able to stagger to my
sleeping bag.

Of all the people I led to adventure that last season,
none stand out so clearly as Julio, Jorge, and Francisco
(pronounced Hoo-lee-oh, Hor-hay, Fran-sees-co). They
hailed from Culiacan, a vegetable growing region on Mexico's west coast, approximately 130 miles north of
Mazatlan. It's a city of around a half-million and is the capital of the state of Sinoloa.

Julio owned a couple of hardware stores, Jorge was a
dentist and rancher, Francisco a top orthopedic surgeon.
All were extremely nice people, courteous and patient and
uncomplaining.

I was, of course, intrigued by our cultural differences.
There was, however, nothing in my Scots Protestant
upbringing, flavored by an Anglo-Saxon work ethic, that

prepared me for their laid-back lifestyle. They would not be hurried—*could* not be hurried. Never mind that we planned to drive seventy miles over a slow and bumpy road, then ride twenty-seven miles over an abysmal trail, those south-of-the-border gents seemed to treat our need for haste as though they planned a day of duck hunting in the marshes around Altata.

Never mind that I got as touchy as a sore-toothed hound. They seemed not to notice, chattering among themselves in their own language, like I wasn't standing nearby, drumming fin-

Jane leading the way across a tough ford near the forks of the river's north and south forks. She's a journeyman outdoor person by now.

gers on a doorjamb and glancing at my watch.

The problem was aggravated by the fact that only Julio spoke English, and then only haltingly. Finally, in dismay that we weren't on our way to the trailhead while they dawdled at breakfast, I tossed a few Latin-sounding words their way; ones I'd picked up while watching "Cisco Kid" in movie matinees a half-century before: *"Andelay! Andelay! Mucho pronto!"*

It had an immediate effect. They looked surprised, then smiled broadly and crowded around, chattering, appar-ently pleased they'd had the foresight to obtain a guide who spoke their language.

I finally threw up my hands and stomped out to load

horses in the stock truck and drive away, leaving Jane to bring our hunters along in our old Chevy station wagon. An hour after I'd reached road's end, the hunters still hadn't arrived. So I jumped in a pickup and headed back down the long winding road to look for them.

Jane and the three Mexicans were sailing blithely along, with Jorge regaling his two compadres with tales of derring-do, when the station wagon hit a pothole and went blank: lights, engine, power steering, power brakes—everything went down.

Fortunately, there was a wide spot in the road and Jane guided the coasting vehicle into it. Gentlemen all, the men jerked flashlights from their saddlebags and jumped out to raise the hood. Nope, battery cables were all right, distributor and coil wires appeared okay. Julio sprawled inside to check the ignition wiring. Still nothing appeared wrong. Finally, the three men gathered off to one side, chattering and gesturing. They shrugged, left the hood up on the stranded vehicle, and piled inside. They turned up their coat collars against the early morning chill. Two of them sprawled into corners to catch up on lost sleep.

"Welcome to Mexico," Julio muttered. ■

Chapter 38

The Full Circle

During the low ebb after the disastrous 1988 season was when Jane and I had made the decision to sell our Skyline Outfit. Though we were to operate the business for two more seasons, the dye was cast, our direction set. We were tired. And disillusioned.

One day in January, between that rocky 1988 operating season and February's Pennsylvania sport show, I sat at my office desk reflecting on life. I leaned back in my swivel chair to stare around the walls at treasures from a lifetime outdoors: the near-recordbook mule-deer head, the six-point bull-elk rack, the bleached buffalo skull from a friend, the wood carvings given by a hunter, the Winchester '73, the original paintings of Bob Marshall Wilderness scenes, the deteriorating Forest Service trail signs I'd rescued from the ground, photos of my dog, my horse, Jane, me.

Sometimes there can be no reconciling the circuits traveled by one's brain while the body is in repose. Such was that day.

There could be little doubt I had, throughout a lifetime, become an accomplished outdoorsman. Though not so swift as some of L'Amour's heroes, I could kindle a fire in a blizzard, track a bull elk through a forest, straddle a rangy bronc, and find my way back to camp during the blackest night. My advice was respected and sound, and even sometimes sought. I'd learned to think like a deer and cast flies to trout. I could move hundreds of pounds of gear for surprisingly long distances in tough mountain country without soring horses or tearing up their tack. My brother and mentor—if he's up there somewhere—should be proud.

Then I wondered how accomplished Hillburn himself would have become—had he lived. When I knew him he was already a superb outdoorsman. But have I surpassed him? Yes, certainly. After all, he was but twenty-three years old when he died. I've had five and a half *decades* of outdoors experience—some in fields he never had an opportunity to enter, such as elk hunting and horse packing. Ah, but what might he have become?

And that's the rub. Hillburn not only was far advanced over his younger brother, he was head-and-shoulders ahead of his outdoors contemporaries in that time. Had he lived, might he still be my mentor? Might he still be a better flycaster, a better hunter, a better woodsman? Who knows, he might have also become an outfitter who leads others on wilderness adventures.

Remnants of Hillburn's plane were recovered from this glacial tarn in the Scottish Highlands. It's a fitting resting place.

One thing is for damn sure. Had he lived and had he entered into such an endeavor, he would've made a success out of it where his younger brother had failed.

But he didn't live. He died in a fiery crash just before his twenty-third birthday on some Godforsaken mountain in Scotland after flying dozens of times over Nazi Germany—for what? What waste is war! Millions died—Hillburn Leon Cheek wasn't the only one.

Millions of the fairest in many lands turned to dust for what? Yes, I know: to stop the triumph of evil. But evil still rages—what good did it do that my brother's life was snuffed before he'd lived it? Isn't there a better way? His life really was given in vain if the world gained no lesson from his death and the death of the evil against which he so gallantly struggled.

And there was this bitterest of all pills: that Hillburn Cheek and his flight mates received no recognition for their valor, their contribution. Killed on the way home, only a few days after hostilities ended, they weren't even accorded the honor of being listed as War Dead.

◦────◦

Jane interrupted my reverie by handing me a handful of mail. In it was a letter from Arlene Fritts, a neighbor from our Oregon days. Arlene's husband, Buck, had recently died, and Arlene was the last of our friends from an earlier life with whom we still corresponded. It was Buck and Arlene who helped us load our furniture when we moved; it was Buck and Arlene who showed up on our Montana doorstep to help us build an addition on our home. I slit the envelope and a clipping from my old hometown newspaper fell out. It was dated January 8, 1989. Attached to the clipping was this note: "I thought you might wish to see this."

> An Englishman who in 1971 at the age of 12 came across the wreckage of an American World War II bomber while walking in the hills of Scotland with his father, has spent considerable time over the past 17 years tracing the history of the aircraft and those aboard.

> One of the airmen who died in the crash, he learned, was a young man from Roseburg by the name of Hillburn L. Cheek.

> To date the Briton, Ian T. Shuttleworth, has been unable to find any of Cheek's surviving relatives. He would like help in doing so.

In a letter to the Oregon Historical Society, which later was forwarded to the Douglas County Library, Shuttleworth described the discovery of the downed plane by him and his father.

"Being only 12 at the time I knew little about WW2 aircraft," he wrote, "but became interested in this one and decided to try and find out more about it. After writing to several record offices both here [England] and the United States, I was informed the plane was a B-24 'Liberator' bomber that had crashed while returning to the states in June, 1945. Sadly, all 15 crewmen aboard were killed ..."

In tracing the history of the airplane and its crew, Shuttleworth said he learned the airmen were not included on the roll of honor for U.S. servicemen killed in Europe during World War II.

"Apparently they were not listed as the accident occurred after hostilities had ceased," he wrote. "This I thought very sad, particularly as my research showed them to have completed a full tour of combat operations while over here, and so I decided to place some form of memorial to them myself."

The memorial placed by Ian Shuttleworth to honor the memory of a fine group of young men who gave all to keep Ian and his countrymen—as well as their own countrymen—free.

Shuttleworth said he obtained permission from the owners of the land where the bomber crashed and subsequently erected a plaque there last year honoring the 15 American airmen.

With the memorial in place, Shuttleworth said he felt he should make an effort to trace any surviving relatives of those who died, "as they have a right to know about it."

"I had not attempted this before," he wrote, "as I was concerned I might upset someone by stirring up sad memories. I am pleased to say, however, that the reaction from those I have traced so far has been quite the opposite and they are delighted that their loved ones are not forgotten over here."

The story ended with a plea for anyone with information on the family to contact Ian Shuttleworth in County Durham, England. I wrote. Ian's reply was dated January 28, 1989:

Dear Mr. Cheek:

... It is wonderful to at last learn something about Hillburn's background, and I am most grateful to you for writing and sending the photograph of your brother. Most of the information that I have concerns his service with the Air Force and has been drawn from the records of his unit, the 44th Bomb Group.

I am enclosing some photographs which I hope will be of interest to you, including one of the memorial plaque. The memorial is in two parts really, the plaque which is bolted to a rock face overlooking the crash site, and a file containing all the information that I have about the fifteen young men who were killed in the accident, along with details of their aircraft....

I was particularly interested to read in your letter, that Hillburn was a keen outdoorsman, skilled at hunting and fishing. Gairloch, where the accident occurred, is located in a fairly wild and remote area on the North West coast of Scotland, which is very popular with sportsmen for its good deer hunting and fly fishing facilities. It is also in my opinion, one of the most beautiful parts of the British Isles. It is perhaps more fitting therefore, that his aircraft went down there ...

A tear rolled out. "Somebody cares," I murmured to

Jane. "Somebody over there cares, even though no one here seems to."

"Roland …"

"Is it so much to ask that they list these men on the honor roll of those killed in the line of duty?"

My wife laid a hand on my shoulder. "Roland, give it up."

I stared up at her.

"Give it up, dear. Don't you think after nearly fifty years that it's time to just give it up?" ■

Technical Sergeant Hillburn L. Cheek somewhere in England, 1945

I found it illuminating to study my brother's photo at the beginning of this book with this one at the end. I fancy there are things etched there most of us are sheltered from ever seeing.

Roland and Jane

Want More of Roland?

Roland's writings can be found weekly in his syndicated column *Wild Trails and Tall Tales*. Here are a few samplings from his hundreds of articles.

Shared Experiences

This could be the most important column I've ever written and I'm afraid that I'll not do it well. The subject is our relations with the less fortunate. It's not about money or care giving or social assistance. Instead, it's one of sharing experiences.

"How is Lyle?" my friend Matt asked.

I shook my head. "Not good. He can no longer see well enough to drive or read, and he can't get much more than just the drift of a football game on television."

Matt shrugged. "A man can only play the cards he's dealt."

Yeah, right. As if this oldest of my friends has too many more cards left to play: emphysema, arthritis, heart bypass, multiple angioplasties, cancer, amputated leg, diabetes. I recalled how he'd once been a superb athlete, an elite member of the 101st Airborne and one of World War II's "Battered Bastards of Bastogne."

Matt and I had taken dozens of horseback packtrips together into some of the most splendid mountain country in the world. We'd coached youth baseball together and built Little League and Legion diamonds that are in use today. We'd worked together and played together and drank beer together.

Now there's not much we can do together but visit about "the old days." Yet here was a guy suffering from multiple afflictions who cared enough to ask about a mutual friend who is losing his eyesight.

"How long has Lyle's eye problems been going on?" Matt asked.

"It came with a rush. Apparently blood vessels ruptured, maybe a couple of months ago. It's been getting progressively worse since."

"And no chance for an operation?"

"His doctors don't hold out much hope. In fact, they say he stands a good chance that an operation would make it worse."

Again, Matt shrugged. I continued: "We rode up Camas Creek in Glacier Park," I continued. "It was during September—a beautiful day, with snow-dusted mountains shining like sentinels all around." I paused in recollection, then went on: "There were some late-blooming harebells growing along the trail and I thoughtlessly said, 'Look at the flowers—aren't they splashes of blue?' Lyle cleared his throat and said in a subdued voice, 'You'll have to tell me about them, Roland. I can't see them.'"

My friend nodded.

"God, Matt, I felt so rotten. Later, I had to slap a hand over my mouth to keep from exclaiming at the magnificent view."

Matt frowned. "You think about …" But I was on a roll. "Jeez, Matt, I have a hard time keeping from telling you about some of the adventures I'm still going on, knowing you can no longer do them."

The frail man pounded his chair arm. "No! Dammit man, you're not thinking right. Don't you realize I know I'll never again be able to do what we once did? But I can still live them and visualize them through your eyes and your body—if only you'll share with me! Don't you see that Lyle still wants to do the things he once did or he'd not been riding with you? Don't you understand that by not sharing what you saw with him, that you diminished his experience?"

I shed a tear while leaving my friend—and decided this bit of wisdom is something that also needs to be shared. ■

Defining the Enemy

The population of America has doubled in our lifetime. My wife and I often commiserate about this regrettable fact while driving down Interstates and through cities. The hordes of other people becomes even more distressing during the holidays, when I'm forced to town to select a Christmas present for a woman who, from the day I met her, deserves more.

My big problem is I'm emotionally and physically ill-equipped to do head-to-head combat with the proletariat masses who've been sale-starved for the previous 365 days. Naturally, traffic leading to all department stores is bumper-to-bumper. And traffic lights merely blink green while staring ugly red for three clicks on the hour hand.

Jane, though not as powerfully designed as I, is imminently more suited for going for the throat when diving into a crowd of screaming women at a sale table. Such carnage I can't even bear to watch.

Not only are roadways clogged, but trails we once enjoyed hiking in solitude now thump with the tread of countless hiking boots. Hitler's storm troopers made less racket marching along Dutch cobblestones while wearing hobnailed jackboots. The damned newcomers even invade eerily quiet ski trails we once glided along with no thought that other folks might be making babies faster than our psyches can adjust.

They built a couple of houses across the highway from us this past summer, and another in the field behind. Such cheek! The next thing you know they'll want to send their kids to the same school for which "my" taxes are paying. And they'll want the fire department to use "my" fire engines if they have a garage fire. And vote in "my" precinct. No doubt some will vote the wrong way.

Not only that, but their dogs will die on "my" highway, and their cats will be after "my" birds. Smoke from their chimneys and exhaust from their autos will pollute "my" atmosphere. It'll be their garbage over-flowing "my" landfills.

All the newcomers will mean more people seeking more jobs that attract more factories and businesses to employ more people that will attract more....

"We're making too many babies," I cried to Jane when they began framing yet another home across the way. "Doesn't anyone else realize what we are doing to the land? Can't they see America cannot sustain unbridled growth? From whence will the natural resources come in another century?"

"The land will be stripped," she said, shedding a tear.

"How will this country feed so many people," I added.

"The water. It's becoming polluted now."

"Animals are endangered. Fish stocks are depleted—even in the ocean."

"It's our fault," she said. "Ours and the generations past."

"Our fathers and mothers had one too many babies," I cried.

That stopped us. Her eyes met mine. "Aren't you the youngest child in your family?" she asked.

"So are you," I replied. Then I added, "Pogo had it right when he said, 'I have met the enemy and he is us.' " ■

Use the order form on the reverse side of this page to order more of Roland Cheek's books.

Dance On The Wild Side 352 pgs. 5-1/2 x 8-1/2 $19.95 (postpaid)
A memoir of two people in love, peppered with wild animals, untamed people, freak weather, and rainbows, set against the backdrop of a magnificent American wilderness. by Roland and Jane Cheek

Phantom Ghost of Harriet Lou 352 pgs. 5-1/2 x 8-1/2 $19.95 (postpaid)
*A key to finding elk with or without a guide; discovery techniques with insight into the habits and habitats of North America's second-most charismatic creatures; a guide to understanding that God made elk to lead we humans into some of **His** finest places.* by Roland Cheek

Learning To Talk Bear 320 pgs. 5-1/2 x 8-1/2 $19.95 (postpaid)
An important book for anyone wishing to understand what makes bears tick. Humorous high adventure and spine-tingling suspense, seasoned with understanding through a lifetime of walking where the bears walk, surviving while smelling the bears' breath. by Roland Cheek

Montana's Bob Marshall Wilderness 80 pgs. 9 x 12 (coffee table size) $15.95 hardcover, $10.95 softcover (postpaid)
97 full-color photos, over 10,000 words of where-to, how-to text about America's favorite wilderness. by Roland Cheek

Telephone orders: Call Toll Free 1-800-821-6784.
Have your Visa, MasterCard or Discover ready.

Postal orders: Skyline Publishing
P.O. Box 1118
Columbia Falls, MT 59912
Telephone: (406) 892-5560   Fax (406) 892-1922

Please send the following books:
(I understand I may return any Skyline Publishing book for a full refund—no questions asked.)

Title	Qty	Cost Ea.	Total
_____	_____	$ _____	$_____
_____	_____	$ _____	$_____
_____	_____	$ _____	$_____
		Total Order:	$_____

Ship to: Name_____

Address_____

City_____ State_____ Zip_____

Daytime phone number (_____)_____-_____

Payment: ☐ Cheque or Money Order

Credit card: ☐ Visa ☐ MasterCard ☐ Discover

Card Nunber_____

Name on card_____Exp. date___/___

Signature:_____